LOVE BETWEEN MEN IN ENGLISH LITERATURE

D1565386

Also by Paul Hammond

JOHN DRYDEN: A LITERARY LIFE

JOHN OLDHAM AND THE RENEWAL OF
CLASSICAL CULTURE

THE POEMS OF JOHN DRYDEN: VOLUME I: 1649–1681 (*editor*)

THE POEMS OF JOHN DRYDEN: VOLUME II: 1682–1685
(*editor*)

SELECTED PROSE OF ALEXANDER POPE (*editor*)

Love between Men in English Literature

Paul Hammond
Reader in Seventeenth-Century Literature
University of Leeds

St. Martin's Press
New York

St. Martin's Press, Scholarly and Reference Division,
175 Fifth Avenue, New York, N.Y. 10010

First published in the United States of America in 1996

Printed in Great Britain

ISBN 0–312–16326–6 (cloth)
ISBN 0–312–16327–4 (paperback)

Library of Congress Cataloging-in-Publication Data
Hammond, Paul, 1953–
Love between men in English literature / Paul
Hammond.
p. cm.
Includes bibliographical references (p.   ) and index.
ISBN 0–312–16326–6 (cloth). — ISBN 0–312–16327–4 (pbk.)
1. Gay's writings, England—History and criticism.
2. Homosexuality and literature—Great Britain. 3. English
literature—History and criticism. 4. Homosexuality, Male, in
literature. 5. Gay men in literature. 6. Love in literature.
I. Title.
PR120.G39H35 1996
820.9'353—dc20   96–8834
                                                           CIP

For Nick

προσεμένου δὲ καὶ λόγον καὶ ὁμιλίαν δεξαμένου, ἐγγύθεν
ἡ εὔνοια γιγνομένη τοῦ ἐρῶντος ἐκπλήττει τὸν ἐρώμενον
διαισθανόμενον ὅτι οὐδ' οἱ σύμπαντες ἄλλοι φίλοι τε καὶ
οἰκεῖοι μοῖραν φιλίας οὐδεμίαν παρέχονται πρὸς τὸν ἔνθεον
φίλον.

Contents

Preface

I was a student of English literature at the college where Byron fell in love with the chorister John Edleston; where Tennyson walked arm in arm with Arthur Hallam; where A.E. Housman dreamt of Shropshire lads; and where the fictional Maurice and Clive first met, blushing and stammering, in E.M. Forster's novel. In spite of such precedents, it was not easy to recognize then (only a few years after homosexual relationships had been partially decriminalized) the degree to which English literature had spoken of the supposedly unspeakable. The present book is one which I wish I had been able to read as an eighteen-year-old embarking on the exploration of literature. But that was in another country.

Today there are many books and articles which discuss the literary representation of emotional and sexual relationships between men, focusing on particular periods or writers, but there is as yet no book for the student and the general reader which offers a guide to the principal expressions of love between men in English literature from the Renaissance to the twentieth century. This book explores the literary resources for the expression of such desire in different periods: the kinds of narrative and imagery which were available; the relationship between expressions of loving friendship and expressions of sexual love; the pretexts for gazing at the male body, and the language which could be used for evoking its beauty; the variety of imagined worlds through which desire dreamt of satisfaction.

The first chapter addresses the question of how such relations have been conceptualized and labelled in different historical periods, and explores two of the most influential myths of love between men, those of Plato and Freud. The discussion of literary texts begins with the late sixteenth century, not because the medieval period is without interest in this connexion, but because it is in the generation of Shakespeare, Marlowe and Barnfield that one finds the first extensive presentation of homoerotic desire in English poetry and drama. Throughout the book my treatment is illustrative rather than exhaustive, and I have not attempted an encyclopaedic survey. While I have made reference to changing social conditions, this is a study of literature rather than a social or cultural history, and it is more interested in the literary resources for expressing love and desire than in hostile characterizations by unsympathetic observers, though these do feature in the eighteenth-century chapter. As well as considering major writers in some detail, I have included some significant minor figures and some less familiar texts, and have quoted more freely from those works which readers may find difficult to obtain. In discussing the nineteenth and twentieth centuries I have had to be particularly selective. The section on Wilde, for example, could have been longer, but plenty has been written about him recently, and there is a risk of his case unduly dominating our sense of the period. Although this book is concerned with English rather than American literature, the importance of Whitman for generations of English writers required his inclusion. Several twentieth-century writers, such as Auden, Isherwood and Spender, could have been added, but their work is relatively familiar, and I have preferred to highlight other writing. The bibliography will direct the reader to other literary texts, and suggest further critical and historical reading. I have brought the book to a close in the 1950s, because after that point (and particularly after the law was changed in 1967) the literature becomes too extensive to be squeezed into a book of this length, and is in any case comparatively accessible.

Page or line references are supplied in the text, and refer to the editions listed in the bibliography. Spelling and punctuation have been modernized in quotations from earlier literature. Wilfred Owen's poem 'I saw his round mouth's crimson' is quoted by permission of the Estate of the author and Chatto & Windus. The diary of Sir Sydney Waterlow is quoted by permission of Professor J.C. Waterlow and the trustees of the Henry W. and Albert A. Berg Collection, The New York Public Library, Astor, Lenox and Tilden Foundations.

I am grateful to the School of English at the University of Leeds for providing research expenses, and to my colleagues Dr David Fairer, Mr David Lindley and Mr Alistair Stead for commenting on chapters in draft.

PAUL HAMMOND

The Desiring Gaze:
A Commentary on the
Illustrations

But even lovers' eyes
Acknowledge boundaries.

W.H. Auden, *Juvenilia* (1994) p. 140

Much homoerotic literature dwells on the desiring gaze, placing the reader in the position of the viewer contemplating male beauty. The gaze is particularly important in circumstances where physical contact with the desired object is potentially dangerous, and so the pleasure which the gaze offers may be the only form of pleasure available. (Indeed, in some Renaissance and Victorian poetry one feels that unending longing is found more desirable than consummation.) The homoerotic gaze is hardly untroubled, however. It may need to find some cultural licence, and represent itself as an aesthetic appraisal of the nude body, or as part of the search for knowledge; it may be aware of an unbridgeable divide between itself and the desired object, a boundary which may frustrate but might also reassure, since it protects the viewer from a response; it may try to entice – or may need to avoid – the man or boy's answering look; it may be reading the other for signs that a sexual advance might be reciprocated.

Caravaggio's David both rewards and wards off the gazer. Particularly if we agree that the head of Goliath is a self-portrait by Caravaggio, the painting speaks of the danger of homoerotic involvement, evoking the Freudian association of decapitation with castration: the older man is rendered powerless by the youth. Like many of Caravaggio's pictures it offers a sado-masochistic pleasure. The lighting invites us to enjoy the boy's flesh, but the light falls equally on the cold steel and the grisly head. The boy has an adolescent torso but an adult's strength, and an unmistakably phallic sword. The image speaks of the danger of desire – and the desire for danger.

The painting of *Two young men* by Crispin van den Broeck reminds us of the difficulty of distinguishing friendship from love; indeed, in the Renaissance and seventeenth century passionate male friendship often spoke a language which we might regard as erotic – and who really knows whether and how that eroticism was recognized at the time? What feelings are expressed in the embrace of these two young men? Their red hair suggests that they might be brothers, but if they are not related then the ease with which they rest their hands on each other signals a relaxed friendship. They enclose each other, but there is also a movement away from complete enclosure since the youth on the left is looking out of the picture, not meeting his partner's gaze even though he returns his smile. Their hands meet at the centre of the painting around an apple; one holds the fruit, while the other touches the forefinger of his friend's hand with the forefinger of his own. The apple has such strong associations with sexuality, being Eve's fatal gift to Adam, that it is difficult to expunge that trace as we read this painting. Does the apple represent a sexuality which they already share with each other? Is it offered by one to the other as a sexual invitation? Or is it a sign of the future sexual relations with women which will inevitably divide them, and complete the movement which their divided gazes have begun? Does the apple unite or separate them? Or is it just an apple? The public symbolic code of the apple invites readings of this private space, but without allowing us to suppose that we can correctly understand the private narrative.

In painting and statuary the nude male was often used to

epitomize the heroic values of a society, and was thus placed at the centre of a public gaze. There was a concerted project to recover classical art in the eighteenth and nineteenth centuries, this recovery being also a form of reinvention as fragments were reassembled and works reconstructed, often somewhat speculatively. Some statues were held to represent anatomical detail to perfection, and were praised for the accuracy of their musculature as well as for their embodiment of heroic values and ideal beauty. But the nude male also allows a private homoerotic gaze which comes at a tangent to officially sanctioned ways of looking. Michelangelo's archers have the vigorous heroic nudity of the quasi-classical warrior, but when they are crowded together naked (instead of being single ideal types) they inhabit an implausible imagined space whose artifice engages the viewer's imagination. The archers' muscular bodies are the main focus of the onlooker's perspective, while their own focus, the object of their onward rush, is the herm. The herm was a Greek figure, often a boundary marker, with a prominent erect penis (though visitors will find that this feature is curiously missing from the examples in the Vatican). As in many paintings of the nude St Sebastian bound to a tree, it is difficult not to see the arrows which pierce the body as arrows of desire. This phallic boundary marker at the edge of the frame, is he also Michelangelo's goal? Is he the viewer's goal?

Ingres' Oedipus is nude as he solves the riddle of the sphinx; his nudity is a sign of his power, his command of knowledge; untroubled himself, his body is oblivious of the viewer's gaze, though we may admire its form as part of our admiration of Oedipus' skill. Wright's painting places the naked gladiator at the centre of attention in a pool of light; two men exchange looks across the sculpture, at the level of his genitals. The discovery of the classical past is imaged here as one of the elements which enlightens the Enlightenment, and Wright's investigators share a space of male comradeship in the pursuit of knowledge. But what focuses their attention is the nude male; once again the expression of social bonding is made via an erotic image.

List's classicism is an elegant contrivance, offering us the young man as an object of beauty but without pretending that we are to take a purely aesthetic pleasure in him. His recumbent pose echoes the generations of reclining female nudes who displayed themselves to the male viewer; instead of their flowers he may hold a sprig of classical laurel or bay, but the gesture indicates that he too is ready to be plucked. His downward gaze patiently allows the viewer to appropriate him at leisure. The texture of the torso contrasts with that of the stone, inviting us to imagine his softness and warmth. List's imagery is a development from the photographs of Italian boys in classical settings made by German photographers such as von Gloeden and Plüshow at the turn of the century. The body rests against part of a temple, and is itself a temple of health and purity. Stephen Spender's semi-fictional memoir *The Temple* includes a character based upon List, and traces the association between the cult of nudity and a re-emerging German identity in the 1920s. Its narrator is frequently photographing his male friends, taking possession of them through the lens rather than through sex.

Bazille's figures inhabit two enclosed spaces, the pool and the sunlit patch of grass surrounded by trees. In contrast to many nineteenth-century poems which focus on bathing scenes, there is no excluded, desiring outsider; the youth leaning against the tree on the left (in a pose suggesting a languid St Sebastian) seems to invite attention, but the other boys are absorbed in their activity. The gaze of the youth resting on his elbow is directed towards the pair in the centre, but it is the gaze of an equal. The two adults are out on the margins: one, stripped to the waist, is helping a lad out of the pool, while the other is taking his clothes off, looking down at the ground; they are not observers, but neither are they quite participants. Right at the centre of the painting are the bright red drawers of the youth with his back to us, who is grasping another youth from behind. It is an embrace which is evidently uninhibited within this setting; perhaps it is a wrestling hold, but it is left to the viewer to define the feelings of the two lads as they hold each other half-naked in the middle of this enclosed, self-sufficient male space. The picture occurs in a period when poetry and painting are offering acute voyeuristic pleasures, and in such conditions 'innocence' is constructed as part of the work of the voyeuristic gaze; innocence is attributed to characters in order to feed the viewer's pleasure.

More blatantly offered to a devouring gaze are the boys in *August Blue*. Compositionally the painting looks as if it originated in a photograph, but any suggestion of photographic realism is countered by the pose adopted by the nude boy standing on the gunwale. His quasi-classical stance requires a piece of drapery (it is not a shirt, and looks too flimsy for a towel) whose artful positioning draws attention to the boy's genitals, which are partly suggested anyway by his hand. The boy in the water dissolves into an enticing blur of colours, teasingly inviting the gaze to penetrate the water and reveal what the ripples have hidden. Tuke frequently called his paintings by colours (like *Ruby, Gold and Malachite*) suggesting a solely aesthetic interest in the colours of sunlit flesh against sunlit sea. A transparent subterfuge, perhaps, but one which permitted the private homoerotic gaze to be satisfied by a painting which was deemed suitable for inclusion in the nation's art collection.

1

The Texture of the Past

Mike: There's no word in the Irish language for what you were doing.
Wilson: In Lapland they have no word for snow.

Joe Orton, *The Ruffian on the Stair*,
in *The Complete Plays* (1976) p. 50

LABELS AND CATEGORIES

During the trial of Oscar Wilde at the Old Bailey in 1895, a debate arose over the interpretation of a literary text. Counsel for the prosecution quoted some lines from a poem by Lord Alfred Douglas called 'Two Loves':

'Sweet youth,
Tell me why, sad and sighing, dost thou rove
These pleasant realms? I pray thee tell me sooth,
What is thy name?' He said, 'My name is Love,'
Then straight the first did turn himself to me,
And cried, 'He lieth, for his name is Shame.
But I am Love, and I was wont to be
Alone in this fair garden, till he came
Unasked by night; I am true Love, I fill
The hearts of boy and girl with mutual flame.'
Then sighing said the other, 'Have thy will,
I am the Love that dare not speak its name'.

Counsel then asked Wilde:

Was that poem explained to you? – I think that is clear.
There is no question as to what it means? – Most certainly not.
Is it not clear that the love described relates to natural love and unnatural love? – No.
What is the 'Love that dare not speak its name'? – 'The Love that

dare not speak its name' in this century is such a great affection of an elder for a younger man as there was between David and Jonathan, such as Plato made the very basis of his philosophy, and such as you find in the sonnets of Michaelangelo and Shakespeare. It is that deep, spiritual affection that is as pure as it is perfect. It dictates and pervades great works of art like those of Shakespeare and Michaelangelo, and those two letters of mine, such as they are. It is in this century misunderstood, so much misunderstood that it may be described as the 'Love that dare not speak its name', and on account of it I am placed where I am now. It is beautiful, it is fine, it is the noblest form of affection. There is nothing unnatural about it. It is intellectual, and it repeatedly exists between an elder and a younger man, when the elder man has intellect, and the younger man has all the joy, hope and glamour of life before him. That it should be so the world does not understand. The world mocks at it and sometimes puts one in the pillory for it. (Loud applause, mingled with some hisses.)

Mr Justice Charles – If there is the slightest manifestation of feeling I shall have the Court cleared. There must be complete silence preserved. (*The Trials of Oscar Wilde*, pp. 235–6)

This is an eloquent and courageous speech, but if considered as literary criticism or social history it is also highly tendentious. For Wilde there is no doubt (at least for his immediate rhetorical purposes) that this love is the same across the centuries and in different cultures. His contemporaries may have misunderstood this love; they may, like the peevish voice in Douglas's poem, call it 'Shame', or like the prosecuting counsel call it 'unnatural', or like the judge impose silence on any expression of feeling: but there is no doubt that it is recognizably the same kind of love, whether in ancient Greece or Victorian England. Yet Wilde's speech is patently a fiction, partly in eliding historical differences, but also in forgetting for the moment the recognition which we find elsewhere in his work that our identities are themselves fictions. In *The Portrait of Mr W.H.* Wilde makes us aware of the precarious fictional status of the story which is woven about Shakespeare's young man, while in aphorisms such as 'The first duty in life is to be as artificial as possible' (p. 1205) he teases us into recognizing that our lives are artifacts, fictions which we make up. Yet the fiction which Wilde weaves so beautifully here would have us believe that all these examples of 'the Love that dare not speak its name' are of the same spirit and temper.

Contrary to Wilde's myth, sexual relations between men have been understood in radically different ways in different cultures: some societies have prescribed them as essential rites of initiation into manhood; others have proscribed them as crimes against nature. Studying the ways in which homoerotic desire has been represented in literature requires an awareness of the mythologies which are at work in different periods, the processes through which behaviour is classified, and the social and ideological pressures which shape those categories through which we represent ourselves to ourselves. And since homosexual acts were outlawed, and homoerotic desire stigmatized, throughout the period discussed in this book, we need to ponder the strategies by which writers may resist both the negative stereotypes of homosexual love, and the predominance in literature of the language of heterosexual experience. What forms of expression are available to a writer within such a culture who wishes to explore homosexual love?

Several typical strategies are employed here by Wilde in his list of impeccably canonical heroes. These are mythic figures for Victorian culture, so at one level they guarantee the innocence and orthodoxy of Wilde's behaviour. At the same time, Wilde is challenging the puritanically selective historiography of the Victorians, which anxiously erased mention of Greek homosexuality or explained as ardent friendship the feelings expressed in Shakespeare's *Sonnets*. To another audience, however, one which has been using references to the Greeks or the *Sonnets* as covert indications of homosexual interests, Wilde's public invocation of a homosexual canon both makes his own sexual interests clear and offers a rousing assertion that such love (to this audience, *our* love) is noble and fine. Silence is eloquent here: by describing this love as pure, intellectual and spiritual, Wilde allows the court to infer that it is not sexual, while many of his hearers will have been used to hearing homosexual desire speak through silences, gaps in texts, moments where language falters and love is left without a name. Such an undoing and remaking of prevailing mythologies is characteristic of many of the texts discussed in this book, and as readers we have to learn that silences may be tongued with meaning, while what is ostensibly open for all to see may be concealing what is unspeakable. At the same time, not every unspeakable secret is a homosexual secret, and not every reference to strange or queer or unnatural behaviour points in this direction; some silences are just silences, or conceal quite different anxieties.

Literary historians and critics may seek to understand the texture of past cultures, but they are themselves caught up in cultural mythologies. These are epitomized in the very vocabulary which is available for discussing erotic relations between men in previous cultures. 'Gay' is perhaps the most widely used adjective today, and it is the word most often chosen for self-description. But it became widespread in its present meaning only in the 1970s; in the nineteenth century it was applied to female prostitutes or 'loose' women. John Boswell used 'gay' in his book *Christianity, Social Tolerance, and Homosexuality* to describe people in the middle ages, but his usage has proved controversial, for it too readily implies historical continuities which are actually debatable. 'Queer' is a term of abuse which has been appropriated by some activists who wish to use it positively as a badge of their difference and opposition, but not every gay man wishes to see his sexuality as dissident or oppositional, nor does every gay scholar see his work as a contribution to 'queer studies'. The words 'homosexual' and 'homosexuality' seem to have originated in 1892 in translations by C.G. Chaddock from the German of works by Krafft-Ebing; 'heterosexual' arrived at the same point, and 'heterosexuality' in 1900. These terms arose within a medical discourse which was attempting to define (and in some cases to cure) a series of 'perversions'. It is interesting that 'heterosexual' was coined simultaneously with 'homosexual', as if it needed the latter for its own definition: only when the homosexual was defined for medical and social purposes as someone other than the norm did that norm itself come so clearly into view. The words 'sodomy' and 'buggery' are more ancient, being present in medieval English, but their meanings are confused: they were used in the Renaissance to mean not only anal intercourse between two men, but also anal intercourse between a man and a woman, intercourse between a human and an animal, and any physical contact between two males which resulted in ejaculation. These were at once legal terms which referred to acts, and moral or theological terms which defined sins. The word 'bugger' comes from 'Bulgar', an inhabitant of Bulgaria where the Manichaean heresy flourished: it thus linked theological and sexual deviancy. Similarly the *Oxford English Dictionary*'s illustrative quotations for 'sodomy' and its cognates show that it was often used in the

Renaissance by Protestant writers denouncing Catholic practices, who thus associated one particular sexual activity with those forms of worship and doctrine which they saw as perversions of the truth. These usages did not map out a consistent, clear categorization of actions or people according to the gender of the partner chosen. This combination of apparent precision and actual instability of meaning is significant, for it suggests how the perception and discussion of sex between men is intricately involved with, and often determined by, social and political imperatives. It becomes difficult, then, to imagine how one might write a history of 'homosexuality', since this category did not exist as a way of conceptualizing experience before the nineteenth century. Instead, one would have to focus on the *representation* of homosexual relationships, to trace the various images, narratives, roles and categories which were available to different cultures in the past.

Since this book is concerned with the literary representation of erotic relations between men from the Renaissance to the twentieth century, the question of what terminology to use is important. I adopt the word 'homosexual' as an adjective, because it is closer to being a neutrally descriptive term than any other. Nevertheless, it is inevitably anachronistic, and should be understood simply as pointing to the general area of sexual attraction between men. I avoid using 'homosexual' as a noun, because it implies a permanent and definitive identity which is often inappropriate and coercive. The word 'homoerotic' is usually applied to feelings rather than acts, and particularly denotes the admiring, desiring gaze which one man may direct at another, or the images which elicit such a gaze. As a wider term than 'homosexual', it applies to feelings which may never be acted upon, and is therefore particularly apposite for literature which articulates longing but rarely describes consummation. Eve Kosofsky Sedgwick in her book *Between Men* introduced the word 'homosocial' to describe that intense male bonding which characterizes so many dominant groups in modern society. There may be a tenable distinction between the homoerotic and the homosocial, but are they part of a continuum or sharply opposed? At what point does one man's admiration of another's masculine physique and prowess pass into desire for sexual possession? The boundary between admiration and desire is often rigorously policed, which points to an anxiety that the distinction may be unstable. Clear dividing lines between the homosexual, homoerotic and homosocial are often blurred or reworked in literary texts, whose primary function as works of art is indeed to refine and enlarge our commonplace modes of perception.

Pondering the social history which is epitomized in this linguistic history, it is apparent that these categories have been neither stable nor clear. In many cases sexual relations between men seem to have been invisible, for people often chose not to see what was going on, or chose a wealth of other terms for what they did see. The mesh through which people of past cultures saw the world was very different from our own.

The differences between the categories through which various cultures perceive sexual relationships between men can be illustrated from two past societies, ancient Greece and Renaissance England. The love which the Greeks most often celebrated was that between adult and adolescent males. The difference in age is important, for Greek texts often specify that the most desirable male body is one which is on the verge of manhood, when the beard is just beginning to grow; moreover, they make it clear that the relationship is partly an educational one. The older man (the *erastes* or 'lover') gives the younger man (the *eromenos* or 'beloved') his knowledge and experience, guiding the youth's intellectual and moral development. It was also important that the adult male should not compromise his honour as a citizen by adopting a subordinate role during intercourse with boys or slaves; nor should he sell himself. The surviving evidence suggests that the Greeks were not concerned about what we would call orientation: they did not feel any pressure to draw a dividing line between men who liked sex with women, and men who liked sex with men. Instead of marking out divisions based upon the gender of a man's partner, they perceived divisions based upon the power relationships involved: it would be demeaning for an adult citizen to be in a subordinate position in *any* sexual relationship or encounter.

Quite different categories were in place in Renaissance England, which located 'sodomy' as one of a series of crimes against nature and God, against the social and divine orders. These were crimes of which anyone was capable if sufficiently dissolute: they were signs not of a specific sexual preference or orientation, but of wickedness. As Alan Bray has shown, sodomy was associated by theologians and jurists with treason and heresy, and these offences against the very order of things revealed a shadow world which threatened to overwhelm Protestant England. The agents of darkness were not only sodomites but witches, werewolves, Jesuits and traitors. Against this picture of sodomy as a subversive and even demonic act, we need to set two contrasting facets of Renaissance life. The first is the everyday domestic fact that men regularly shared beds and slept naked. Beds were expensive, privacy was a luxury. Masters and servants, tutors and students, and men who were just good friends might share beds, and the bed no doubt became a companionable private space in which secrets were exchanged, and the bonds of affection and obligation which cemented Renaissance society were nurtured. Whatever else happened when men shared beds was normally no one else's business. It was chiefly when other personal grudges or wider social and political pressures arose that an adverse construction could be placed upon the companionship of two men. If a social climber shared a bed with a powerful aristocrat, and began acquiring power himself, those courtiers whom he displaced might well find that charges of sodomy became convenient. The perception that affectionate physical closeness between men denoted 'sodomy' seems to have been discontinuous. The second point is that Renaissance literature offered a repertoire of homoerotic narratives, dramatic roles and poetic expressions which might be relished by readers and provide them with imaginative spaces which they could inhabit, temporary private worlds which no one could police.

The problem for a modern reader confronted by a culture which is mapped out in these terms is that it seems to lack not simply clarity in its conception of homosexual behaviour, but any possibility of giving the individual a single or coherent sexual identity. Today it may well have cost a gay man a lot to arrive at the point of being able to say 'I am gay', and such a mode of self-definition, once achieved, is not lightly surrendered, even in our imaginative transactions with the past. But it would be anachronistic to expect a Renaissance reader to seek his sense of identity primarily through his sexual behaviour. Ultimately, what gave the Renaissance world its sense of coherence was religion, and this shaped a man's self-understanding; secondarily, the hierarchical social order provided the roles for everyday living. It may not have mattered that the categories through which homosexual behaviour was conceptualized did not altogether mesh: a man might fulfil his social duties as husband and father and still enjoy the erotic pleasures of sleeping with his friend, and reading Barnfield's *The Affectionate Shepherd*. One needs to allow Renaissance readers multiple sources for their sense of themselves, and perhaps a more discontinuous sense of identity than we might now envisage.

The question at issue here might be phrased very simply as 'What did they see?'; or more fully as 'What were the most important fields of meaning which were brought into play when they thought of two men making love?'. The Greeks looked and expected to see *eros* at work (a complex notion to which we shall return); to see an educative relationship which would lead the younger partner into citizenship and wisdom, while the older partner came to understand the Beautiful and the Good through his delight in the beautiful body of the youth. Renaissance Englishmen looked and often saw nothing; or saw two friends whose male bonding was a proper part of a strong society; or saw pleasurable experimentation which was a temporary variation from the duties of marriage; or they saw a vile, demonic threat to the very fabric of godliness and government. What you see depends upon what you need to see.

The most influential modern work on how categories of sexual behaviour have been constructed and reconstructed is that of Michel Foucault. In the introductory volume to his unfinished series *The History of Sexuality*, he contests the assumption that sexual desire is a strong disruptive force which is simply repressed or contained by the power of the state and official culture. Power does not operate simply through prohibition and blockage, he says, but in a more far-reaching way by making sexual desire visible and articulate in terms which then make it manageable. The categories through which this happens changed between the Renaissance and the present, with a shift from an interest in acts to an interest in persons:

> As defined by the ancient civil or canonical codes, sodomy was a category of forbidden acts; their perpetrator was nothing more than the juridical subject of them. The nineteenth-century homosexual became a personage, a past, a case history, and a childhood, in addition to being a type of life, a life form, and a morphology, with an indiscreet anatomy and possibly a mysterious physiology. Nothing that went into his total composition was unaffected by his sexuality. It was everywhere present in him . . . less as a habitual sin than as a singular nature . . . The sodomite had been a temporary aberration; the homosexual was now a species. (*The History of Sexuality, Volume I*, p. 43)

Nineteenth-century medicine developed specialized categories in which these deviants were described and contained: classification builds an elaborate conceptual prison.

Foucault insists that man was compelled to become a confessional animal, made to admit his 'perversions' not as acts which anyone might perform, but as elements which defined his very existence as a person. It is now through sex that an individual becomes intelligible to society and to himself; sex provides the ultimate meaning of a life. Foucault sees power as anything but monolithic, as inhabiting a whole network of relationships which make up society. Potentially there should therefore be innumerable sites of resistance to the pressures of categorization through which power operates, and yet the rhetoric of Foucault's writing tends to imply that we are caught within a giant prisonhouse. His idea of confession, for instance, does not allow for the creative dislocation which an individual may apply to the words which are given him. Foucault makes considerable use of the notion of the subject, describing the kinds of subjectivity which are fashioned through an individual's relations with power; and yet once again we miss a recognition of the space which individuals create for themselves through their acknowledgement of other kinds of authority, especially their reading of literature. No culture is efficiently hermetic or monolithic, and both individuals and groups play intricate games of self-fashioning through the imaginative resources which are made available by art.

The remainder of this chapter will consider two mythologies of homosexual love and desire which have been particularly influential: Plato's linking of homoerotic love with the pursuit of philosophy, and Freud's analysis of how homosexual orientation comes about.

PLATO'S MYTHS

Because the ancient Greeks regarded homosexual relationships as an ordinary part of life, and because their culture had such a high standing in England, writers who sought a language and a justification for love between men often travelled to Greece, either literally or in their imaginations. Greek statues of the nude male form helped

to fashion eighteenth-century taste, and Greek or vaguely Mediterranean settings became common in homoerotic poetry in the nineteenth century. But a recurring attraction for writers was the praise
of homosexual love which could be found in the pages of Plato
(*c.* 429–347 BC). To Renaissance writers he was known chiefly via
the Neo-Platonism of Marsilio Ficino and others, whose translations and commentaries emphasized Plato's spiritual teaching and
fashioned an accommodation between his philosophy and Christianity. A few scholars read him in Greek, but it was not until the
early nineteenth century that Shelley's rendering of the *Symposium*
made that text readily accessible, while Benjamin Jowett's translation of the complete dialogues appeared in 1871. As Wilde's reference to Plato suggests, he became the point of origin for a
homosexual canon, but he could also be a pretext for courtship: in
Maurice Clive prepares the ground for his declaration of love by
urging his friend to read the *Symposium*, while in *The Charioteer*
Laurie receives a copy of the *Phaedrus* from the head prefect as a
scarcely coded message.

In the all-male world which provides the settings for Plato's
dialogues, it is assumed that adult men naturally desire beautiful youths, and in the *Protagoras*, the *Charmides* and the *Lysis* the
pleasures and pains of such love are made the starting point for
philosophical discussion. The pursuit of wisdom evidently does not
entail any rejection of the body, or the suppression of its desires:
rather, the reader is seduced into philosophy through erotic invitations, and encouraged to see that a knowledge of (and a delight
in) the body is the starting point for other kinds of knowledge.
Love of male beauty leads to love of beauty and truth in their
abstract forms, and so to wisdom.

Plato's most extended discussion of love between men is found
in the *Symposium*. During a banquet at the house of Agathon the
participants take it in turns to speak in praise of *eros*. This word
means 'strong desire' as distinct from *philia*, which is affection. The
speeches offer varied – and indeed incompatible – understandings
of *eros*, which (except in the contribution by Aristophanes) is always
taken to apply to love between men. Phaedrus begins (178a–180b)
by saying that while the poets write hymns of praise for other gods,
no one has yet offered proper praise to Eros. (Eros was depicted by
the Greeks as a god, but was also thought of as a strong feeling in
an individual: the same is true of other feelings such as courage or
madness. Since the Greeks wrote only in capital letters, there is no

ready distinction between *Eros* the divinity and *eros* the feeling.) Phaedrus tells us that lovers wish to live 'beautifully', which may conjure up visions of Wildean aesthetes until we recall that in the Greek moral vocabulary the beautiful and the good were closely linked. The lover will be ashamed to be seen doing anything shameful by his beloved, he says, and so this desire to live beautifully in the eyes of the loved one is an important source of moral conduct.

The next speech, by Pausanias (180c–185c), argues that there are two kinds of *eros*, the vulgar one and the heavenly one; the latter is called *Ourania* (from *ouranos*, 'heaven'), a name which was revived by the Uranian poets of the later nineteenth century. The vulgar form of *eros* lacks discrimination: it leads men to love women no less than boys, to love bodies rather than souls, and to have no care for any beauty in the act of love. The heavenly form leads men to the male, delighting in what is 'by nature stronger and possessed of more intelligence'; men inspired by such an *eros* 'do not love boys except when they begin to get intelligence, that is, when they are on the verge of getting a beard'. For Pausanias this form of love seeks a life-long commitment, such lovers being 'prepared to be with them through the whole of life and pass their lives in common, rather than deceiving them by catching them in the thoughtlessness of youth and then contemptuously abandoning them and running off to someone else'. (This life-long relationship is apparently what Pausanias enjoys with Agathon, and it seems to have been unusual in Athenian society.) Pausanias recognizes, however, that other societies take a different view: in many places ruled by barbarians such love is held shameful – as is philosophy, for rulers do not like their subjects to have lofty ideas or strong associations.

For Pausanias the dividing line runs between those who value the soul and the intellect along with physical beauty, and those on the other hand who are capable of no such discrimination. The gender of the partner is not in itself an issue, but the sort of man who is drawn by *eros* to women is heedless of the intellectual and moral dimension to love, which can only be at work in *eros* with boys. The category of the unacceptable 'other' which Pausanias creates here contains men who love only women, men who seduce boys and abandon them, barbarians who disapprove of homosexual love, and tyrants who hate philosophy. By contrast, 'we' are the Athenian intellectuals (and perhaps specifically the followers of Socrates) who conduct our erotic affairs on a higher plane. Even so, Pausanias admits that some Athenians make sure that their sons' tutors protect them from any erotic approaches from men, so apparently there were Athenians who distrusted both homosexual relations and Socratic teaching. There is no single philosophy of *eros* operating either in Athens or in the *Symposium* itself.

The speech of Aristophanes (189c–193e) provides a remarkable myth for the origin of love, and one which seems to divide human sexual attraction into homosexual and heterosexual categories. Once upon a time, he says, human beings were round, with four arms, four legs, and two faces. They were of three sexes, male, female and androgynous. These humans tried to storm heaven and displace the gods, so as a punishment Zeus decided to cut each of them in two. The separated halves rushed to embrace each other, and this is what humans have been doing ever since: 'Eros then is a name for the desire and pursuit of wholeness'. Much of Aristophanes' speech is comic in its imagination and vocabulary: a modern human 'is but the token [that is, tally, a notched stick split in two] of a human being, sliced like a flatfish', while the original humans, far from being sublime and beautiful in their wholeness, were comical creatures, spherical and eight-limbed, who ran by tumbling in somersaults.

Aristophanes' myth seems to provide an explanation (a 'just so story') for how it happened that some human beings are heterosexual and others homosexual. But his account is clearly tendentious. The humans who result from the original hermaphrodite will tend to be adulterers, he says, so they can hardly provide a norm for sexual behaviour, nor is there any suggestion that heterosexual love can provide a happy fulfilling marriage. The women who are halves of the original woman will turn out to be lesbians, and this category may well have struck Athenians as strange, for this is the only extant reference to lesbians in Attic prose: at the very least readers will have been unaccustomed to any mention of lesbian sex in a serious treatment of *eros*. Aristophanes' account of the men who seek their lost half in other men is also peculiar. First, it attributes an active sexual desire to the boys themselves, those junior and supposedly passive partners who according to this account positively delight in sex with men. These, he says, are the most manly sort of men, because they seek out what is masculine, and are not to be called shameless; and yet the Old Comedy of which Aristophanes is a representative had poked fun at eminent politicians for allegedly submitting as youths to homosexual advances either shamelessly or

for money. A further irony is the suggestion that it is difficult to
know what lovers of any kind actually want to achieve:

> No one can think it is for the sake of sexual intercourse that the
> one so eagerly delights in being with the other. Instead, the soul
> of each clearly wishes for something else it can't put into words;
> it divines what it wishes, and obscurely hints at it.

In this suggestion that what lovers seek is not sexual satisfaction
but something more elevated, we may hear Aristophanes mocking
the Platonic idealization of love – and perhaps at the same time
hear Plato mocking Aristophanes as one whose vision was too limited. What Aristophanes offers is a myth of the origin of *eros* which
is often eloquent but is also comic in its tone, tendentious in its
classifications, and limited in its vision. Like the other speeches in
the *Symposium*, it presents only one version of *eros*.

Socrates himself avoids the appearance of providing a definitive
account of *eros* by disclaiming any personal insight, and presenting
what he has to say in the form of a conversation which he recounts
between himself (in the role of the slow pupil seeking enlightenment)
and the wise woman Diotima (201d–212a). She tells him that Eros
is neither god nor human but a *daimon* midway between the two.
He is a lover of the beautiful, and so he is a philosopher (literally,
'a lover of wisdom'), for wisdom is among the most beautiful of
things. *Eros* is also the love of immortality: some men express this
through the procreation of children, but others are pregnant in their
souls. Such a man desires something beautiful in which he may
beget his intellectual offspring, and so seeking a beautiful soul in
a beautiful body he undertakes the task of education. But this relationship is in part physical, for 'in touching the beautiful person
and holding familiar intercourse with him, he bears and begets
what he has long since conceived'. Such offspring are poems, and
laws, and philosophy. But this is not an end in itself. Diotima explains that the lover who is guided rightly will progress as it were
up a ladder: he will move from love for a single beautiful body to
love for all kinds of physical beauty, then to the beauty of the soul,
to the beauty of various forms of human knowledge, and finally to
the Beautiful itself; and it is in the contemplation of the Beautiful
itself that human life is to be lived.

This lofty vision – of *eros* as the motivating force which impels
us in an ascent towards contemplation of those ultimate realities, the

'Ideas' or 'Ideal Forms' which Plato held to be the true and eternal forms of the world – would be the climax of the *Symposium* were it not for the abrupt entry of the drunken Alcibiades. Now the love between Alcibiades and Socrates is brought into play, with Socrates complaining that ever since he fell in love with Alcibiades it has been impossible for him even to look at another pretty boy without Alcibiades becoming madly jealous. This teasingly alters yet again the expected picture of Greek homosexual relations, and more surprises are to follow. Instead of speaking in praise of *eros*, Alcibiades speaks in praise of Socrates; instead of speaking in praise of beauty and youth, he speaks of Socrates as being like a *silene*, a clay model which on the outside represents an ugly or grotesque old man, but when opened reveals the golden figure of a god. So despite all this cult of beauty and youth, the wisest of men is old and ugly. Alcibiades also tells us of his repeated attempts to seduce Socrates: proud of his own beauty, and confident that he is irresistibly attractive, Alcibiades has defied the passivity conventionally assigned to the younger partner and set out to acquire the most prestigious possible *erastes*; but in spite of all Alcibiades' most blatant advances, Socrates has remained unmoved. Amid this cult of sexually-based friendships between adults and adolescents, the wisest of men turns away from the beautiful boy's offer.

The *Symposium*, then, provides an anthology of views of *eros*, most of which are at once imaginative and moving, yet also partial and tinged with absurdity. *Eros* has led the speakers into blindness as well as insight, and each attempt to build conceptual frameworks has revealed the inadequacy of such structures, however appealing they may seem. Even the speech of Diotima seems to have departed some way from the usual notion of *eros*, and to be recommending a kind of life which not even Socrates has achieved. There is no conclusion. Eventually Socrates argues and drinks the others into submission, and as dawn breaks he leaves them asleep, steals out, and starts his day.

In the *Phaedrus*, the practical problem of constructing a convincing speech to persuade a boy to submit to his lover is made the starting point for a philosophical enquiry into the nature of the soul. Phaedrus has acquired a copy of a speech by the rhetorician Lysis which argues that it is better for a handsome boy to submit to someone who is not in love with him than to one who is. As Socrates reclines in the shade to the sound of the cicadas, Phaedrus reads him the speech. Socrates is not impressed, and is persuaded to make a better one himself. But after finishing his own speech he is anxious that it may be considered an affront to the god Eros, and so he makes amends in a speech arguing the opposite case. This oration is much longer and more philosophical than the first one, and centres on the nature of the soul.

The soul, says Socrates, is like a chariot pulled by two horses, one black, one white, and driven by a charioteer (253c–256e). The white horse is tractable, a lover of glory, temperance and modesty; the black horse is hot-blooded, wanton and hard to control. What happens when the lover approaches the beloved? Before the soul entered the human body, it had enjoyed the contemplation of true being, and some faint memory of that vision remains in the more enlightened souls. When such a soul now sees a beautiful form, it responds first with reverence, then with ferment. When the driver of the soul's chariot sees the loved one, a sensation of warmth suffuses the soul. The white horse is constrained by modesty, but the black horse rushes ahead and drags the chariot close to the beloved. As he approaches, the charioteer's sight of the beautiful boy stirs his memory of the earlier vision of Beauty itself and evokes reverence; the unruly black horse forces the chariot to approach the beloved, but is restrained from making a violent assault by the white horse and the charioteer. The beloved receives services from the lover, welcomes his companionship, and gradually comes to feel an emotional response: 'as he continues in this converse and society, and comes close to his lover in the gymnasium and elsewhere, that flowing stream which Zeus, as the lover of Ganymede, called the "flood of passion", pours in upon the lover'. This stream turns back and enters the eyes of the beloved, filling his soul in turn with love: 'he feels a desire – like the lover's, yet not so strong – to behold, to touch, to kiss him, to share his couch, and now ere long the desire, one might guess, leads to the act'. The black horse in the beloved's soul also swells with desire, though without knowing what this is for. If the charioteers and the white horses keep control, then the two will enjoy a philosophical life of self-mastery and inward peace; if the black horses are occasionally given their head, the pair will still be dear friends, though their bond will be less profound. Even so, they too have taken a crucial step on the road to the good life.

In this myth the black horse of sexual desire needs to be controlled if the relationship is to achieve its philosophically satisfying potential. Yet the black horse is instrumental in bringing the two men

together, for without it the lover would merely admire the beloved
from afar, and the whole speech is devoted to the proposition that
it is *eros*, not mere friendship, to which the boy should respond, for
'he who is not a lover can offer a mere acquaintance flavoured with
worldly wisdom'. This, of course, is Socrates' view as represented
by Plato for the purposes of this rhetorical display; it is not necessarily Plato's view, and certainly not a normative Athenian or Greek
view. But it has proved to be a highly influential myth, and has a
marked resemblance to the triple structure of the psyche (id, ego
and super-ego) delineated by Freud.

FREUD'S MYTHS

Sigmund Freud (1856–1939) was the principal contributor to the
understanding of selfhood which twentieth-century man employs,
and his writings about sexuality have significantly influenced the
structures of thought through which we interpret homosexual relations. Though based upon an analysis of a small sample of disturbed patients from Vienna before the First World War, Freud's
ideas have attained a much wider, mythic power. His thought was
not monolithic, however, and the texture of those works in which
he discusses homosexuality reveals uncertainties and contradictions, significant complications of the ostensibly clear lines of presentation. Moreover, Freud's unresolved struggles with his own
homosexual feelings complicated his closest professional relationships, notably those with Wilhelm Fliess and Carl Gustav Jung. A
brief exploration of Freud's treatment of this subject may identify
both the strengths and the fissures in what is still the dominant
modern mythology of homosexuality.

'We ourselves speak a language that is foreign' (xiv, 341) said
Freud. It is one of those sentences which for a gay reader italicizes
itself on the page. If the language of the ordinary world is foreign
to its users because it does not arise from their own point of origin
but is always something other than their own – a framework into
which they must enter, and through which their sense of themselves is created – then so much the more is a gay man compelled
to speak a language that is foreign. Particularly pertinent, then, are
the moments when Freud explores the cluster of ideas associated
with the home and the point of origin.

In his essay *The 'Uncanny'* (1919) the meanings of the 'homely' and the 'uncanny' (*heimlich* and *unheimlich*) are shown not to be opposites, but to generate and qualify each other in a weird movement. In one definition, 'everything is *unheimlich* that ought to have remained secret and hidden but has come to light' (xiv, 345). In another usage, *heimlich* may mean something which is hidden and therefore dangerous, in other words, *unheimlich*. This lexical instability which gathers around the ideas of self/not self, homely/strange, safe/dangerous, has implications for the understanding of sexuality: the genitals are called *heimlich*. Perhaps, then, our sense of the self (and our communal definitions of what is homely and acceptable) may be unstable, and the place of safety may also be the place of danger. In Freud's analysis of the semantic field of the *heimlich*, language is seen to patrol the boundary between self and non-self, insisting that some things are homely, others alien, while at the same time being unable to make these categories watertight.

The image of the disrupted home – and the consequent search for unconventional compensations for this in adult life – features prominently in Freud's essay *Leonardo da Vinci and a Memory of his Childhood* (1910). Many of the documents upon which Freud draws are of questionable status: Leonardo's notebooks are only partly legible; some information and conjectures are supplied from a novel by Merezhkovsky; and much hinges upon Freud's dubious perception of a bird-like form in the folds of the Madonna's drapery in the painting 'Madonna and Child with St Anne'. Not only is Freud writing without first-hand contact, he is interpreting texts which he himself has selected and partly created, instead of listening to the stream of free association produced by a patient. If anything, this makes the edifice of interpretation which Freud constructs all the more revelatory of his attitudes towards male homosexuality.

For Freud, Leonardo's early home shows both a lack and an excess. He was an illegitimate child, and suffered from having an absent father. However, he had two mothers, first his natural mother, with whom he spent his early years and to whom he was intensely close, and second the childless wife of his father, into whose care he had been transferred by the age of five. The factual accuracy or otherwise of Freud's account is less significant for us than the mythological power of the pattern which he creates: the homosexual man comes from a home which is unhomely, in that it lacks a father; he is then displaced into a second home where he belatedly meets the father (who is, but should not be, a stranger); the stepmother redoubles the maternal influence while displacing the original mother, who is now herself made a stranger. The *heimlich* and the *unheimlich* exchange places. Thus the homosexual man is formed: an intense, erotic attachment to the mother, along with the lack of the father who should have been able to 'ensure' the 'correct' choice of sexual object by his son.

> The child's love for his mother cannot continue to develop consciously any further; it succumbs to repression. The boy represses his love for his mother: he puts himself in her place, identifies himself with her, and takes his own person as a model in whose likeness he chooses the new objects of his love. In this way he has become a homosexual. What he has in fact done is to slip back to auto-erotism: for the boys whom he now loves as he grows up are after all only substitutive figures and revivals of himself in childhood – boys whom he loves in the way in which his mother loved *him* when he was a child. He finds the objects of his love along the path of *narcissism*, as we say; for Narcissus, according to the Greek legend, was a youth who preferred his own reflection to everything else. (xiv, 191–2)

In its aetiological form this explanation has its obvious deficiencies, and Freud himself says that 'we are far from wishing to exaggerate the importance of these explanations of the psychical genesis of homosexuality . . . What is for practical reasons called homosexuality may arise from a whole variety of psychosexual inhibitory processes' (xiv, 192). But despite Freud's own explicit acknowledgement in *Three Essays on the Theory of Sexuality* that the heterosexual object-choice requires explanation just as much as the homosexual one (vii, 57), the need to explain origins and causes arises primarily with homosexual cases. Freud was a doctor seeking the cause of psychic conditions which generate physical symptoms, but he was also a mythmaker fashioning a myth of origins for homosexuality. This deploys a repertoire of images of deviation, for 'inhibitory processes' produce the homosexual by preventing the natural course of growth. Freud's pathology seems to deploy images from fluid mechanics: Leonardo

> had merely converted his passion into a thirst for knowledge . . . and at the climax of intellectual labour, when knowledge had been won, he allowed the long restrained affect to break loose and

to flow away freely, as a stream of water drawn from a river is allowed to flow away when its work is done. (xiv, 164)

So the childhood of Leonardo is marked by both lack and excess; the usual forward movement of the child along the course of life is impeded, and there is a regression into a previous state. When the adult male loves other males, Freud sees these others only as versions of the earlier self; these lovers are called boys, not men; they replicate the disadvantaged child, locking him into a state of immaturity and auto-eroticism. Various important possibilities are excluded here: that it might be the boys' otherness that attracts, their difference in physique or temperament from either the adult or the juvenile Leonardo; or that these 'boys' are young men whose virile masculinity attracts him. To Freud they are androgynous figures, 'beautiful youths of feminine delicacy' (xiv, 210). Freud's perception of adolescent males as feminized boys similarly colours his account of Greek homosexuality, for he claims that in ancient Greece 'what excited a man's love was not the *masculine* character of a boy, but his physical resemblance to a woman as well as his feminine mental qualities – his shyness, his modesty and his need for instruction and assistance' (vii, 56).

In Freud's account the home which Leonardo fashioned for himself as an adult male repeated both the excess and the incompleteness of his own childhood. Leonardo was a prolific artist, but Freud stresses the number of his works which remained incomplete, as if this were an inevitable or at least a wholly appropriate characteristic of a life which lacked sexual completion. Freud notes that 'when he had become a Master, he surrounded himself with handsome boys and youths whom he took as pupils ... we may take it as ... probable that Leonardo's affectionate relations with the young men who – as was the custom with pupils at that time – shared his existence did not extend to sexual activity. Moreover a high degree of sexual activity is not to be attributed to him' (xiv, 162). Freud provides no argument for thinking that Leonardo's relationships with his apprentices were unconsummated, nor does he explore the historically particular conditions which made certain kinds of sexual behaviour likely or acceptable: governing his analysis is an overriding myth of lack. That Leonardo carefully kept track of his apprentices' expenses is interpreted as a sign of a 'particularly strict and parsimonious head of household'. But why is this construed as parsimony rather than prudence? Instead of sensible management, it is seen as an anxious hoarding of resources by one who cannot spend in love or in sex. Yet even this household failed in its principal artistic purposes: Leonardo's works were left unfinished, while his preference for pupils who were beautiful rather than talented meant that he had no worthy successors. Neither paintings nor protégés turned out to be satisfactory offspring.

But the myth of wholeness which Freud implicitly invokes is itself suspect. Few childhoods are exempt from some form of emotional lack or excess, and aspects of those ideals of wholeness which the child inherits from his parents often need to be fragmented and refashioned in adult life. The link between emotional fulfilment and finished works of art is also dubious, for there is no necessary causal link (and only an imprecise metaphorical one) between the two kinds of completion. This is not to say that Freud's essay on Leonardo is wrong or even implausible, simply that it enacts a myth of emotional lack, arrested development and the need for compensation which has had a powerful and not wholly beneficial influence upon our period's understanding of homosexual men.

The origin and development of homosexual inclinations is given most extended treatment in Freud's *Three Essays on the Theory of Sexuality* (1905). He begins by questioning two important preconceptions about 'inversion' (the late nineteenth-century term which Freud generally uses). Inversion should not be regarded as a form of degeneracy, because the physiological functioning of the body is not impaired, and because it is found in people 'who are indeed distinguished by specially high intellectual development and ethical culture'. Moreover 'inversion was a frequent phenomenon – one might almost say an institution charged with important functions – among the peoples of antiquity at the height of their civilization', and 'even amongst the civilized peoples of Europe, climate and race exercise the most powerful influence upon the prevalence of inversion and upon the attitude adopted towards it' (vii, 49–50).

This leads to the question of whether inversion is innate or acquired. Freud classifies inverts into three groups: those whose sexual objects are always of their own sex; those whose sexual objects are sometimes of their own and sometimes of the opposite sex; and those 'contingent inverts' who under external conditions (for example, in prison) take satisfaction from a partner of their own sex. Freud asserts that only in the case of the first group, the 'absolute inverts', might their object-choice be innate, and even among this group there are many cases where a tendency to homosexuality can be traced to a sexual impression in early childhood, or some other external influence. But since many people are subjected to the same sexual influences with different consequences, Freud rejects the idea that a homosexual object-choice is always acquired. 'We are therefore forced to a suspicion that the choice between "innate" and "acquired" is not an exclusive one or that it does not cover all the issues involved in inversion' (vii, 51). Freud halts the explicit search for origins at this point, but continues to pursue this issue in other ways.

The model which he offers for the original state of human sexuality is 'polymorphous perversity': 'a disposition to perversions is an original and universal disposition of the human sexual instinct and . . . normal sexual behaviour is developed out of it as a result of organic changes and psychical inhibitions occurring in the course of maturation' (vii, 155). In this original state the child makes no distinction in its choice of sexual object; it exists in the psycho-analysts' equivalent to the political theorists' state of nature, in which all men have rights to anything. The disposition to perversions of every kind is therefore a universal human characteristic. According to this model, human sexuality is like a stream which at first spreads out promiscuously over the landscape, and requires to be dammed and channelled in order to produce 'normal' object choices. The perverse is original, the normal is acquired. This 'freedom to range equally over male and female objects – as it is found in childhood, in primitive states of society and early periods of history, is the original basis from which, as a result of restriction in one direction or the other, both the normal and the inverted types develop' (vii, 57).

What, then, produces a homosexual object choice in later life? The intervention of a boy's father to prevent his sexual experimentation, together with the competitive Oedipal relationship with him, deflects him from an interest in his own sex (vii, 153). Where this paternal intervention is lacking, the necessary deflection may not occur. Perversions arise 'as a collateral filling of subsidiary channels when the main current of the instinctual stream has been blocked by "repression"' (vii, 156). Here the image of the stream reappears: if, instead of meeting the dams which direct its course towards normal maturity, it now encounters blockages in its path, it will spill over into the secondary channels of perversity. Perversion is again imaged as both excess and lack: excess in that it is a flooding of instinct into alien territory, lack in that it constitutes a stalling of progress at (or even a reversion to) an early stage in development. Perversions, says Freud, either '(a) *extend*, in an anatomical sense, beyond the regions of the body that are designed for sexual union, or (b) *linger* over the intermediate relations to the sexual object which should normally be traversed rapidly on the path towards the final sexual aim' (vii, 62). Perversions are thus a kind of perpetual fore-play. They are also fixations upon infantile sexual interests which ought to have been left behind on the road to adulthood.

Despite Freud's challenging idea that the normal is a development from the perverse, rather than the other way round, many elements in his discussion of homosexuality represent a man's choice of another man as his sexual object as a parodic version of heterosexual choice. He says that '*paedicatio* with a male owes its origin to an analogy with a similar act performed with a woman' (vii, 65). In some cases the invert feels that he is a woman in search of a man, but many others retain masculine mental qualities, and 'what they look for in their sexual object are in fact feminine mental traits' (vii, 55). In this account the desire of a man for another man is imagined as anything but desire by the masculine for another version of masculinity: it is the love of mother for child, of feminine for masculine, of the masculine for femininity in boys, of a man for his own image – but never the desire of one adult male for another autonomous adult male. This insistence shapes Freud's depiction of Greek homosexuality, which makes the *erastes* and *eromenos* analogous to a nineteenth-century husband and his child-bride, like David and Dora Copperfield.

In some respects, however, Freud's mythology creatively challenges the stability of contemporary classifications. The normal is achieved as a product of the perverse; heterosexual object-choice needs explanation; homosexual orientation cannot be explained as simply innate or simply acquired. Moreover, homosexuality is neither a crime nor a disease, as nineteenth-century theorists asserted. In a letter written in 1935, in English, to an unknown American lady who had sought advice about her son's homosexuality, Freud said:

> Homosexuality is assuredly no advantage, but it is nothing to be ashamed of, no vice, no degradation; it cannot be classified as an illness; we consider it to be a variation of the sexual function, produced by a certain arrest of sexual development. Many highly respectable individuals of ancient and modern times have been

homosexuals, several of the greatest men among them (Plato, Michelangelo, Leonardo da Vinci, etc.). It is a great injustice to persecute homosexuality as a crime – and a cruelty, too. (*Letters*, pp. 419–20)

For its date it is an enlightened and generous statement.

Freud was fascinated by archaeology, by the treasures which it uncovered but also by its grand project to recover the structures of the past. Indeed, he saw himself as an archaeologist of the mind. Discussing the psychoanalyst's role, he wrote:

Imagine that an explorer arrives in a little-known region where his interest is aroused by an expanse of ruins, with remains of walls, fragments of columns, and tablets with half-effaced and unreadable inscriptions . . . he may start upon the ruins, clear away the rubbish, and, beginning from the visible remains, uncover what is buried. If his work is crowned with success, the discoveries are self-explanatory: the ruined walls are part of the ramparts of a palace or a treasure-house; the fragments of columns can be filled out into a temple; the numerous inscriptions, which, by good luck, may be bilingual, reveal an alphabet and a language, and, when they have been deciphered and translated, yield undreamed-of information about the events of the remote past, to commemorate which the monuments were built. *Saxa loquuntur!* (*Standard Edition*, iii, 192)

Saxa loquuntur: the stones speak. But they rarely do speak, not without interpretation. Whatever the merits of this haunting image as an analogy for the work of psychoanalysis, it prompts us to realize how different from such a work of reconstruction is the process of understanding those literary texts which speak – or can be made to speak – of homoerotic desire. Freud imagines that once upon a time there was a complete and coherent fabric whose shape can be deduced from the fragments that remain; that there was a language which is preserved in legible records and can even be translated into other known tongues by the aid of bilingual inscriptions; that these were public monuments, the work of an official culture. The process of deciphering is easy, because the cipher is so open. By contrast, the literary texts which address homoerotic desire often use a language which cannot easily be deciphered because it is not complete and coherent: it lives within known languages, at a tangent to them; it is a tissue of quotations and silences, an undertow of strangeness within a language which we thought we knew. Instead of recovering complete and familiar forms from fragments, we may need to fragment completed literary forms in order to read the desires half-hidden in them. And if it seems to us that instead of a legible literary history we have a pile of fragments which we cannot fit together into imaginable ways of living, we may have to acknowledge that the power of heterosexual culture has made much of our history irretrievable. 'We ourselves speak a language that is foreign.' It has been one of the achievements of literature to mitigate that foreignness which has been imposed upon homosexual readers by creating imagined spaces for them to inhabit; and it is the aim of the remainder of this book to make those spaces accessible, at least partially, to modern readers, to challenge and to enhance our own imagined worlds.

2
The Renaissance

Ma: You mean Ed's a friend-friend or a euphemism-friend?
Arnold: He used to be a euphemism, now he's just a friend.
Harvey Fierstein, *Torch Song Trilogy* (1984) p. 59

THE BONDS OF MASCULINITY

Freud's excavations in the psyches of his patients generally took
him back to buried incidents and desires of a sexual nature (the
'secrets of the alcove', his mentor Charcot called them). Partly as
a result of Freud's work, our contemporary mythologies about ourselves include the assumption that hidden sexual feelings or behaviour could, if brought to light, reveal some ultimate, definitive truth
about a person: our identity is often thought to be, at root, our sexuality. When a tabloid newspaper drags someone out of the closet,
the 'truth' about them is 'revealed'. We might therefore expect the
presence of homosexual feelings or anxieties in literary texts to be
signalled through silences and secrecies, which may be uncovered
through ingenious readings, much as buried trains of thought may
be elucidated through the 'Freudian slips' mapped in his study *The
Psychopathology of Everyday Life* (1901). These are not assumptions
which apply readily to the culture of the English Renaissance. A
man's sense of himself, of his identity and his meaning, was derived
principally from his religious belief and his social position, and
there is no evidence that men defined themselves according to the
gender of their sexual partners. Such classification would be at odds
with the kinds of erotic pleasures which we meet in Renaissance
literature, where there is often a variety of viewpoints and desires.
Indeed, many works are open texts which invite the reader to engage
in a range of imaginative erotic pleasures.

Among these pleasures, explicitly sexual desire between men was
articulated in many classical texts which were freely available to
Renaissance readers. Some of these texts speak openly of homosexual
attraction, and many allow the reader the pleasurable contemplation

25

of youthful male beauty. Ovid's *Metamorphoses* (read by every school-boy) included the stories of Adonis, Narcissus and Hermaphroditus, all beautiful youths who resisted advances by women, while Ovid also tells how Orpheus, after the loss of his wife Eurydice, turned away from women and took pleasure only in boys. Orpheus sings of the love of Jove for Ganymede, Apollo for Hyacinthus, and Sylvanus for Cyparissus. Virgil's *Eclogue* II tells of the shepherd Corydon's unrequited love for Alexis. This poem was widely read, though it was evidently the subject of some anxiety, for Erasmus advised teachers not to use it, and several editors and translators interpreted it allegorically to refer to Virgil's poetic ambitions. Readers of Latin would also have come across lyrical homosexual desire in Horace's *Odes*, epigrams about sex between men in Martial, stories of the homosexual debauchery of the Roman emperors in Suetonius, and satires against a whole gamut of sexual behaviour in Juvenal. Classical literature (normally read and discussed within an all-male milieu) would have represented a wider variety of sexual desires and pleasures than vernacular texts, and the *Metamorphoses* in particular would have suggested that identities are not fixed, and desire not single. For those who were philosophically inclined, Plato's works were available in Greek, or in Latin translations, though Ficino's commentary on the *Symposium* elevated *eros* to something almost unrecognizably mystical. Besides providing readers with imaginative enjoyment, these texts furnished writers with narratives, images and allusions which could be explicitly reworked, or deployed less overtly to give a homoerotic subtext to writing which was ostensibly concerned with heterosexual love.

Renaissance culture also provided various kinds of private space for the reader and his imagination. Elizabethan architecture offered new opportunities for privacy: small chambers or closets, secret alcoves, large window recesses, seats and bowers within the gardens. The medieval habit of reading aloud even when alone was displaced by the practice of silent reading, enveloping the reader in the privacy of silence. Private notebooks were used for recording favourite texts. Books were cheap enough for a man to own an Ovid or a Horace which he could annotate, slip into a pocket or lock away in a chest. Renaissance readers had many places of privacy in which their imaginations could play freely. They were also taught ways of engaging with their texts which made readers into editors, commentators and writers. Most Renaissance editions of the classics surrounded the words of the original text with an apparatus of notes and paraphrases, multiple interpretations from which the reader could select for himself. He would have been encouraged at school to note down maxims, images and striking examples for use in his own compositions, but the texts which a reader composed might be imaginary, emotionally charged dreams, not just formal written compositions. A reader would have a repertoire of images, narratives and roles from which to construct imaginative possibilities for himself. But the construction of a single, coherent 'self' might not be a part of such a reader's project, for there seem to be discontinuities in the fabric woven by Renaissance writers at just those points where we might look for wholeness and singleness of purpose. The 'I' of Renaissance love poetry is a persona, a mask or an assumed voice, not the private interior self of the man writing the lines. When Donne in his *Songs and Sonnets* says 'I' or 'we', there is no means of knowing what autobiographical element (if any) there may be in such poems: the 'I' and the 'we' are experimental roles which are tried out, developed and discarded.

The Renaissance male was brought up within a society where many of his most important relationships were with other men, and within this masculine culture the bonds of affection, loyalty and obligation were often passionate. 'Love' was what bonded friends, neighbours, kinsmen and households. In some societies the boundary between the homosocial and the homosexual is rigorously policed, and any expression which could be construed as hinting at erotic desire between men would disrupt the masculine world. It appears that this may not have worried men in Renaissance England, who freely shared beds, embraced and kissed, and used highly-charged language for their bonds of friendship and social obligation. Perhaps a range of emotion and erotic feeling was allowed, and seen as enhancing rather than endangering the masculine milieu. For example, an eroticized version of an educational relationship is seen in the elegies which Richard Crashaw wrote as a student for the Cambridge don William Herrys, in which the blazon of physical features (a familiar poetic technique for describing female beauty) is deployed in order to display Herrys' learning; but his physical beauty is attractive in itself, and the love which he inspires in other men is not simply love of virtue and scholarship:

> in the centre of his breast
> (Sweet as is the phoenix' nest)
> Every reconcilèd grace

> Had their general meeting place . . .
> His mouth was rhetoric's best mould,
> His tongue the touchstone of her gold . . .
> . . . to his sweetness, all men's eyes
> Were vowed love's flaming sacrifice . . .
> [he died] Ere Hebe's hand had overlaid
> His smooth cheeks with a downy shade.

('His Epitaph', ll. 17–46)

The acceptance of such eroticism may also have extended to physical sex: Nicholas Udall's career as a headmaster was not ruined when it became known that he was buggering the boys at Eton. There were indeed anxieties, but they seem to have been local and occasional rather than universal and structural. The picture which one gleans from historians is of a culture where bonds between males of unequal social status (James I and the Duke of Buckingham, Francis Bacon and his servant) were sometimes given sexual expression; this may have disconcerted those whose sleep or whose prospects of advancement were disturbed, but did not generally lead to the terrible punishment for 'sodomy'. At the same time, it is necessary to remind ourselves that the death penalty lay in wait for anyone convicted of sodomy, and some satirists (like 'T.M.' in *Microcynicon*) made clear their hatred of sodomites, ingles and catamites. It is not surprising in such a climate that literary texts sometimes blurred distinctions between different kinds of male relationship, or offered alternative, safer, ways of reading homoerotic images and narratives. The capacity to deny that anything untoward was intended could be (quite literally) vital.

An example of the discontinuous, or even contradictory, character of writing about homosexual relations is provided by the classical figure of Ganymede. This boy was desired by Zeus ('Jove' to the Romans), who took the form of an eagle and carried him up into heaven to be his cupbearer. Sometimes 'Ganymede' is used contemptuously in Renaissance English as a pejorative term for the younger, passive partner in a relationship, as in several satires on London life and in some poems on the relationship between James and Buckingham. In Henry Peacham's emblem book *Minerva Britanna* (1612) there is an image of Ganymede with these verses:

> Upon a cock here Ganymede doth sit,
> Who erst rode mounted on Jove's eagle's back;

One hand holds Circe's wand, and joined with it
A cup top-filled with poison, deadly black;
　The other medals, of base metals wrought,
　With sundry monies, counterfeit and nought.

These be those crimes abhorred of God and man
Which Justice should correct with laws severe:
In Ganymede the foul sodomitan;
Within the cock vile incest doth appear;
　Witchcraft and murder by that cup and wand,
　And by the rest, false coin you understand.

(p. 48)

Ganymede is seated not on the imperial and divine eagle, but on a bird which parodies it, a farmyard cock; he carries a cup of poison instead of wine or nectar, along with the wand of Circe, the enchantress who in the *Odyssey* turned men into swine. In his other hand he carries a collection of counterfeit coins and medals made from base metals. All these images which cluster around Ganymede associate him with parody and counterfeit. The second stanza construes these emblems as representing crimes which merit the severest punishment from a ruler. By contrast, George Wither's *A Collection of Emblemes* (1635) uses a picture of Ganymede mounted on the back of an eagle, and explains how the boy was washing himself when Jove 'his naked beauty spying/ Sent forth his eagle'; the interpretation this time is spiritual:

By Ganymede, the soul is understood,
That's washèd in the purifying flood
Of sacred baptism . . .
The eagle means that heav'nly contemplation
Which after washings of regeneration
Lifts up the mind from things that earthly be
To view those objects which faith's eyes do see.

(p. 156)

This translates the Greek myth into an allegory of Christian immortality, completely erasing any sexual implication. Two writers looking at the Ganymede myth saw different meanings; similarly, the actual male friendships which flourished in this period were (and still are) capable of multiple interpretations (see Plate 2).

Within the network of male social bonds, many men evidently found emotional satisfaction in a passionate relationship with another man which they did not find with women. Construing those relationships, and interpreting the ways in which they were represented in literature, leads us into areas where certainty is impossible, and indefinition actually seems to have had important advantages. If we try to pin down the difference between love and friendship, we find that the vocabulary for such relationships in Renaissance English is significantly ambiguous, with different terms covering similar semantic fields. The point can be made with some examples from Shakespeare.

'Friend' could be used to greet a stranger, particularly a social inferior: thus Viola greets the Clown in *Twelfth Night* (III. i. 1). It could mean 'relation' (*OED* 3): a lady in *The Two Gentlemen of Verona* (III. i. 106–7) has been promised in marriage 'by her friends/ Unto a youthful gentleman'. It could mean someone of the same sex with whom one is specially intimate, a relationship implying comradeship, loyalty and trust (the word echoes through *The Two Gentlemen of Verona* as Valentine is betrayed when his friend Proteus steals his girl). The word can be used between men and women who are in love, but not yet married or sexual partners: thus the virginal Perdita calls Florizel 'my fairest friend' and 'my sweet friend' (*The Winter's Tale* IV. iv. 112, 128). But 'friend' can also mean 'sexual partner' (*OED* 4): Caesar says that Antony is Cleopatra's 'friend' (*Antony and Cleopatra* III. xii. 22); in *Measure for Measure* Claudio 'hath got his friend with child' (I. iv. 29). In these last two examples 'friend' may be an ironic euphemism, slyly suggesting how the relationship has moved beyond friendship. But it can also be used with full, unironic force, as Juliet – aching with love and longing as Romeo is forced to leave after their first and only night together – calls him 'Love, lord, ay husband, friend' (*Romeo and Juliet* III. v. 43). In this case the last of those names cannot be an anticlimax. The ambiguities of this word can be richly exploited to imply meanings without being committed to them, to avoid definition. What kind of 'friend' is the friend in Shakespeare's *Sonnets*? In what sense is Antonio in *The Merchant of Venice* Bassanio's 'friend'? When Iago assures Roderigo that he is his 'friend' (*Othello* I. iii. 337), the two are of similar social status and comrades in skulduggery; but when Othello calls Iago –

who is his military subordinate – 'my friend' (V. ii. 155) this signi-
fies the depth of dependency into which Othello has sunk. And
when Iago tells Othello that Desdemona has been 'naked with her
friend abed/ An hour, or more' (IV. i. 3–4), he can be sure that
Othello will understand what sort of 'friend' to his wife Cassio has
become. The web woven by these usages delineates the shifting
bonds of trust within and between the sexes.

'Lover' applies to a similar range of relationships. It can simply
mean 'well-wisher' (*OED* 1): when Ulysses says to Achilles 'I as
your lover speak' (*Troilus and Cressida* III. iii. 213) he is simply
claiming to give him helpful advice. More strongly, 'lover' can mean
'one in love with someone' (*OED* 2; the *OED* tells us that this only
happens between people of opposite sexes). Shakespearean comedy
is full of besotted 'lovers' who moon around looking melancholy
and dishevelled, courting their loved ones. But could 'lover' also
mean 'sexual partner' in Renaissance usage as it does today? The
OED is ignorant of this usage in any period, but Shakespeare seems
to use the word with these implications. 'Lover' moves towards its
modern sense in *Measure for Measure*, when Claudio's sister Isabella
is told that 'your brother and his lover have embraced' and that
his lover is consequently pregnant. In this instance 'lover' might
still mean 'one who is in love' or 'one who is being courted', but
it clearly has a sexual meaning when Antony says that he will run
towards death 'as to a lover's bed' (*Antony and Cleopatra* IV. xiv. 101),
or when Juliet longs for the night which will bring her first love-
making with Romeo, and says: 'Lovers can see to do their amorous
rites/ By their own beauties' (*Romeo and Juliet* III. ii. 8–9). As with
'friend', the ambiguities of 'lover' proliferate creatively. In which
of these senses is the poet of Shakespeare's *Sonnets* using 'lover'
about himself in relation to the young man (32.4; 55.14; 63.12)? In
what sense is Antonio the 'dear . . . lover' and even the 'bosom lover'
of Bassanio (*The Merchant of Venice* III. iv. 7, 17)? The semantic
ambiguity is important in creating multiple possibilities. We cannot
decide on a single meaning without careful reference to the context,
and in the case of male/male relationships the context may be a
society where civilized neighbourliness and passionate sexual love
inhabited the same continuum and spoke the same language. Literature which exploits the variousness of such terms is not concealing desire behind gestures of secrecy or obfuscation, but speaking
of desire within an open (and yet almost indecipherable) fabric.

Some works include gestures which would contain homoerotic

material within a socially acceptable framework, or would cancel out what has just been said. Richard Barnfield's *The Affectionate Shepherd* enacts (as we shall see) a blatantly homosexual courtship, and yet the preface to his subsequent collection *Cynthia* (whose title invokes Diana, goddess of chastity) attempts a disclaimer: addressing 'the courteous gentlemen readers' he says:

> Some there were that did interpret *The Affectionate Shepherd* otherwise than (in truth) I meant, touching the subject thereof, to wit, the love of a shepherd to a boy; a fault the which I will not excuse, because I never made. Only this, I.will unshadow my conceit ['idea']: being nothing else but an imitation of Virgil, in the second *Eclogue* of Alexis. (pp. 115–16)

Yet *Eclogue* II is a clearly homosexual poem, and Barnfield's own poems which follow this preface to *Cynthia* are no less explicit about their sexual passion and the gender of its object than those in his first collection. It is almost a gesture which confirms while appearing to cancel. In Spenser's *The Shepherd's Calendar* (1579), dedicated to Sidney, there is a note by the editor 'E.K.' (who may be Spenser's friend Edward Kirke, or may be Spenser's fictional persona) concerning the character Hobbinol in the eclogue 'January':

> In this place seemeth to be some savour of disorderly love, which the learned call *paederastice*, but it is gathered beside his meaning. For who that hath read Plato his dialogue called *Alcibiades*, Xenophon, and Maximus Tyrius of Socrates' opinions, may easily perceive that such love is much to be allowed ['approved'] and liked of, specially so meant as Socrates used it: who saith that indeed he loved Alcibiades extremely, yet not Alcibiades' person but his soul, which is Alcibiades' own self. And so is *paederastice* much to be preferred before *gynerastice*, that is, the love which enflameth men with lust toward womankind. But yet let no man think that herein I stand with Lucian or his devilish disciple Unico Aretino, in defence of execrable and horrible sins of forbidden and unlawful fleshliness, whose abominable error is fully confuted of Perionius and others. (p. 17)

Later on, E.K. identifies Hobbinol with Gabriel Harvey, so perhaps he felt that some explicit denial of homosexual interest was needed if readers were drawing parallels with living people. But the invocation of the Greeks fails to answer the questions which are raised. Not only does E.K. oversimplify Greek love, and unjustifiably seek to remove its physical dimension, he also sets up a ludicrous interpretation of Hobbinol's love for Colin, who had said that albeit

> my love he seek with daily suit,
> His clownish gifts and curtsies I disdain,
> His kids, his cracknels, and his early fruit.

(p. 16)

The parallel between Hobbinol and Socrates is comically inappropriate; the obvious parallel has actually been provided by E.K. in his previous note which refers us to Virgil's *Eclogue* II. Whether this is E.K.'s ineptitude or Spenser's wit, it is clear that the homosexual content of the eclogue is not cancelled by the invocation of the Greeks. The gesture of denial and containment undoes itself, leaving the text open to the reader – indeed, inviting him to ponder the possible significance of what E.K. has so usefully drawn to his attention. Ineffective closure actually opens the text.

THE MALE BODY IN THE READER'S GAZE

The reader who delights in the male body can create a safe area in the mind for this contemplation, free from censorship and interruption. In some cases this imaginative contemplation of the male body will be carried out in response to clear invitations from the text that a homoerotic engagement is expected; in other cases, the reading will be against the grain of the text, a pleasure derived in spite of clear signals that a heterosexual interest is presupposed.

Many passages in Christopher Marlowe's *Hero and Leander* (1598) imply not simply a male reader, but one who takes a homoerotic interest in Leander. Marlowe's descriptions of the two lovers are markedly different in focus. The account of Hero concentrates on her clothing, emphasizing its fantastic artifice and highlighting details which signal that a woman's beauty is deceitful and dangerous (i. 9–36). The description of Leander, by contrast, focuses on his naked body and makes it the object of masculine interest (i. 51–90). His hair is uncut (a sign of masculine strength, like Samson's), but we are told that if it had been shorn, and available as a separate object of desire, it would have allured those Greek heroes who sailed with Jason in pursuit of the Golden Fleece. Hippolytus (the youth who rejected the advances of his stepmother Phaedra) would also have desired Leander, while both 'the rudest peasant' and 'the barbarous Thracian soldier' sought his favour: he appeals, then, to a spectrum of masculinities from the rough to the virginal. Further mythological references guide our responses: Jove might have sipped nectar from his hand as if Leander were another cupbearer like Ganymede, while Leander's beauty exceeds that of Narcissus, another emblem of male/male desire and of the rejection of woman. Diana, the virgin goddess of the moon and of chastity, grows pale because she cannot be embraced by him, so the only woman in this passage represents a wan, unsatisfied desire. The framework of allusions constructs Leander unambiguously and almost exclusively as an object of men's interest and longing. At the same time there is danger here too: Leander's back is like Circe's wand in the *Odyssey*, which can transform men into animals, unlocking their desires and fantasies.

The reader's gaze is led delightedly into the erotically enticing details of Leander's naked form. First the unshorn hair, then the straightness of the body; an implicit invitation to sip nectar with the tongue from Leander's hand, followed by the suggestion that his neck is 'as delicious meat is to the taste'. His creator's

> immortal fingers did imprint
> That heavenly path with many a curious dint
> That runs along his back,

> (i. 67–9)

and as the reader's eye follows this path the fingers trace it too. The word 'curious' meant 'beautifully wrought' (*OED* 7) and 'dainty, delicate' (of food or clothing: *OED* 7b), so this is a wondrous work of art which can be displayed and perhaps consumed. In contrast to Hero's elaborately artificial costume, Leander's naked body is a true work of art, created lovingly by the gods. By making Leander 'all that men desire', and celebrating his power to attract gods and all kinds of men, Marlowe suggests that he will be irresistible to the reader also. At the same time, the passage clearly inhabits a mythological world, so that this desire is framed and removed from the everyday. Thus the male reader's desire for Leander is encouraged and confirmed, yet placed safely within the world of the imagination, that private sphere of enjoyment and experimentation.

A second episode of homoerotic pleasure is offered to the reader in the description of Leander swimming the Hellespont to reach Hero. When Leander has 'stripped him to the iv'ry skin' (ii. 154) and jumped in, the sea god Neptune plays around the youth as he swims:

> He clapped his plump cheeks, with his tresses played,
> And smiling wantonly, his love bewrayed.
> He watched his arms, and as they opened wide
> At every stroke, betwixt them would he slide
> And steal a kiss, and then run out and dance,
> And as he turned, cast many a lustful glance,
> And threw him gaudy toys to please his eye,
> And dive into the water, and there pry
> Upon his breast, his thighs, and every limb,
> And up again, and close beside him swim,
> And talk of love. Leander made reply,
> 'You are deceived, I am no woman, I.'
> Thereat smiled Neptune . . .

> (ii. 181–93)

And the reader smiles too, understanding that Neptune knows exactly what he is doing, and sharing the pleasure which the god derives from playing around the youth's naked body. To seduce the youth, Neptune tells him the story of a shepherd's love for a boy, but Leander will not listen. The angry god throws his mace at the boy, but recalls it and it strikes his own hand. Leander's pity for Neptune's wound is interpreted by the god as love; men in Elizabethan texts regularly implore women to have 'pity' on them, meaning to reciprocate their sexual passion. But Neptune has mis-read Leander's feelings, and the boy remains unresponsive. Marlowe writes:

> In gentle breasts
> Relenting thoughts, remorse and pity rests.
> And who have hard hearts and obdurate minds,
> But vicious, harebrained, and illit'rate hinds?

> (ii. 215–18)

Obdurate hearts are associated with uncouth and illiterate people, so to return sexual passion is a sign of a virtuous and civilized man – like the implied reader of this poem. Marlowe does not offer the reader any homosexual consummations, and weaves into his text a strand of unfulfilment. The poem itself remains unfinished. But there is an imaginative consummation offered to the reader, who is invited to explore Leander's naked body not only with the eyes, but with hand and tongue as well. The act of reading invited by Marlowe's text is an explicitly homoerotic pleasure.

The reader is differently situated in Francis Beaumont's *Salmacis and Hermaphroditus* (1602), a retelling of the story from Ovid's *Metamorphoses* in which the fifteen-year-old son of Hermes and Aphrodite is pursued by Salmacis, a nymph who lives in a pool. The description of Hermaphroditus stresses the boy's rosy face and white skin (conventional in Elizabethan accounts of female beauty) and brings in another kind of eroticism by saying that 'his leg was straighter than the thigh of Jove': adolescent male beauty would seem to combine feminine colouring with masculine strength. Purity is one of his characteristics, and he seeks 'clear watery springs to bathe him in/ (For he did love to wash his ivory skin)' (ll. 87–8). Hermaphroditus is attracted by the nymph, but as he gazes on her he is much more attracted by the reflection of himself in her eyes. She warns him about the fate of Narcissus, and begins to touch him: his hand is whiter than mountain snow, whereas her palm is moist (a sign of lechery):

> Then did she lift her hand unto his breast,
> A part as white and youthful as the rest,
> Where, as his flowery breath still comes and goes,
> She felt his gentle heart pant through his clothes.

> (ll. 797–800)

She continues to explore his face, but he resists and she pretends to leave. Up to this point Hermaphroditus has been explored by female hands, and the reader finds Salmacis intruding between himself and the youth. When Hermaphroditus thinks that he is alone,

> he did begin
> To strip his soft clothes from his tender skin,

When straight the scorching sun wept tears of brine,
Because he durst not touch him with his shine,
For fear of spoiling that same ivory skin
Whose whiteness he so much delighted in;
And then the moon, mother of mortal ease,
Would fain have come from the antipodes
To have beheld him, naked as he stood
Ready to leap into the silver flood,
But might not; for the laws of heaven deny
To show men's secrets to a woman's eye.

(ll. 837–48)

We are explicitly made voyeurs, because we are told that the boy is behaving as if no one saw him. The waters weep because they do not wholly possess him; the sun weeps because he cannot touch him for fear of spoiling that very beauty in which he delights; and the moon would have come to gaze on the naked youth were this not forbidden. These secrets are for men's eyes alone. Salmacis sees him, however, and is 'almost mad' with desire:

When young Hermaphroditus as he stands,
Clapping his white side with his hollow hands,
Leapt lively from the land whereon he stood,
Into the main part of the crystal flood.
Like ivory then his snowy body was,
Or a white lily in a crystal glass.

(ll. 859–64)

Salmacis jumps in after him but Hermaphroditus still resists her, and so the gods grant Salmacis the fulfilment of her prayer that they should not be separated, and the two are fused into one, the first hermaphrodite.

This poem articulates the anguish of the desiring gazer who can do no more than gaze. It offers some voyeuristic pleasures, but no details specifically reward homosexual desire. When Hermaphroditus stands on the riverbank, sun and moon are equally enamoured, and if the reader is as interested in the boy as the sun is, then his desiring gaze is just one more amongst several others: Beaumont creates no special place for it as Marlowe had done, even though he says that men's secrets are for men alone. Perhaps the poem speaks primarily to a homosocial audience about the voraciousness of a woman's sexual desire, which has resulted here in the destruction of the lad's purity and his masculinity. In this instance a homoerotic gaze has to insert itself into a text which makes no special provision for it, but which permits it as one possible response amongst other kinds of masculine interest in the story.

Richard Barnfield's *The Affectionate Shepherd* (1594) is the most explicitly homoerotic text from the English Renaissance. It expresses the unrequited love of the shepherd Daphnis for the boy Ganymede. 'Daphnis' is not only the name of the poem's speaker, it is also the name which Barnfield uses to sign the preface dedicated to Penelope Rich (the Stella of Sidney's *Astrophil and Stella*): author and persona are thus associated in an unusually explicit way. Barnfield presents a rudimentary narrative framework in which Ganymede is also being courted by Queen Gwendolen, who is herself being courted by an old man, though this attempt to create a rivalry for possession of Ganymede (or a choice for Ganymede himself between suitors of different genders) is not developed. There is also a confusing drift into moralizing advice at the end of the first poem, when Daphnis appears to resign himself to not winning Ganymede, and instructs him on how to live a good married life. *The Affectionate Shepherd* therefore presents us with several structural confusions or uncertainties. What is unambiguously clear about this work, despite Barnfield's disclaimer in the preface to *Cynthia*, is that it voices an adult male's sexual passion for a beautiful young man, urges him to reciprocate, and seeks physical consummation. Is there a link between the structural incoherence of the work and the clarity with which the homosexual desire is expressed? Has Barnfield reached the limits of what can be said? Barnfield is only an intermittently accomplished poet, but lack of literary skill will not account fully for his failure in certain crucial areas: his inability to create a convincing persona for Daphnis, who ages and changes, but not as part of any emotional or psychological narrative which we can follow; his hesitation over the relationship between author and persona, as if he knows that some disguise is necessary, but is uneasy with a distanced, fictionalized 'I'; his difficulty in developing a narrative of sexual desire between men; and his confusion over how to end the story, for Daphnis' despairing farewells in *The Affectionate Shepherd* are followed by a series of passionate sonnets in *Cynthia*.

There seems to be a barrier in the way of imagining the narrative consequences of such an explicit and overwhelming homosexual passion. Perhaps these dislocations and irresolutions within Barnfield's text result from him coming perilously close to forcing the reader into construing this love as 'unlawful and forbidden fleshliness', in E.K.'s phrase.

There is no doubt about the nature of the desire which Barnfield's text expresses: this is not affection or friendship, but a courtship which seeks physical satisfaction. The object of Daphnis' passion is described in terms which are familiar from the Elizabethan poets' praise of female beauty:

> If it be sin to love a sweet-faced boy,
> (Whose amber locks trussed up in golden trammels
> Dangle adown his lovely cheeks with joy,
> When pearl and flowers his fair hair enamels)
>   If it be sin to love a lovely lad,
>   O then sin I, for whom my soul is sad.
>
> His ivory-white and alabaster skin
> Is stained throughout with rare vermilion red,
> Whose twinkling starry lights do never blin
> To shine on lovely Venus, beauty's bed,
>   But as the lily and the blushing rose,
>   So white and red on him in order grows.

> (pp. 79–80)

The reader is invited to reply, 'this is no sin'. This is not an anxiety which is attached only to homosexual love, for Sidney raises a comparable question in *Astrophil and Stella* (sonnet 14), where he insists that his love loathes 'all loose unchastity'. Yet the sin of Astrophil's potentially adulterous devotion to Stella, and the sin of Daphnis' infatuation with Ganymede do not fall into the same category, even though Barnfield's protective dedication to Lady Rich might wish us to think so. Daphnis wants his beloved to respond with 'pity':

> O would to God he would but pity me,
> That love him more than any mortal wight;
> Then he and I with love would soon agree,

That now cannot abide his suitor's sight.
　O would to God (so I might have my fee)
　My lips were honey, and thy mouth a bee.

Then shouldst thou suck my sweet and my fair flower
That now is ripe, and full of honey-berries;
Then would I lead thee to my pleasant bower,
Filled full of grapes, of mulberries and cherries;
　　Then shouldst thou be my wasp, or else my bee,
　　I would thy hive, and thou my honey be.

I would put amber bracelets on thy wrists,
Crownets of pearl about thy naked arms . . .
. . . by a silver well with golden sands
　I'll sit me down, and wash thine ivory hands.

　　　　　　　　　　　　　　　　　　　　　　(p. 82)

This elaborates on the offerings of the love-lorn shepherds in Virgil's
Eclogue II and Marlowe's 'The Passionate Shepherd to his Love',
with additional erotic language which may have been informed by
the hymn to male beauty in the biblical *Song of Songs*. Barnfield's
eroticism delights in images of ripeness and consumption (taste is
a dominant sense), in the abundance of precious metals, and in
intimate private spaces, the 'cool cabinets' which the lovers will
share. The domestic and the exotic, the natural and the artificial, are
mingled. The longed-for consummation (which never arrives as part
of the narrative) is already present here in this imagined world. It
is an impossible place, of course, an over-abundant and bejewelled
romance space, which in itself seems to signal the impossibility of
fulfilment; and it is also a fragmented, discontinuous space, for
unlike Spenser in fashioning the Bower of Bliss or the Garden of
Adonis in *The Faerie Queene* (II. xii; III. vi) Barnfield cannot imagine
a single coherent space which could be the scene of love's consummation, but instead deploys a series of separate images. Neither
do Daphnis' images of consummation suggest any equality or reciprocity between the two, for if Ganymede were to accept Daphnis'
offers, then Daphnis would only adorn Ganymede's limbs, and
gaze on him as he sleeps or bathes. The imagination remains that
of the gazer: consummation would consist of an eternal courtship.
Fruits are offered, but none received. Yet any other representation of
homosexual consummation is unthinkable in this period, and what

the poem offers through its narrative gaps is space for the reader to imagine satisfaction. The tense of the verb in 'Then shouldst thou suck my sweet and my fair flower/ That now is ripe' ostensibly signals the deferment of pleasure to an unrealizable future, yet the reader will have no difficulty in translating this into an image of consummation in the present – and no difficulty in imagining the kind of sexual satisfaction which those images figure.

Barnfield occasionally tries to suggest that the love is other than physical, but the attempts collapse. Daphnis argues that while Gwendolen loves Ganymede for his beauty, he loves him for his 'qualities divine' and for his 'virtue' (p. 85). Yet Daphnis' sexual interest in the boy has been plain enough: he has asked him to be 'my boy or else my bride' (p. 88), and offered to 'hang a bag and bottle at thy back' (p. 87) – which is not simply providing him with a packed lunch. Not for nothing is this described as a 'prick song' (a technical term for a melody or descant accompanying a simple tune). Little has been said about Ganymede's beauty of soul; indeed, he has been rebuked for being mercenary: 'Thou suck'st the flower till all the sweet be gone,/ And lov'st me for my coin till I have none' (p. 83). When Ganymede's beauty fades, Gwendolen will lose interest, whereas Daphnis 'will still admire with joy those lovely eyen' (p. 85); eyes may disclose the soul, but the phrasing suggests that Daphnis' interest is still physical. Such gestures attempt to place the love on a more exalted, quasi-Platonic level, but fail to displace the overwhelmingly erotic interest.

The second lamentation heaps yet more gifts at Ganymede's feet (including a golden tennis racket and a fan of phoenix feathers), but Daphnis soon turns to despair. He interprets Ganymede's lack of interest as pride, moves on to a moral sermon against pride, and then offers Ganymede advice on how to live happily with his wife. As in *Hero and Leander* and Shakespeare's *Sonnets*, the sexual consummation between men is half-hidden: consummation looks like courtship, bawdy jokes and sensual images speak of physical intimacies, but on the narrative level the boy is given up to women.

If extended narrative caused Barnfield problems, a collection of sonnets might have been easier, since they allow a focus upon a single mood or argument. In sonnets from his second collection, *Cynthia* (1595), the lack of reciprocity and the impossibility of consummation remain dominant themes: merely the dream of a kiss rejuvenates the ageing speaker in sonnet 6, while in sonnet 8 the unsatisfied gazer is still longing for a kiss:

> Sometimes I wish that I his pillow were,
> So might I steal a kiss, and yet not seen . . .

(p. 126)

Only in sonnet 11 is there some exchange between the two, when the speaker admits to his beloved that love is the reason for his sorrow:

> 'And what is she', quoth he, 'whom thou dost love?'
> 'Look in this glass', quoth I, 'there shalt thou see
> The perfect form of my felicity.'
> When, thinking that it would strange magic prove,
> He opened it: and taking off the cover
> He straight perceived himself to be my lover.

(p. 127)

But this revelation leads nowhere, and no narrative follows this disclosure. The last sonnet in the sequence (20) speaks of a muse 'toiled with continual care' who has no power to speak persuasively; the speaker still craves reciprocity from his beloved, but this plea for 'pity' – which is the poem's last word – goes unanswered. In the following 'Ode', Daphnis' love for Ganymede has been overwhelmed by another passion:

> Love I did the fairest boy
> That these fields did ere enjoy;
> Love I did fair Ganymede,
> Venus' darling, beauty's bed;
> Him I thought the fairest creature,
> Him the quintessence of nature:
> But alas, I was deceived
> (Love of reason is bereaved),
> For since then I saw a lass,
> Lass that did in beauty pass
> Pass fair Ganymede as far
> As Phoebus doth the smallest star.

(p. 133)

This may seem to describe how an unsatisfied, immature homo-sexual passion is displaced by a more adult heterosexual one, until we find that the woman's name which is written on the shepherd's heart is 'Eliza': it is the Queen who has attracted Daphnis' devotion. Thus we have an ending which is not an ending, for although the shepherd dies broken-hearted, it is not through despair of Ganymede; Ganymede is displaced from the shepherd's affections, but not by a woman who can reciprocate sexually. This form of closure may leave desire unsatisfied on a narrative level, but it leaves intact the world of homoerotic play in a perpetual present which the reader has helped to construct.

By contrast with the private spaces fashioned by individual readers, the Renaissance theatre provided a playing area in which single and collective imaginations came together. The English stage used only male actors, and consequently the great passionate dramas of Antony and Cleopatra or Romeo and Juliet were, at one level, played out between men. The first encounter of Romeo and Juliet calls for the two actors to join hands, and then join lips:

> *Romeo*: . . . let lips do what hands do . . .
> Thus from my lips, by thine, my sin is purged.
>
> (I. v. 102–6)

The lovers' speeches delicately weave together into a sonnet which charts the meeting of hands palm to palm, and then the meeting of lips. The gradual achievement of physical contact is the focus of our attention. Shakespeare could have kept the lovers apart (as he does in the balcony scene) if he or his actors had felt any embarrassment about such physical contact, but he chose not to. Likewise, when Cressida says to Troilus 'Stop my mouth' (*Troilus and Cressida* III. ii. 132) he does so with a kiss; and all through this scene between the two lovers, Pandarus, as a voyeuristic audience on stage, calls our attention to what the pair are doing, or what they may be about to do. In *Cymbeline*, when Iachimo gazes at Imogen's body while she is asleep, and sees 'On her left breast/ A mole cinque-spotted' (II. ii. 37–8) we agree that it is a woman's body which has been thus revealed to him, and on stage the coverlet on the bed would have to be drawn back enough to make his perception plausible; yet we also know that the actual body whose nakedness is being read is that of an adolescent male. At such moments of physical display an audience must either choose to be unaware that these bodies are male, or choose to perceive this maleness, and perhaps enjoy the resulting homoerotic pleasures: probably many did the former, some the latter.

For John Rainolds, the puritan scholar who denounced the practice of men wearing women's clothing on stage, such kissing was an incitement to sin:

> as certain spiders, if they do but touch men only with their mouth, they put them to wonderful pain and make them mad, so beautiful boys by kissing do sting and pour secretly in a kind of poison, the poison of incontinency. (Binns, 'Women or transvestites', p. 102)

And Rainolds thought that for a male actor to don a female costume was a step towards 'that sin against nature [which] men's natural corruption and viciousness is prone to' (Binns, p. 101), citing biblical and classical examples of homosexual behaviour. However, he also thought that 'a woman's garment being put on a man doth vehemently touch and move him with the remembrance and imagination of a woman; and the imagination of a thing desirable doth stir up the desire' (Binns, p. 103). Rainolds' arguments envisage that these actors are in danger of being provoked to lust equally for either boys or women.

Would audiences also be aroused? Rainolds believed that for a man to gaze on a beautiful boy who is dressed as a woman would incite him to lust after *women*, just as much as if he were looking at a real woman:

> Can you accuse yourself, or any other, of any wanton thought stirred up in you by looking on a beautiful woman? If you can, then ought you beware of beautiful boys transformed into women by putting on their raiment, their feature, looks and fashions. For men may be ravished with love of stones, of dead stuff, framed by cunning gravers to beautiful women's likeness, as in poets' fables appeareth by Pygmalion. (Binns, p. 103)

Another puritan who distrusted the theatre, Philip Stubbs, wrote that after watching theatrical performances, 'everyone brings another homeward of their way very friendly, and in their secret conclaves covertly they play the sodomites, or worse' (Levine, *Men in Women's Clothing*, p. 22). However, in Lady Mary Wroth's *Urania*, a man who is unmoved by a woman who is wooing him is said to be 'no

further wrought than if he had seen a delicate play-boy act a loving woman's part, and knowing him a boy, liked only his action'
(Shapiro, 'Lady Mary Wroth', p. 187). So, according to Rainolds and
Stubbs, theatrical transvestism can encourage actors and spectators
to lust after boys or women; according to Lady Mary Wroth, discriminating audiences can admire (and be moved by) the histri-
onic skill of a boy actor, without ever quite forgetting that it is a
performance.

It would seem likely, then, that men in the audience could have
taken erotic pleasure in the boy actor as boy or as woman, and so
imagine the amorous encounters on stage as either homosexual or
heterosexual ones. It is for spectators to decide what it is that they
see, even though playwrights may from time to time wish to remind
them of the boy actor behind the female role. But we should not
underestimate the erotic attractions of androgynous figures, or the
excitement (an excitement fuelled partly by the threat to ordinary
identities) which is generated by cross-dressing, especially when it
is left incomplete and so offers a suggestive juxtaposition of the
masculine and feminine. An episode in Sidney's *Arcadia* suggests the
kind of double vision, and doubled pleasure, which might be
available to a male spectator viewing an attractive adolescent male
actor in female costume. Musidorus is helping his friend Pyrocles
to disguise himself as a woman; this is part of a long description:

> Upon his body he ware a kind of doublet of sky-colour satin, so
> plated over with plates of massy gold that he seemed armed in
> it; his sleeves of the same, instead of plates, was covered with
> purled lace. And such was the nether part of his garment; but
> that made so full of stuff, and cut after such a fashion that, though
> the length fell under his ankles, yet in his going one might well
> perceive the small of the leg which, with the foot, was covered
> with a little short pair of crimson velvet buskins, in some places
> open (as the ancient manner was) to show the fairness of the skin.
> (*Old Arcadia*, p. 24; the revised version in *New Arcadia*, pp. 130–1,
> presents this as a description of a woman.)

Here the reader's gaze is invited to admire the richness of fabric
and metal, the mixture of masculine and feminine attire, and the
glimpses of fair male skin. Musidorus smilingly warns Pyrocles not
to fall in love with himself like Narcissus, and admits that for his
part, 'if I were not fully resolved never to submit my heart to these

fancies, I were like enough while I dressed you to become a young Pygmalion'.

Many plays deploy a double transvestism by having female characters dress as men, usually as pages. This allows female characters to escape from danger (Imogen in *Cymbeline*) or pursue their beloved (Rosalind in *As You Like It*) or adopt social roles otherwise reserved for men (Portia as a lawyer in *The Merchant of Venice*). But it also opens out new erotic possibilities – that a female character might fall in love with such a woman in her male disguise (as Olivia does with Viola in *Twelfth Night*), or that men may find the beauty of such a boy alluring, as Orsino is drawn to Viola in her disguise as Caesario. Such double disguises, where the male actor impersonates a female character impersonating a male, allow a range of responses both to the characters and to the audience, and the playwright's refusal to define identity and feeling makes such episodes particularly enticing – and particularly unsettling. If a male character finds such a disguised woman attractive, is he responding to the masculinity, the boyishness, the androgyny, the femininity? Pleasure mixes with danger; the uncertainties are unresolved, because we know that the boy is 'really' a woman, yet is also 'really' a boy actor. In Middleton and Dekker's *The Roaring Girl*, Sebastian finds an additional pleasure in kissing his girlfriend Mary when she is dressed as a boy:

> *Moll*: How strange this shows, one man to kiss another.
> *Sebastian*: I'd kiss such men to choose, Moll;
> Methinks a woman's lip tastes well in a doublet.
> ... Troth, I speak seriously:
> As some have a conceit their drink tastes better
> In an outlandish cup than in our own,
> So methinks every kiss she gives me now
> In this strange form is worth a pair of two.
>
> (IV. i. 45–55)

And in the same play, Laxton (that is, 'Lack-stone', implying castration) is attracted by Moll Cutpurse, the roaring girl, partly because of her masculine behaviour and dress (II. i. 261–84). These plot motifs register the homoerotic undercurrents which may be at work in ostensibly heterosexual relationships, and permit the representation of homosexual desires whose overt staging would have been too dangerous: apart from Gaveston and Edward in Marlowe's *Edward II*, explicitly sexual desire is never articulated between men on the Renaissance stage unless one of the 'males' is actually a female character in disguise.

THE STORY OF EDWARD II

Several Renaissance writers told the story of Edward II and Piers Gaveston, and a comparison of the different ways in which their relationship was imagined illustrates the variety of categories through which love between men might be perceived.

In the chronicle of Raphael Holinshed (1587) the relationship between the two men is not made explicitly sexual. Edward 'set his heart upon' Gaveston and had a 'fervent affection' for him, and under Gaveston's tutelage he indulged in 'wantonness', 'voluptuous pleasure', 'riotous excess' and even 'most heinous vices'. But the nature of what Holinshed repeatedly calls Edward's 'lewdness' (which at this date just means 'wickedness') remains unspecified. Indeed, the description of Gaveston as Edward's 'procurer' casts him in the role of pimp rather than lover. Throughout Holinshed's account runs a thread which characterizes Edward as a counterfeit of true kingship, even a player-king. He had 'lightness' rather than weight, and 'counterfeited a kind of gravity, virtue and modesty'; he then began to 'play divers wanton and light parts . . . and that covertly'. Gaveston made Edward 'forget himself, and the state to which he was called', and Edward's lack of self-government is linked by Holinshed with his inability to rule the country. The court lost its decorum, and Gaveston

> furnished his court with companies of jesters, ruffians, flattering parasites, musicians, and other vile and naughty ribalds, that the king might spend both days and nights in jesting, playing, banqueting, and in such other filthy and dishonourable exercises. (p. 318)

The way Edward and Gaveston blurred social distinctions emerges as their principal offence, for the king elevated his cronies while both Edward and Gaveston 'began to have his nobles in no regard'; Gaveston even invented rude nicknames for them.

Gaveston is cast by Holinshed as the disrupter of social hierarchy, who diverted Edward's attention from the business of government. His chief crime was ambition, and his violation of national propriety is epitomized when he appropriates from the king's treasury a table and a pair of gold tressels which were popularly supposed to have belonged to King Arthur, and sends them home to Gascony. Symbolically the English state suffers from this upstart Frenchman, who holds so much power because he is the king's 'dearly beloved familiar' – a word which had a range of meanings from 'member of a household' (*OED* 1) to 'intimate friend' (*OED* 2) to 'attendant demon' (*OED* 3; from 1584). What seems to be diabolical about Gaveston is that he is close to Edward without holding a position recognized by the social hierarchy.

Holinshed's text directs our attention to the two crucial matters: government of the self and of the state. Homosexual behaviour is available as a meaning (and may be implied by the interwoven references to the Templars, as Bruce Smith suggests, and by the image of counterfeiting, which is how sodomy is represented in Peacham's emblem of Ganymede) but it is not made explicit. For Holinshed it is Edward's 'lewdness' and the way private interests have triumphed over public ones which brought about chaos, not one particular form of wickedness.

Marlowe's *Edward II* (1594) opens with Gaveston receiving a letter from the king:

> 'My father is deceased; come, Gaveston,
> And share the kingdom with thy dearest friend.'
> Ah, words that make me surfeit with delight!
> What greater bliss can hap to Gaveston
> Than live and be the favourite of a king?
> Sweet prince, I come. These, these thy amorous lines
> Might have enforced me to have swum from France,
> And, like Leander, gasped upon the sand,
> So thou wouldst smile and take me in thy arms.

> (I. i. 1–9)

Immediately the audience understands that the relationship is more than that of master to servant or friend to friend: it is overtly erotic, since there is no mistaking the tenor of 'amorous' or the allusion to Leander, which is clear enough as a myth of sexual passion even without the additional homoerotic overtones of Marlowe's version.

Indeed, when Gaveston says of Edward 'upon whose bosom let me die', the pun on the secondary meaning of 'die' as 'reach orgasm' seems in this case to be the word's primary meaning. Gaveston will arrange erotic pleasures for the king, including 'Italian masques by night' (Italians' reputation for sodomy was an Elizabethan commonplace), while the daytime entertainments which he plans seem no less enticing:

> Like sylvan nymphs my pages shall be clad . . .
> Sometime a lovely boy in Dian's shape,
> With hair that gilds the water as it glides,
> Crownets of pearl about his naked arms,
> And in his sportful hands an olive tree
> To hide those parts which men delight to see,
> Shall bathe him in a spring; and there, hard by,
> One like Actaeon, peeping through the grove . . .

(I. i. 57–66)

Here the myth of Actaeon spying on the goddess Diana as she bathes is transformed into a drama of all-male pleasure, with delighted attention directed at the boy's half-hidden parts; for this illicit pleasure the offending voyeur receives a somewhat ambiguous punishment, as he is 'pulled down, and seem[s] to die' (I. i. 69). But this expectation of pleasure is interlaced by Marlowe with indications of Gaveston's danger: he surfeits with delight; he will be the king's 'favourite'; no longer will he stoop to the peers; and he envisages that his musicians will 'draw the pliant king which way I please' (I. i. 52). These details are markers of excess, and warn us that Gaveston will exploit his relationship with Edward in order to gain power.

When Edward welcomes Gaveston, there is similarly little doubt about the homosexual character of his feelings, and there are further signs that this relationship will disturb England's social and political fabric. 'Kiss not my hand,/ Embrace me, Gaveston, as I do thee', says Edward, and he calls himself

> Thy friend, thy self, another Gaveston!
> Not Hylas was more mourned of Hercules
> Than thou hast been of me since thy exile.

(I. i. 142–4)

This reference to the love of Hercules and the boy Hylas would have been explicit enough to a classically educated audience. Edward showers Gaveston with titles and offices as if they were red roses, and when his brother objects that such preferments are too extravagantly bestowed on one of Gaveston's lowly birth, Edward responds with a rhetoric which could have come from Shakespeare's *Sonnets*:

> Thy worth, sweet friend, is far above my gifts;
> Therefore to equal it, receive my heart.

> (I. i. 160–1)

But Edward and Gaveston do not live in the enclosed, private world of the Elizabethan sonneteers. When Edward says that kingly power pleases him solely because it allows him to honour Gaveston (I. i. 163–4), and when he gives Gaveston his royal seal to command 'what so thy mind affects or fancy likes' (I. i. 169), such capricious disregard for the interests of the country can only spell trouble.

The barons are offended by Gaveston's rapid advancement, and their insults harp on his low social origins. Several times Gaveston is described as Edward's 'minion', a word which has a range of meanings from 'sexual lover' (*OED* 1a) to 'favourite friend, child or servant' (*OED* 1b) and 'favourite of a prince' (*OED* 1c). The semantic range of this word suggests that its sexual meanings could come in and out of focus as the context demanded, and this is what happens in the barons' perception of Gaveston's role. When Edward makes Gaveston sit by his side as if he were his consort, Lancaster chooses to see this not as a sexual but as a social outrage:

> Your grace doth well to place him by your side,
> For nowhere else the new earl is so safe.

> (I. iv. 10–11)

and the elder Mortimer bursts out:

> What man of noble birth can brook this sight? . . .
> See what a scornful look the peasant casts.

> (I. iv. 12–14)

Gaveston is seen as one who like Phaeton 'aspir'st unto the guidance of the sun' (I. iv. 16–17). But the focus of attention shifts when
young Mortimer asks Edward, 'Why should you love him whom
the world hates so?' (I. iv. 76). 'Love' here could simply refer to the
bonds between master and servant, ruler and subject, but where
Mortimer had left its meaning open, Edward's reply defines the
word romantically: 'Because he loves me more than all the world'
(I. iv. 77). Mortimer now acknowledges Edward's definition, but
transfers it to a mocking key: 'The king is lovesick for his minion'
(I. iv. 87).

Later the two Mortimers, uncle and nephew, discuss Edward's
relationship with Gaveston. The elder Mortimer says:

> The mightiest kings have had their minions:
> Great Alexander loved Hephaestion;
> The conquering Hercules for Hylas wept;
> And for Patroclus stern Achilles drooped.
> And not kings only, but the wisest men:
> The Roman Tully loved Octavius,
> Grave Socrates, wild Alcibiades.
> Then let his grace, whose youth is flexible,
> And promiseth as much as we can wish,
> Freely enjoy that vain light-headed earl,
> For riper years will wean him from such toys.
>
> (I. iv. 390–400)

Mortimer suggests that this is a weakness which even the greatest
warriors, kings and philosophers have indulged in, and is little
more than a youthful folly. His nephew, however, is concerned not
about Edward's 'wanton humour' but about the influence of the
upstart, and he highlights Gaveston's extravagant style of dress:

> . . . Midas-like, he jets it in the court
> With base outlandish cullions at his heels,
> Whose proud fantastic liveries make such show
> As if that Proteus, god of shapes, appeared.
> I have not seen a dapper jack so brisk;
> He wears a short Italian hooded cloak
> Larded with pearl, and in his Tuscan cap
> A jewel of more value than the crown.
>
> (I. iv. 407–14)

This speech presents Gaveston not as effeminate, but as outlandish, changeable, foreign, extravagant – the very antithesis of sober traditional Englishness.

Though Mortimer's perception is prejudiced by self-interest and class interest, we cannot avoid seeing how Edward's desire for Gaveston generates an irresponsibly casual attitude to government: after trying to placate the barons by handing out more titles, he exclaims:

> ... if this content you not,
> Make several kingdoms of this monarchy,
> And share it equally amongst you all,
> So I may have some nook or corner left
> To frolic with my dearest Gaveston.
>
> (I. iv. 69–73)

But there can be no such space. The two men are hardly ever alone together, and when we hear descriptions of their intimacy from others, the accounts are inevitably partial: Warwick says of Gaveston:

> Thus leaning on the shoulder of the king,
> He nods, and scorns, and smiles at those that pass.
>
> (I. ii. 23–4)

while Queen Isabella says that Edward

> ... dotes upon the love of Gaveston.
> He claps his cheeks and hangs about his neck,
> Smiles in his face and whispers in his ears,
> And when I come, he frowns, as who should say
> 'Go whither thou wilt, seeing I have Gaveston'.
>
> (I. ii. 50–4)

Both these speeches represent the lovers as conscious (contemptuously or resentfully) of the onlooker's gaze. When Gaveston is banished, Edward cries: 'Thou from this land, I from my self am banished' (I. iv. 118). The two men exchange pictures, a substitute for that private possession of each other which is denied them. This is a poignant scene, but like the rest of the play it is verbally re-strained, with little of the extravagant lyricism which Marlowe uses in other plays and poems. When Edward is resisting the barons' demands that Gaveston be banished a second time, he imagines living with Gaveston in defiance of the rest of the world:

> Do what they can, we'll live in Tynemouth here.
> And, so I walk with him about the walls,
> What care I though the earls begirt us round?

> (II. ii. 220–2)

But this lovers' haven is no more than a small port under siege.

Marlowe has not given us a lyrical celebration of homosexual love, or a tragedy of such love thwarted by society: *Edward II* is not a homosexual version of *Romeo and Juliet*, and it would be anachro-nistic to expect such a play to be conceivable on the Elizabethan stage. The love between Edward and Gaveston is represented as doomed not so much because it is between two men, as because it places private satisfaction before public duty, and employs the state's resources of honour and office as love-tokens. Gaveston is manipulative, Edward is irresolute. But the barons too are seeking their own advantage, while Isabella, displaced by Gaveston from her role as Edward's companion, turns to the younger Mortimer for sexual satisfaction and political influence. The play is remarkable for its sympathetic evocation of a homosexual relationship, but its conception of tragedy is common to Renaissance representations of the fall of princes, in that it shows the dire consequences which follow from the misgovernment of the passions by those entrusted with the government of the realm.

The treatment of the passion of Edward and Gaveston by Michael Drayton in his poem *Piers Gaveston Earl of Cornwall* (1593–4) offers a complex picture of an erotic attachment which seems to speak almost the same language as heterosexual love. The poem is spoken by the ghost of Gaveston, released from hell with a 'tormented heart', and so a first-person narrator is used both to voice desire and to offer moral reflections on his tragic story. Gaveston describes his young self as a paragon of beauty, a heavenly creation which combined all nature's gifts:

> A gracious mind, a passing lovely eye,
> A hand that gave, a mouth that never vaunted,
> A chaste desire, a tongue that would not lie,
> A lion's heart, a courage never daunted . . .

(p. 162)

And yet he compares his exceptional beauty to a comet or meteor, whose evanescent brilliance presages disaster. Gaveston's account of the love between himself and Edward continues to weave two threads together, for on the one hand he says that he used his beauty exploitatively as a bait to angle for Edward's love, on the other he describes the bond which results as a heavenly union:

> With this fair bait I fished for Edward's love,
> My dainty youth so pleased his princely eye:
> Here sprang the league which time could not remove,
> So deeply grafted in our infancy
>   That friend, nor foe, nor life, nor death could sunder,
>   So seldom seen, and to the world a wonder.
>
> O heavenly concord, music of the mind,
> Touching the heart-strings with such harmony . . .

(p. 163)

Gaveston muses on what it was that drew Edward to him – his beauty, or heavenly influence, or natural sympathy (a strong word in the Renaissance for the force which joins two things which belong together in nature); he reflects that the soul can be more clear-sighted than we commonly recognize in her choice of 'that which is pure and pleasing to her kind' (p. 164; 'kind' here means 'nature'). In this passage the bond between the two men is presented as entirely natural, for they are two creatures seeking out their appointed kin. And yet despite these strong assertions of mutuality and reciprocity, Gaveston also indicates that this relationship was not one between equals. Edward as prince was like Jove to Gaveston's Ganymede, and yet in the following stanza Gaveston images the difference of power between them in the opposite way: Edward took Gaveston's word as law, he was like his shadow, and was merely the echo of his voice; 'my hand the racket, he the tennis ball' (pp. 164–5). Thus we have the manipulative Gaveston becoming the power behind the throne. Drayton's poem keeps this double vision in play: love as reciprocal, beauty as exploitative; love as part of nature, lust as the force which disrupts society.

The passages in which Gaveston evokes the development of their relationship into sexual passion draw on a language which is scarcely distinguishable from that commonly used for heterosexual desire: the two men entwine their bodies like the ivy around the oak (though there may be a suggestion here that the 'wanton' ivy is a parasite on the royal oak); they act like Venus and Adonis; and they indulge in sensual delight:

> The table now of all delight is laid,
> Served with what banquets beauty could devise,
> The Sirens sing, and false Calypso played.
>
> Fraught with delight, and safely under sail,
> Like flight-winged falcons now we take our scope,
> Our youth and fortune blow a merry gale,
> We loose the anchor of our virtue's hope:
> Blinded with pleasure in this lustful game.

> (p. 166)

So the pursuit of sensual pleasure leads to the loss of virtue and innocence, a new fall of man from paradise; 'what act so vile that we attempted not?' (p. 167). What is striking about this presentation of mutual homosexual desire is that nowhere does Drayton use language which he would not have used about some illicit heterosexual affair: when the two are tempted by the Sirens of sexual pleasure, and go 'wandering in the labyrinth of lust' (p. 167), they might be Antony and Cleopatra. Indeed, this is exactly the comparison which Drayton makes (p. 191).

Nor is this moral self-condemnation the only language which Drayton allows Gaveston, for when he recounts his banishment he compares himself poignantly with the turtle dove, a favourite Elizabethan image of marital fidelity, since it mates for life:

> ... as the faithful turtle for her make ['mate']
> Whose youth enjoyed her dear virginity,
> Sits shrouded in some melancholy brake
> Chirping forth accents of her misery ...

> (p. 170)

Edward is given lines of broken-hearted farewell, more lyrical than
the equivalent in Marlowe:

> Farewell, my love, companion of my youth,
> My soul's delight, the subject of my mirth,
> My second self (if I report the truth)
> The rare and only Phoenix of the earth:
>   Farewell, sweet friend, with thee my joys are gone,
>   Farewell my Piers, my lovely Gaveston.

(p. 172)

But the tone changes again, as Gaveston admits to pride and ambition which lead him to war with the barons. Drayton's Edward goes
further than Marlowe's in surrendering his kingly power and dignity
to his lover:

> Oft would he set his crown upon my head,
> And in his chair sit down upon my knee;
> And when his eyes with love were fully fed,
> A thousand times he sweetly kissèd me.

(p. 180)

The idea that this relationship might constitute 'sodomy' is attributed to malicious enemies:

> Some slanderous tongues in spiteful manner said
> That here I lived in filthy sodomy,
> And that I was King Edward's Ganymede,
> And to this sin he was enticed by me.

(p. 194)

But this is not a classification which the poem itself seems concerned to establish. The reader's imagination is engaged by erotic
descriptions of masculine beauty and homosexual embraces, evocations of intense sensual pleasure and of profound spiritual union;
and interwoven with this extraordinarily intense narrative is an acknowledgement of the power of lust and ambition which destroyed
the two lovers and tore apart the kingdom. It is thus a story with

a clear moral content, but the homosexual character of the relation-ship is not denounced *per se*.

Drayton frequently brings in classical examples: Edward laments his exiled Gaveston as Hercules did his lost Hylas (p. 187); when they are reunited Edward clasps Gaveston as Hero clasped Leander's 'billow-beaten limbs,/ And with sweet kisses seizeth on his lips', and the two embrace like the twin gods Castor and Pollux (p. 198). Here Drayton moves without difficulty between images of classical homosexual lovers, male and female lovers, and two divine brothers. These three different kinds of relationship are, apparently, equally appropriate as ways of understanding the intense bond which united Edward and Gaveston, and this suggests a way of thinking about love between men which proceeds by means of adding together examples from different categories rather than sharply splitting off one kind of love from another. When Gaveston recounts his death at the hands of the barons, he sees himself as Adonis, his blood erotically 'staining his fair and alabaster skin' (p. 202). This myth can be made to speak about the attractiveness of Gaveston to Edward as easily as it can speak about their tragic destiny. There is no sign of discontinuity here, no suggestion that the love of Edward and Gaveston is anything but love: intense, misguided, lustful, tragic – but love. Gaveston's soul, finally conscious of sin, flies to God in true contrition (p. 203). But this is the kind of moralizing ending which we might expect from any Renaissance tale of destructive passion; nothing in Drayton's account suggests that this particular example is to be thought of as belonging to another world: in Drayton's imagination, erotic love between men is easily figured by classical stories of heterosexual lovers. No doubt other men made similar translations when constructing their own imagined worlds, reading the stories of Hero and Leander or Venus and Adonis to figure other desires.

3

Shakespeare

The course of true love never did run straight.
Alan Hollinghurst, *The Folding Star* (1994) p. 322

EDEN WITHOUT EVE

Keats described a quality 'which Shakespeare possessed so enormously – I mean *negative capability*, that is when man is capable of being in uncertainties, mysteries, doubts, without any irritable reaching after fact and reason' (letter of 21–7 December 1817). This ability to accept, even to foster, uncertainties and contradictions without always insisting on definitions and resolutions, characterizes Shakespeare's handling of relations between men. He explores 'love' between men across the full gamut of the Renaissance meanings of that word, charting the range and temper of the feelings which draw men to one another, and protecting these relationships from the tyranny of classification. Shakespeare often accentuated those passionate relationships between men which he found in his sources, working into these stories an interest in the complexities of male/ male passions. Homoerotic attraction is part of this reimagined world, colouring it at many points, but such desires are hardly ever marked out as different, let alone deviant. Only once in the entire canon is homosexual desire ridiculed, and that mockery comes from the scurrilous Thersites in *Troilus and Cressida*, to whom everything is filth. Shakespeare's imagination explores how the homoerotic can be part of the homosocial worlds which men create for themselves. As for Shakespeare's own feelings, there is simply no evidence. There are no letters or journals by him, and even the apparently personal *Sonnets* are not straightforwardly autobiographical. This has not stopped people pronouncing on how the national bard ought to have behaved and felt, but all that survives is his work, and the imagined worlds which it creates.

The idea that men might be able to inhabit an all-male world, an Eden without Eve, is a recurring dream in Shakespeare's plays.

From the outlaws in *The Two Gentlemen of Verona* who establish a new society in the forest, to the shipwrecked noblemen in *The Tempest* who are thrown together as an all-male commonwealth, Shakespeare imagines men inhabiting a timeless paradise without women. The king and his nobles in *Love's Labours Lost* vow to shut themselves away for three years to pursue their studies free from even the sight of ladies, while the deposed duke in *As You Like It* goes off into the forest with his 'co-mates and brothers in exile' to enjoy a life of pastoral innocence without 'the penalty of Adam', that change of seasons which replaced Eden's eternal summer (II. i. 1–6). Such imagined worlds are never permanent, nor are they free from tensions, for the all-male society proves incapable of being wholly self-enclosed or self-sufficient. But the regularity with which Shakespeare returned to this motif points to the power which it had over his thinking and that of his contemporaries: there was evidently a recurring need to revisit this place, to keep reflecting on why it was both necessary and impossible.

The bonds between men which flourish in these all-male worlds are frequently passionate and sometimes erotic. When Romeo's infatuation with Juliet removes him from the company of his male friends, led by Mercutio, they mock him in bawdy punning which seeks to re-establish a comfortable male subculture. Their puns show a particular interest in Romeo's 'prick' which will be 'beat . . . down' (I. iv. 28) and his 'spirit' (that is, erect penis) which Mercutio tries to 'raise up' (II. i. 24–9). When Mercutio imagines Juliet as a medlar he chooses the fruit's dialect name and says: 'O that she were/ An open-arse and thou a poperin pear', simultaneously evoking both vaginal intercourse and sodomy (II. i. 37–8). His subsequent teasing of Romeo after what he imagines to have been Romeo's night of sexual activity is full of punning references to Romeo's penis, and he offers to give Romeo an affectionate nibble on the ear for a particularly good jest (II. iv. 38–99). Homosocial play includes homoerotic play.

There is a comparable ambiguity about the interest which the voyeuristic Pandarus takes in the love-making of Troilus and Cressida. When Pandarus provides Cressida with a commentary on the Trojan soldiers who are returning from battle (I. ii.), he runs his eye over them one by one, describing their prowess and noting their 'beauty, good shape' and other qualities. Pandarus calls them 'meat', and although he is ostensibly imagining them as meat for Cressida's consumption, this is nevertheless a male gaze which is weighing up the men's sexual potential. Pandarus is partly the audience's proxy on stage, so there is an implicit invitation to male spectators to take a similar pleasure in the soldiers. Pandarus is not alone in looking on soldiers with a sexually appraising eye. Achilles says that he has 'a woman's longing,/ An appetite that I am sick withal,/ To see great Hector in his weeds of peace' (III. iii. 236–8), and when he does see Hector without his armour on he scrutinizes him 'joint by joint', wondering 'in what part of his body/ Shall I destroy him – whether there, or there –' (IV. v. 230–42). Achilles says that he has 'fed mine eyes on thee' and 'As I would buy thee, view thee limb by limb'. This scrutiny of Hector's body disturbingly fuses soldierly appraisal, erotic pleasure, and the prospect of consumption. When Achilles a few moments later amicably feasts not on Hector but with him, the shift of tone only adds to the complexity of feeling, as Hector temporarily becomes a comrade.

Achilles' sexual love for Patroclus had been a feature of classical legend, and Shakespeare alludes to it here when Thersites says to Patroclus:

> Thou art said to be Achilles' male varlet.
> *Patroclus*: . . . What's that?
> *Thersites*: Why, his masculine whore.

> (V. i. 14–16)

The rest of the play neither confirms nor refutes the idea of a sexual relationship between Achilles and Patroclus. Although Patroclus is nowadays acted by an adult, both Thersites and Achilles refer to him as a 'boy' (V. i. 13; V. v. 45), so Shakespeare may be imagining a classical Greek relationship of *eromenos* and *erastes*. Achilles is also known to be in love with the Trojan princess Polyxena, and the two loves are linked by Patroclus when he says to Achilles:

> A woman impudent and mannish grown
> Is not more loath'd than an effeminate man
> In time of action. I stand condemn'd for this:
> They think my little stomach to the war
> And your great love to me restrains you thus.
> Sweet, rouse yourself; and the weak wanton Cupid
> Shall from your neck unloose his amorous fold.

> (III. iii. 216–22)

Ulysses has rebuked Achilles for his infatuation with Polyxena, which has kept him out of the war: Achilles has become 'effeminate' (in the Renaissance sense of being too susceptible to women) since he is swayed more by his love for a woman than by his manly duty to his Greek comrades. At the same time he has been influenced by his love for Patroclus, who hates the fighting. Though Patroclus blames himself, the Greek generals do not: they are indeed outraged by his mocking impersonations of them, but never cast aspersions on the nature of the love between the two men. What endangers the homosocial coherence of the Greek army is not Achilles' love for Patroclus, but his love for the enemy princess, together with his encouragement of Patroclus' subversive satire.

In *Julius Caesar* it is 'love' which binds together the principal male characters, and the significance of the word modulates with the ethical and emotional tensions which arise when civic and military duties conflict with private feeling. The feelings of Brutus for Caesar (who looks set to become a dictator) and for Cassius (who is resolved to assassinate Caesar) are alike described as 'love'. Cassius complains that Brutus no longer treats him with his usual 'gentleness / And show of love' (I. ii. 32–3); Brutus says of Caesar, 'I love him well' (I. ii. 81), while also speaking about his 'love' for Cassius (I. ii. 160, 164). Cassius comments that Caesar 'loves Brutus' (I. ii. 310), while Mark Antony likewise says that Brutus was 'dearly ... lov'd' by Caesar and was his 'angel' (III. ii. 178, 183–4). In their quarrel after the assassination Cassius complains to Brutus, 'you love me not', alleging that he is 'hated by one he loves' (IV. iii. 88, 95). On the eve of the final battle, Cassius recalls that he and Brutus used to be 'lovers in peace' (V. i. 95). The word 'love' is used over fifty times in this play, and for Brutus in particular it signals his conflicting obligations: he killed Caesar 'not that I loved Caesar less, but that I loved Rome more ... I slew my best lover for the good of Rome' (III. ii. 22–3, 46). Nowhere does this vocabulary suggest sexual relationships between the men (though many of Shakespeare's audience would have known the story told by the Roman historian Suetonius that Caesar had been the King of Bithynia's catamite) but it does delineate passionate commitment, tenderness, jealousy and mistrust, feelings which give the homosocial bonds an almost erotic intensity.

Symbolizing these shifting relationships are the shifting ways in which the body of Caesar is imagined by other men: it is a feeble body which could not swim the Tiber and had to be carried by

Cassius (I. ii. 99–114); a feverish body which is as weak as a sick girl
(I. ii. 118–27); a colossus under whose legs men walk about in awe
(I. ii. 133–6); a statue spouting blood (II. ii. 76–89); a dish carved for
the gods to eat (II. i. 173); a body of which Antony is only a limb
(II. i. 165); a dead body exhibited by Antony to the people, where
every wound is made to signify a friend's betrayal (III. ii. 176–99);
and finally an avenging ghost which haunts the imagination of
Brutus (IV. iii. 274–85). The bodies of the conspirators are also drawn
into the drama. When Cassius believes that Brutus no longer loves
him, he rips open his tunic and asks Brutus to tear the heart from
his 'naked breast' (IV. iii. 99–106). Eventually Brutus and Cassius
turn 'our swords/ In our own proper entrails' (V. iii. 95–6). To bring
themselves to carry out the assassination it was necessary for the
conspirators to reimagine Caesar's body as either unmanly or too
threatening; to defeat the plot Antony had only to produce the
actual corpse and make its wounds speak of the man's betrayal by
those whom he had loved. This fascinated reimagining of the male
body gives both emotional and symbolic focus to the homosocial
political world, and reminds us that Shakespeare and his contemporaries could be unafraid of the proximity between (or even
the continuity of) the homosocial and the homoerotic. The stress on
the male body in *Julius Caesar* is also part of Shakespeare's way of
imagining a republican community, for it is a new version of that
imagery of society as the body politic which was already familiar
to his contemporaries in its hierarchical and monarchical form: the
king was said to be the head of the body, and father and husband
of his people. Caesar's crime was (in part) to turn lateral homosocial
bonding into a hierarchical relationship of superior and dependant;
the conspirators tried to keep it a republican union of equals.

   In *Coriolanus*, where the body politic is also threatened, the male
body takes on an even stronger homoerotic significance as soldiers
embrace with a rapture which now has an explicitly sexual charge.
Coriolanus, covered in blood, greets his comrade Cominius with
these words:

> Oh! let me clip ye
> In arms as sound as when I woo'd; in heart
> As merry as when our nuptial day was done,
> And tapers burn'd to bedward.

> (I. vi. 29–32)

The comparison with Coriolanus's excitement on his wedding night is startling; startling too is the word 'our' where one would expect 'my': it is the wedding of Coriolanus and Virgilia which is being referred to, yet 'our' momentarily creates an imaginary wedding of Coriolanus and Cominius. Later, when Coriolanus exiles himself from Rome and defects to the Volsci, he is greeted by their general Aufidius in imagery which echoes his own earlier speech:

> Let me twine
> Mine arms about that body, where against
> My grained ash an hundred times hath broke,
> And scarr'd the moon with splinters. Here I clip
> The anvil of my sword, and do contest
> As hotly and as nobly with thy love
> As ever in ambitious strength I did
> Contend against thy valour. Know thou first,
> I lov'd the maid I married; never man
> Sigh'd truer breath; but that I see thee here,
> Thou noble thing, more dances my rapt heart
> Than when I first my wedded mistress saw
> Bestride my threshold ...
> I have nightly since
> Dreamt of encounters 'twixt thyself and me –
> We have been down together in my sleep,
> Unbuckling helms, fisting each other's throat –
> And wak'd half dead with nothing.

(IV. v. 107–27)

It is not only the overt comparison with the excitement of the wedding night which signals an erotic element in Aufidius's passion for Coriolanus: the lance splintering into fragments against his body (scarring the moon, the symbol of chastity), and the dream of the couple wrestling on the ground are also obvious sexual images. In making this consummation so clearly sexual, Shakespeare has discerned an erotic element in that bond between soldiers which fashions a world from which others are excluded. It is only with great reluctance that Coriolanus exhibits his battle-scars to the people when he is standing for office, as if these are secret tokens from a world elsewhere which those who are not soldiers have no right to see. By contrast, the people are likened unerotically to a body suffering rebellion from its mutinous limbs (I. i. 95–159), and to 'the dead carcasses of unburied men' (III. iii. 122). The ecstatic meeting of bodies in combat gives a purpose to Coriolanus's life which is stronger than his commitment to Rome, for he can more readily embrace his enemy Aufidius than submit to the power of the Roman mob. Aufidius in turn 'makes a mistress of him, sanctifies himself with's hand' (that is, considers the touch of his hand holy: IV. v. 200–1). When Aufidius subsequently vows revenge on Coriolanus for failing to press home his attack on Rome, he uses an image which again links martial and sexual encounters: 'my sinews shall be stretch'd upon him' (V. vi. 45). Editors reassure us that 'upon' here means 'against', but the idea that Aufidius desires to stretch himself *upon* Coriolanus seems present as well.

Coriolanus is undone because he heeds his mother's plea to spare Rome, despite having steeled himself to stand firm and act 'As if a man were author of himself/ And knew no other kin' (V. iii. 36–7). Within the all-male world of the army he is looked upon as 'son and heir to Mars' (IV. v. 197), and such an exclusively male lineage is part of Shakespeare's dream of masculine self-sufficiency, male self-generation. It is a dream of which Shakespeare is seldom uncritical, however, and the misogynistic element in this desire becomes most evident in Posthumus's ranting attempt to locate and destroy 'the woman's part' which his mother has contributed to the making of his body and spirit (*Cymbeline* II. iv. 171–80). But even in its calmer moods the longing for an all-male form of reproduction still casts woman as the destroyer of innocence. In *The Two Noble Kinsmen* the imprisoned friends Palamon and Arcite initially lament that they are likely to die unmarried and without heirs, but Arcite suggests that they should reimagine their prison as a 'holy sanctuary' which will keep them free from corruption. The temptations of 'liberty and common conversation . . . might like women/ Woo us to wander from' the 'ways of honour', but their imaginations can fashion an innocent world where 'We are one another's wife, ever begetting/New births of love' (II. i. 125–35). Tragically, a woman does separate them, and the momentary all-male world of mutual love is destroyed.

Similarly the arrival of women is said to have fractured the pastoral world of male innocence in *The Winter's Tale*. Polixenes recalls that he and his boyhood friend Leontes had once been

> as twinn'd lambs that did frisk i' th' sun,
> And bleat the one at th' other: what we chang'd

Was innocence for innocence: we knew not
The doctrine of ill-doing, nor dream'd
That any did . . .
Temptations have since then been born to 's: for
In those unfledg'd days was my wife a girl.

(I. ii. 67–78)

The woman who intrudes into this Eden may be loved, but she will not readily be forgiven for precipitating this fall from paradise. Even comedy seems to be in no hurry to leave the masculine paradise: marriage is postponed in *Love's Labours Lost* while the men learn maturity; it is postponed in *The Merchant of Venice* while Bassanio attends to the duties of his relationship with Antonio; it is postponed in *Much Ado about Nothing* when Claudio believes his comrade's slanders against his fiancée; and in *Twelfth Night* the marriage of Orsino and Viola cannot take place until she removes her male disguise, which she has not done by the time the play finishes: the drama ends on the very brink of marriage, but with the inevitable heterosexual consummation still – perhaps reassuringly – deferred.

It is Othello's tragedy that even after marriage he still belongs to the male world of the army more than to the strange heterosexual world of Venice into which he has married, but in which he never really lives. Like a more tragic version of Claudio, he trusts his male adjutant Iago more than he trusts his wife Desdemona, and he is readier to believe Iago's allegations of her adultery than Desdemona's protestations of incomprehension and innocence. This is the bond which has the strongest power over him, the bond of soldier to soldier. The vow which Othello and Iago swear echoes the marriage vow which we suppose Othello and Desdemona must have exchanged, though we have never actually heard it; what we hear and see instead is its parodic displacement into a male/male version:

Othello [*kneeling*]. . . . Now by yond marble heaven,
In the due reverence of a sacred vow,
I here engage my words.
Iago. Do not rise yet. [*Iago kneels.*]
Witness, you ever-burning lights above,
You elements that clip us round about,

> Witness that here Iago doth give up
> The excellency of his wit, hand, heart,
> To wrong'd Othello's service . . .
> *Othello*. I greet thy love.

(III. iii. 467–76)

As Othello and Iago weave a story about Desdemona's unfaithfulness, they fashion between them an imagined world which they alone inhabit, and to which Desdemona has no access. There is scarcely any private space or intimate language which husband and wife share, and it is significant that Othello imagines his loss of Desdemona not as the loss of one woman, or of domestic happiness, but as the loss of military comradeship:

> O now for ever
> Farewell the tranquil mind, farewell content:
> Farewell the plumed troop, and the big wars . . .
> Farewell, Othello's occupation's gone!

(III. iii. 353–63)

This is the milieu which has given him his identity. One of Iago's contributions to this imagined world is a teasing, partly homoerotic, fantasy in which he describes to Othello what happened one night when he and Cassio were sleeping together:

> In sleep I heard him say 'Sweet Desdemona,
> Let us be wary, let us hide our loves;'
> And then, sir, would he gripe and wring my hand,
> Cry out, 'Sweet creature!' and then kiss me hard,
> As if he pluck'd up kisses by the roots,
> That grew upon my lips, then laid his leg
> Over my thigh, and sigh'd, and kiss'd, and then
> Cried 'Cursed fate, that gave thee to the Moor!'

(III. iii. 425–32)

For the purposes of his plot Iago could have invented any moment of privacy: the shared space did not have to be a shared bed. The

narrative of Desdemona's betrayal is interwoven with a homoerotic scenario, as it is in miniature when Othello says 'I found not
Cassio's kisses on her lips' (III. iii. 347). Momentarily, a homoerotic
contact is made between Cassio and Iago, and between Cassio and
Othello. What Desdemona and Cassio seem to have broken is
not only Othello's marriage, but also the emotionally charged
but unthreatening male comradeship which flourished before her
arrival. As in *Troilus and Cressida* and *Coriolanus*, the eroticism in
the way military comradeship is envisaged strengthens rather than
disrupts it.

In the plays discussed so far, Shakespeare has fashioned spaces in
which an all-male world can flourish, albeit temporarily. Such a
space may be an army, a prison, a forest; it is also a symbolic space,
a place shaped by the masculine imagination. This can be described
(in a term from the book *Playing and Reality* (1971) by the psy-
chologist D.W. Winnicott) as 'potential space': it is the area which
is neither wholly the territory of the self, nor wholly that of the
other, but a space shared between self and other in which creativity
can come into play. Here the individual neither imposes his own
terms on the other, nor surrenders himself wholly to the other's
demands: the two share the space, jointly defining it and each other.
The tragedy in *Othello* is generated because Othello cannot allow
Desdemona into this space as a partner in its shaping, and instead
insists on defining her (and defining their marriage) only in his
terms – and these all too easily become Iago's terms. In Shakespeare's
imagination, men can readily join other men in this creative shaping
of a potential space: they share a language, and share common (or
at least mutually comprehensible) aims. But to share such a space
with a woman is to encounter a disruptive otherness instead of a
comforting version of one's self. Sexual desire for her is liable to
disrupt the continuum of male society, whereas emotional and even
erotic desire for another man can be made to enhance the masculine
paradise.

But sometimes Shakespeare invents spaces in which he can
experiment with the gendered roles which people play. In *As You
Like It* the forest into which the characters escape becomes an arena
for play and discovery. Banished from court as a traitor, Rosalind
dresses up as a boy and calls herself 'Ganymede'. Meanwhile, her
beloved Orlando is also an exile in the forest, where he is besottedly
pinning poems about her on to the trees. When they meet he fails

to recognize her. 'Ganymede' suggests that he can cure Orlando of his infatuation with Rosalind by pretending to be Rosalind while Orlando courts him: the capricious responses which Ganymede will make on behalf of Rosalind will, he says, so infuriate Orlando that he will be cured of his love. 'I would not be cured' says Orlando (III. iii. 413), but nevertheless agrees to the treatment.

The scene in which the actor playing Orlando woos the actor playing Rosalind playing Ganymede playing Rosalind, is full of homoerotic possibilities. Does an audience choose to see Ganymede/Rosalind as male or female? Might it take pleasure in the very ambiguity and androgyny of the image? Is Orlando simply wooing Rosalind via Ganymede, or is he also interested in wooing Ganymede for his own sake? When Ganymede asks Orlando how he would begin courting Rosalind, Orlando replies 'I would kiss before I spoke' (IV. i. 69). Though there are various ways of playing this scene, one possibility is that Orlando is actually interested in getting a kiss from this pretty boy. When Orlando and Ganymede go through a form of marriage on stage, with Orlando taking Ganymede's hand and calling him Rosalind, the scene is teasingly complex: verbally a marriage of man and woman, but visually the marriage of man and boy. This is a potential space in which the status of the characters, their desires and their actions are ambiguous; various erotic possibilities are unfolded which the play will ultimately have to leave behind at the end, when Hymen sorts the characters into conventionally marriageable couples who prepare to return to the everyday world.

HOMOSEXUAL ATTRACTION IN *TWELFTH NIGHT* AND *THE MERCHANT OF VENICE*

In two plays Shakespeare allows a more explicit homosexual attraction to become visible. The love of Antonio for Sebastian in *Twelfth Night*, and the love of another Antonio for Bassanio in *The Merchant of Venice*, are seen as part of a continuum of homosocial bonding, and yet at the same time are marked out as special. The spaces in which these relationships take place are spaces of experimentation and trial, as if Shakespeare is moving beyond the representation of homoerotic feelings as part of an undisturbed male world, and focusing instead upon the awkward, disruptive demands which powerfully homosexual feelings may make.

Before we meet Antonio and Sebastian, *Twelfth Night* presents us
with Sebastian's twin sister Viola, shipwrecked on the coast of Illyria,
who disguises herself as a boy under the name Caesario. 'He' makes
his way to the court of Duke Orsino, who is ostensibly in love with
Olivia: his passion for her remains distanced from its unattainable object, and results in melancholy posturing. One of Orsino's
retainers comments on his sudden interest in Caesario: 'he hath
known you but three days, and already you are no stranger' (I. iv.
2–4). Caesario wonders whether there is any reason to doubt 'the
continuance of his love' (I. iv. 6), and at this point we do not know
where on the spectrum of meanings this 'love' belongs, whether it
might mean more than just a master's approval of his servant. When
Orsino enters he makes his entourage stand back, creating a semi-
private space on stage which he shares with Caesario alone. 'Thou
know'st no less but all' he says to him, 'I have unclasp'd/ To
thee the book even of my secret soul' (I. iv. 13–15). The secret which
Orsino has shared with Caesario is his love for Olivia, so an intimate homosocial bond has been established between the two, and
Orsino promises Caesario that if he successfully woos Olivia on his
behalf his reward will be equality with Orsino and complete freedom
to share Orsino's wealth: 'thou shalt live as freely as thy lord/ To
call his fortunes thine' (I. iv. 39–40). Yet this dream of intimate male
friendship on an equal footing is at variance with the actual relationship which is developing, for they are not equal in years or in
status. Moreover, when Orsino reflects on Caesario's youth, his
blazon of Caesario's body has a homoerotic colouration, for it is
the androgynous ambiguity of Caesario which attracts him:

> Dear lad . . .
> . . . they shall yet belie thy happy years
> That say thou art a man; Diana's lip
> Is not more smooth and rubious: thy small pipe,
> Is as the maiden's organ, shrill and sound,
> And all is semblative a woman's part.

> (I. iv. 28–34)

Shakespeare seems to be inviting us to understand the relationship
between Orsino and Caesario through the paradigm of *erastes* and
eromenos.

Later, Orsino talks to Caesario about love, while music plays in the background:

> Come hither, boy. If ever thou shalt love,
> In the sweet pangs of it remember me:
> For such as I am, all true lovers are,
> Unstaid and skittish in all motions else,
> Save in the constant image of the creature
> That is belov'd.

(II. iv. 15–20)

Orsino wonders whether Caesario has experienced love, and asks: 'What kind of woman is't?'. 'Of your complexion' and 'About your years' Caesario replies. The desires figured here are extraordinarily mobile, in spite of Orsino's assertion of constancy to the image of his beloved. The scene has erotic potential, as the Duke and his page talk about love to the accompaniment of music (and according to Renaissance thinking, music had the power to provoke men to act on their hidden feelings); the Duke asks Caesario to think of him when he is in love with another; Caesario describes his beloved as being like the Duke. And so a homoerotic text is interwoven with the overt heterosexual text in which Orsino is presenting himself as the constant lover of Olivia and as the disinterested adviser to Caesario on his choice of women. We know that Viola is in love with Orsino, but 'Viola' is not quite present here, since she has been partly displaced by Caesario. In this temporary space, where at one level two men are defining their desires for women, the possibilities of other desires arise: that of Viola for Orsino – which can only be represented on stage through what appears as the desire of Caesario for Orsino, and through the voice of the male actor playing Viola – and that of Orsino for Caesario.

This is one of the ways in which *Twelfth Night* opens up before us more complex erotic possibilities than we might have expected, and these possibilities are extended when we encounter Sebastian, who enters with the sea-captain Antonio. Sebastian shares the name of the martyr whose nude male body pierced by arrows was a familiar Renaissance icon, an object of religious devotion which might also serve to arouse homoerotic devotion. In his first scene he draws attention to his (perhaps androgynous) beauty by recalling his sister's: 'though it was said she much resembled me, [she] was

yet of many accounted beautiful' (II. i. 24–5). Antonio had res-
cued Sebastian from the shipwreck, and cannot now bear to lose
him, saying that he will die if parted from him. He is quite explicit
about his feelings for the young man, saying after Sebastian has left,
'I do adore thee so' (II. i. 46), and deciding to follow him even at
risk of being imprisoned by his old enemies in Illyria. Catching up
with Sebastian, he confesses: 'my desire,/ More sharp than filed steel,
did spur me forth' (III. iii. 4–5). It seems as clear as Shakespeare
could possibly make it on the public stage that the 'love' to which
Antonio twice refers in this speech is a homosexual desire in the
older man for the younger, and perhaps in Sebastian's reply there
is a recognition of Antonio's longing, with an admission that he
cannot reciprocate by giving Antonio any physical satisfaction: 'My
kind Antonio,/ I can no other answer make, but thanks,/ And
thanks, and ever thanks' (III. iii. 13–15). Antonio gives Sebastian
his purse in case anything catches his eye while sightseeing, and
goes off to arrange lodgings where they will spend the night. His
purse may be the only thing which Antonio can in practice get the
boy to accept from him, but it figures another offering, since the
purse symbolizes the genitals, not only in Freudian psychology but
in Elizabethan slang.

Later on, Antonio rescues Caesario (whom he takes to be Sebastian) from a fight, and is immediately arrested as an enemy of the
state by the Duke's officers. Asking Caesario to return his purse, he
is devastated when the youth disclaims all knowledge of him.
Bitterly, Antonio reflects on how his love for the boy has been
misplaced:

> This youth that you see here
> I snatch'd one half out of the jaws of death,
> Reliev'd him with such sanctity of love;
> And to his image, which methought did promise
> Most venerable worth, did I devotion . . .
> But O how vile an idol proves this god!

> (III. iv. 368–74)

This is not the language of a man outraged by his friend's in-
gratitude, but the cry of a lover spurned by the man upon whom
he had lavished his worship. In the play's final scene Antonio tells
the story again to Orsino, who is standing next to Caesario:

A witchcraft drew me hither:
That most ingrateful boy there by your side,
From the rude sea's enrag'd and foamy mouth
Did I redeem. A wrack past hope he was.
His life I gave him, and did thereto add
My love, without retention or restraint,
All his in dedication. For his sake
Did I expose myself (pure for his love)
Into the danger of this adverse town . . .
[he] grew a twenty years' removed thing
While one would wink . . .
. . . for three months before
No int'rim, not a minute's vacancy,
Both day and night did we keep company.

(V. i. 74–94)

Here we must recognize the anguish of a lover upon discovering that the man with whom he shared three months' companionship, day and night, has turned so quickly and so coldly into a 'twenty years' removed thing'.

By the final scene Olivia has married Sebastian (thinking him to be Caesario), and when Orsino discovers that Caesario is actually Viola, he proposes marriage to her. She is still dressed as a boy, and remains so at the end of the play, and although Orsino knows her to be a woman he still chooses to call her 'boy' and 'Caesario' (V. i. 265, 384) as he takes her hand: is he reluctant to give up the idea that his Caesario is an attractive boy? The interweaving of masculine and feminine descriptions of Viola/Caesario here reminds us that the actor playing Viola is himself a boy, and the theatrical image of Orsino leaving the stage hand in hand with the boy Viola/Caesario defers heterosexual consummation, keeping alive the fantasy of homosexual union. Meanwhile, Antonio has been reunited with Sebastian, and the misunderstandings have been cleared up, but Sebastian is now married to Olivia, leaving Antonio on one side. As Janet Adelman observes, 'we arrive here at a core of loss, the consequence of a felt necessity to choose between homosexual and heterosexual bonds; the central fantasies of the play attempt momentarily to deny that core of loss by denying the need for choice' ('Male Bonding' p. 89). The play suggests that Antonio's three months by Sebastian's side were, and could only be, an interval:

the boy may not have betrayed him as brutally as Antonio once thought, but his misapprehension was a warning of the desertion to come. The closing theatrical tableau of Antonio without a partner, while Orsino stands hand in hand with Caesario, simultaneously offers and withholds the possibility of homosexual union.

The Merchant of Venice opens with a question: why is the merchant Antonio so melancholy? His male friends Salerio and Solanio suggest that he may be worried about his trading ventures, but he dismisses this explanation with detailed reasons why they are wrong. Their second suggestion – that he is in love – is countered only with 'Fie, fie!' (I. i. 46). We may wonder why there is no comparably detailed rebuttal in this case. Soon Bassanio arrives on the scene, and the other characters recognize that they should leave the two friends together, for within the male world of mercantile Venice there is an inner space which Antonio and Bassanio share.

Antonio may play a melancholy role on the world's stage, but there is no sign of this sadness when he is alone with Bassanio. He soon broaches a subject which Bassanio seems to be avoiding: 'Well, tell me now what lady is the same/ To whom you swore a secret pilgrimage' (I. i. 119–20). Bassanio has in mind an expedition which will be both pleasurable and profitable, the pursuit of the rich and beautiful Portia. But for this he needs money, and he is already in debt to Antonio. Antonio's reply offers Bassanio the necessary cash in language which simultaneously makes a sexual offer:

> My purse, my person, my extremest means
> Lie all unlock'd to your occasions.

> (I. i. 138–9)

Like the other Antonio, this one offers both purse and person, but since his purse is insufficient for Bassanio's needs, Antonio puts his person at risk by borrowing money from Shylock and entering into a bond by which he will forfeit a pound of flesh if he fails to repay the money on time.

The parting of the two friends when Bassanio leaves to woo Portia is not staged, but is described by Salerio to Solanio; the focus is on Antonio:

> his eye being big with tears,
> Turning his face, he put his hand behind him,
> And with affection wondrous sensible
> He wrung Bassanio's hand, and so they parted.

(II. viii. 46–8)

And Solanio replies: 'I think he only loves the world for him'. These two representatives of masculine Venice are entirely sympathetic to Antonio's emotion, and do not regard it as in any way strange. The friendship of Antonio and Bassanio is part of the masculine ethos, even though it is recognized as a special bond within that milieu. There is no secrecy here.

But there is secrecy in Belmont, the home of Portia, where suitors have to undertake the trial of choosing between caskets of gold, silver and lead, only one of which contains Portia's image and with it the prize of Portia herself in marriage, while the other two contain symbolic revelations of the suitors' folly. Portia can only be won by the unlocking of a secret. The contest for Portia is fraught with hazard for the suitors, since they must forswear women if they choose wrongly. The fact that Portia is contained within a casket (and contained by the whole game which her father had devised) speaks of men's need to contain women, and the risks to men which arise at the frontier where the male world meets the female. There is another form of danger within the male world, figured in Antonio's predicament. Antonio's love for Bassanio, which goes beyond friendship, makes him vulnerable when he proves unable to repay the loan, and Shylock claims his pound of flesh; but he is vulnerable only to the outsider Shylock, for no one within his own Venetian circle exploits him or considers him deviant: he may call himself 'a tainted wether of the flock' (IV. i. 114), but they do not. He epitomizes Venetian masculinity.

Antonio appears in court, surrounded by the men of Venice, and prepares to have his body revealed and then cut open by Shylock. It is a scene which permits sadistic eroticism: in Shakespeare's source story the merchant is stripped naked as the Jew prepares his razor; on the Elizabethan stage Antonio's bosom is bared to Shylock's knife. Antonio is about to give his body for Bassanio in a displaced act of sexual surrender, in what threatens to be a double revelation of Antonio's heart, both figuratively and literally. Antonio's farewell to Bassanio is at once measured and passionate:

Commend me to your honourable wife . . .
Say how I lov'd you, speak me fair in death:
And when the tale is told, bid her be judge
Whether Bassanio had not once a love:

(IV. i. 269–73)

The word 'love' here must be a strong word: a passionate, self-sacrificing lover. Bassanio protests that his wife, his own life, and all the world are not as dear to him as Antonio: 'I would lose all, ay sacrifice them all/ Here to this devil, to deliver you' (IV. i. 282–3). Later, when Portia (disguised as a male lawyer) has extricated Antonio from his predicament, Bassanio is forced to consider whether he really means this, as Portia, still in disguise, demands as her payment the ring which Bassanio had received from her earlier. Bassanio has to choose: does he (as he had claimed in what he thought was an all-male gathering) really prize Antonio above Portia? He does; he gives away the ring.

Here we seem to have a variant of the problem which Shakespeare maps in *Twelfth Night*: does a man have to choose between his male and female lovers? Is it possible to have both homosexual and heterosexual relationships? In *The Merchant of Venice* Shakespeare makes Antonio's love for Bassanio clearly more than friendship, and once again seems to be thinking in terms of the *erastes/eromenos* model. In the source story the merchant is a father-figure, and his love for the boy is purely paternal. Antonio's age is not specified, but he is clearly old enough to be an established merchant, while Bassanio is just launching out into speculation and matrimony. If there is probably a difference of age between the two men, there is certainly a difference of power and status. The two are friends, yet without that comradely equality which was so strong a feature of the Renaissance ideal of friendship. It is Gratiano, not Antonio, who accompanies Bassanio on his quest for Portia. At the end of the play Antonio appears at Belmont alongside Portia and Bassanio; indeed, when Portia returns the ring to Bassanio, she does it via Antonio, making him her proxy in this second engagement. Yet this gesture through which Antonio momentarily stands in for Portia only underlines his exclusion from the charmed circle. Neither *Twelfth Night* nor *The Merchant of Venice* quite manages to imagine a permanent place for an older man in love with a youth.

THE SECRECIES OF THE *SONNETS*

It is this unresolved question with which Shakespeare wrestles in the *Sonnets*. The world which he creates in the *Sonnets* is a half-secret world of homosexual infatuation which unfolds within other worlds which are more open to the view. The poems were made public in 1609 in circumstances which are still mysterious. Whether or not Shakespeare acquiesced in this publication, he did not leave the usual authorial traces over its text and introductory material, for the book was poorly proof-read and carried a riddling (perhaps deliberately indecipherable) dedication, not from Shakespeare but from the publisher, to an unknown 'Mr W.H.'. Francis Meres' reference in 1598 to Shakespeare's 'sugared sonnets among his private friends' tells us that the poems had previously had some limited private circulation in manuscript, but we cannot now recover the circumstances in which they were composed and shown to their first readers. This teasing mixture of openness and secrecy which attended the origin and publication of the *Sonnets* is rather appropriate for a collection which fashions various forms of secrecy while paradoxically promising eternal fame to the anonymous beloved.

Much ink has been spilt over the identities of Mr W.H., of the young man to whom sonnets 1 to 126 are addressed, and the 'dark lady' with whom both the young man and the poet seem to be sexually involved in numbers 127 to 152, but we actually know nothing beyond what the poems themselves tell us. Many stories have been woven around these poems by readers determined to impose their own interpretations, and much effort has been devoted to denying any possibility that Shakespeare's sonnets speak of homosexual desire. The first of these attempts to deflect such an interpretation was the second edition of the *Sonnets*, published by John Benson in 1640 under the title *Poems: Written by Wil. Shakespeare, Gent*, in which the poems were rearranged, given titles which referred to the poet's mistress, and had some masculine words changed to feminine ones. The erasure of homoerotic content is by no means systematic, but it is sufficiently deliberate to indicate discomfort with the implications of the original text. The poems then suffered a period of critical neglect, during which attitudes to emotional and sexual relations between men changed significantly, and in 1790 the great Shakespearean editor Edmond Malone felt it necessary to explain that Elizabethan men often addressed one another in emotive language which might sound indecorous to eighteenth-century readers. Subsequently the nature of the relationship described in the *Sonnets* was debated by nineteenth-century commentators, who frequently reassured one another that the love was purely idealistic, and that Shakespeare's work contained 'not even an allusion to that very worst of all possible vices', as Coleridge insisted. By contrast, Joseph Pequigney has recently argued that the *Sonnets* are a detailed account of a fully sexual relationship between the poet and the youth. However one reads the *Sonnets*, it is fruitless to guess at some supposed autobiographical story behind the poems – 'what actually happened' – since we have no means of knowing which actions and desires of his own Shakespeare drew on in fashioning these poems: 'what actually happened' was that Shakespeare, obviously deeply committed emotionally and imaginatively to the subject, though for reasons which we can no longer trace, created a sequence of poems which explore the delight and despair which may attend one man's love for another.

The sequence begins within a clearly homosocial milieu, with seventeen poems urging the young man to marry and beget an heir. Out of this emerges a different discourse, impassioned and utterly committed, which charts the poet's obsession with this beautiful but ultimately untenable youth. The early sonnets urging marriage do not expound the delights which might await the young man if he fell in love with a woman whom he could make his wife: the woman is imagined only as the medium which is necessary if the young man is to produce an heir, and she is variously described as a field to be ploughed, and a phial holding his precious liquid (3.5–6; 6.3). The sole requirement is that the young man should be reproduced, and leave copies of himself. The poet, therefore, is not inviting the young man to savour the delights of heterosexual love, but rather urging him to attend to his homosocial duty of reproducing the male. Yet already within these early poems a theme is sounded which will return later in a darker key: the young man is too satisfied with his own beauty, too self-enclosed and Narcissus-like to contemplate giving himself to another person. Later that self-sufficiency will torment the poet as he finds that he cannot hold the young man in any fully-assured, mutual love.

Ominously, the word 'love' occurs first in the *Sonnets* in the charge that the young man has 'no love toward others' (9.13) if he refuses his obligations of marriage. In the next sonnet 'love' slides into a different register as the poet asks:

> Make thee another self for love of me,
> That beauty still may live in thine or thee.

(10.13–14)

Now we see that the poet has a personal interest in the young man's beauty and its continuation. The idea that the young man should make 'another self' fits with the message of these first seventeen poems, but also anticipates the language later in the sequence in which the poet regards the young man as another self: the idea of creating another self in the form of a son will be displaced by the idea that the poet himself, as lover, is the youth's other self, and will ensure the youth's immortality through his poetry. By sonnet 13 'love' and 'dear my love' have become the terms in which the poet refers to and addresses the young man; by sonnet 19 the tone in which 'my love' is spoken of has become protective and celebratory; and so out of this talk of self-reproducing masculinity has emerged another language, that of male/male love.

Is this sexual desire or passionate friendship? The youth is occasionally described as the poet's 'friend', a designation which is often favoured in modern discussions of the poems because it is taken to signal that the relationship lacks an erotic charge. But the argument that the feelings expressed in these poems would have been construed by Shakespeare's contemporaries as friendship confronts the problem that the essential characteristics of Renaissance male friendship do not figure in this relationship. We would expect equality, reciprocity, sharing and trust; instead we find a difference of age, and probably of social status, between the poet and the young man; the poet's feelings for him are not reciprocated in their consistency or intensity; and the sharing of a mistress by the two men generates in the poet a jealousy which is more concerned at the loss of the man than of the woman (42). Trust is repeatedly given by the poet, repeatedly betrayed by the youth. In every area where we would expect stability, the *Sonnets* register instability: they are almost an extended definition of what classic Renaissance friendship was not. Moreover, the poet's passion is acknowledged to be stirred by the youth's physical beauty, yet without any suggestion of the Platonic ideal that love of beauty is a path to moral and spiritual insight. On the contrary, the poems articulate the exhilaration and despair of raw passion, and sonnet 93, for example, casts the poet in the role of the man who has been sexually betrayed by his wife:

So shall I live, supposing thou art true
Like a deceivèd husband . . .
   How like Eve's apple doth thy beauty grow,
   If thy sweet virtue answer not thy show!

(93.1–2, 13–14)

Eve's apple was recognized to represent temptation of a specifically sexual kind. The sonnet sequence itself was a semi-private genre for the exploration of passionate love, typically of a kind which faced some prohibition (as in Sidney's courtship of Penelope Rich in *Astrophil and Stella*), and Shakespeare's poems repeatedly stress the difficulties of speech, the importance of privacy, the rarity of possession. Friendship did not face such difficulties, nor seek out such secrecies.

But the argument that what is figured in the *Sonnets* is erotic love also confronts a problem – sonnet 20. Here the young man's beauty is described as androgynous:

A woman's face with Nature's own hand painted,
Hast thou, the master-mistress of my passion . . .
A man in hue all hues in his controlling,
Which steals men's eyes, and women's souls amazeth.

(20.1–2, 7–8)

The language teases us. What does 'master-mistress' mean? And what does 'passion' mean? Contemporary senses of 'passion' included both 'strong feeling' and 'sexual desire'. The poem seems to be saying the unsayable – that the poet desires the youth as other men do their mistresses – while at the same time providing an alternative, safe meaning. It then imagines that the young man was at first intended by Nature to be a woman:

Till Nature as she wrought thee fell a-doting,
And by addition me of thee defeated,
By adding one thing to my purpose nothing.
   But since she pricked thee out for women's pleasure,
   Mine be thy love, and thy love's use their treasure.

(20.10–14)

Here the poem apparently makes an unequivocal distinction between the poet enjoying the young man's love, and women enjoying the use of him sexually. But a delight in the equivocal is characteristic of Shakespeare, even when he is not treading on dangerous ground. The unsayable ('I wish to have the use of your prick') lurks within these lines. Why mention the young man's 'thing' if it is of no interest? Such a disclaimer is an old rhetorical trick ('Far be it from me even to mention . . .'). The possibility of the poet having sexual desire for the young man has now been brought into the language of the sonnets, and it haunts the rest of the sequence, altering the range of lexical and emotional possibilities which unfold from the poems' imagery. These sonnets are also fragments of a dialogue in which only one speaker is heard, but where answers or actions are often implicit between the poems. Is there an implicit invitation here for the young man to reply: 'You can have the use as well as the love'? If we turn on to sonnet 21 expecting some development of this topic, we are disappointed: the gap between 20 and 21 is one of the sequence's most eloquent yet indecipherable silences.

The tone of sonnet 20 presupposes at least the kind of intimacy which permits homoerotic teasing, but there now follows a transition to a different kind of intimacy, a reciprocal emotional bond. By sonnet 22 some kind of exchange is imagined to have taken place. The youth's beauty is now envisaged as the covering for the poet's heart, as each heart lives within the other's breast. Sonnet 23 poignantly registers that hesitant speech and anxious scanning of the other's intentions which attend the early stages of love. Shakespeare may have been a consummately skilled playwright, but here he imagines himself stranded without a script, like an imperfect actor struck dumb with fear, or like a creature made speechless with rage:

> So I, for fear of trust, forget to say
> The perfect ceremony of love's rite,
> And in mine own love's strength seem to decay,
> O'ercharged with burden of mine own love's might.
> O, let my books be then the eloquence
> And dumb presagers of my speaking breast,
> Who plead for love and look for recompense
> More than that tongue that more hath more expressed.
>   O, learn to read what silent love hath writ;
>   To hear with eyes belongs to love's fine wit.

(23. 5–14)

The difficulty of voicing love is caught here in the deployment of paradoxes and linguistic awkwardness: the dumb writing speaks on behalf of the 'speaking breast' which has been struck dumb. The young man must learn that special kind of discriminating intelligence ('fine wit') which is necessary for the interpretation of such a difficult form of lovers' discourse. Other tongues which speak more volubly in praise of the youth actually speak less and expect less in return, for the poet pleads for more recompense than do any of the youth's other admirers. On one level this is a poem about a writer seeking reward from his patron for his professional services, and being jealous of his rivals for employment; but although the poem retains a contact with this world of publicly acknowledged relationships, such possible definitions of 'love' and 'recompense' are denied by the anxiety, the sheer difficulty of articulation, the stress on the creation of a private code of expression and interpretation. The youth is asked to join the poet in the shaping of a private world within those public spaces (both social and linguistic) which they share with others.

But any private world which the two lovers might fashion seems transitory, and those very poems which first register mutual love register also uncertainty and instability. When the ideas of sonnet 22 are reworked in 24, that poem concludes with the unsettling reflection that eyes can see only the outside, and cannot know the heart. Sonnet 25 celebrates an unexpected gratification, the discovery of joy where there had previously simply been honour ('I . . . unlooked for joy in that I honour most': 25.3–4), and the poem ends with a couplet which enacts perfect balance and reciprocity:

> Then happy I that love and am beloved
> Where I may not remove nor be removed.

> (25.13–14)

The expressive redundancy of this repetition says that there is no point in striving for elegant verbal variation where love is so stable and equal. Yet the opening of the next poem immediately undoes that equanimity by figuring the relationship in terms of power:

> Lord of my love, to whom in vassalage
> Thy merit hath my duty strongly knit . . .

> (26.1–2)

Henceforward the inequalities between the two men in their feeling, in their fidelity, in their social status, and in the ease with which they move on the public stage, are never out of sight for very long.

The sonnets do not build up into a narrative, or into a dialogue, or into a shared language; instead each sonnet seems to mount yet another attempt to understand the lover and the poet's feelings for him. The sonnets repeat images and ideas obsessively, yet without advancing; the concluding couplet is as likely to refute the rest of the poem as to bring it to a satisfying close, and one poem is liable to undo the work of its predecessors. As we read through the sequence we are struck by the discontinuities, the repetitions, the lacunae. What this poetry enacts so poignantly is the persistence of devotion in spite of the lack of assured possession. It is as early as sonnet 33 that the time of mutual possession is presented as already past: 'he was but one hour mine' (33.11). The youth has been like the sun whose radiance flattered and kissed the landscape, images which imply (but never quite reveal) that the relations between the two men included flattery and kisses. Now this sun is obscured by clouds. Whether this is an image for some emotional or sexual betrayal of the poet by the young man (and much depends on how strongly one interprets the image of his 'stain'), it is certainly an image for the poet's loss of exclusive, private possession of the youth, even though we cannot know (because the *Sonnets* will not, dare not, tell us) whether such possession includes sexual possession. In 34 the poet laments that the young man's promises have tempted him to 'travel forth without my cloak' (and so without, for once, disguising his feelings?) into a storm for which he was unprepared, a sobering reversal of the unexpected joy celebrated in sonnet 25. This poem speaks about venturing beyond one's usual territory, risking a revelation of love which might lead to a matching response, but might also expose one to rejection, to betrayal, and to 'vulgar scandal' (112.2).

Many of the sonnets delineate the complexity of the relationship through the way in which they imagine versions of private space. In 48 the poet has carefully locked 'each trifle under truest bars' to keep them away from 'hands of falsehood' (are these trifles love tokens?), while the youth himself is left exposed to the risk of being stolen by others; only in the poet's heart can he be locked safely away in the 'gentle closure of my breast', a phrase which seems to evoke the gentle closures of erotic embraces. In 46 the young man is imagined to lie in the poet's heart away from others' gaze in 'A closet never pierced with crystal eyes' (46.6). In 52 this image is reworked as the young man is represented as a treasure locked up in a chest, or a fine suit of clothes kept in a wardrobe until a 'special instant' is made 'special blest' and the clothes can be unfolded. This image of an unfolding which can only happen in a special moment of privacy speaks poignantly of the kind of possession which the poet has: it is a 'seldom pleasure' (52.4). But it also evokes the difficulty of writing, of unfolding such feelings into a language which can never quite be private, and where being too open might be dangerous. The sonnet ends:

> Blessèd are you whose worthiness gives scope,
> Being had, to triumph, being lacked, to hope.

> (52.13–14)

The moment of triumphant possession, when the poet has had the young man (and the sexual sense of 'had' was common in Shakespeare's time: cp. 129.9) gives way in this couplet to a renewed sense of lack: any consummation is unstable.

In sonnet 43 the principal space in which the poet is able to see the youth clearly is the space of his dreams, and so the nights give him clear sight, whereas the days are dark: 'All days are nights to see till I see thee, / And nights bright days when dreams do show thee me' (43.13–14). This is but one instance of the *Sonnets'* recurring idea that the poet's love for the young man changes altogether the way he experiences time. Sonnet 57 represents the poet's time as worthless compared with the lover's:

> Being your slave, what should I do but tend
> Upon the hours and times of your desire?
> I have no precious time at all to spend,
> Nor services to do, till you require.

> (57.1–4)

The tone of these poems is often complex and elusive, but there is no mistaking a bitterness in the poet's perception of his relationship with the youth as that of servant to master, a relationship so unequal that the poet is completely deprived of his own time, which is given up to wondering what the lover is doing:

> Nor dare I question with my jealous thought
> Where you may be, or your affairs suppose,
> But like a sad slave stay and think of naught
> Save where you are how happy you make those.

(57.9–12)

In the public world which the young man inhabits he brings joy to others, but this is evidently not a space or a time which the poet can share with him. Meanwhile, the poet waits in agony:

> Be where you list, your charter is so strong
> That you yourself may privilege your time
> To what you will . . .
> I am to wait, though waiting so be hell.

(58.9–13)

Sonnet 56 attempts to represent the lover's absence as being only a 'sad interim', a temporary season:

> As call it winter, which being full of care
> Makes summer's welcome thrice more wished, more rare.

(56.13–14)

In that phrase 'call it winter' there seems to be a recognition that the image is a piece of wishful thinking, and at any rate it suggests how difficult it is for the poet to find a language for this relationship. To call the absence winter would at least locate it within a recognizable framework, make it part of a comprehensible rhythm which promises a future harvest. The imagery is recalled in numbers 97–8, where the poet's absence from the youth in summer (97) or in spring (98) have both seemed like winters: the calendar by which others live is at variance with the poet's experience.

Running through the *Sonnets* is the problem of finding, or forging, a language which is suited to the poet's feelings for another man. Like Barnfield, Shakespeare could have turned to the resources of homoerotic pastoral, but he is not interested in sensuous physical description and teasing courtship; instead he makes the problem of the lack of a suitable precedent into one of the major themes of the sequence. In 59 (and again in 106) the poet reflects that there is no pre-text for his account of the young man, no text already written which can provide an apt vocabulary. He is not like writers 'stirred by a painted beauty' (21.2). When attempting to represent the youth's beauty, Shakespeare evokes both male and female images: he is a 'master-mistress' who has 'a woman's face' but is 'a man in hue' (20.1–2, 7). In 53 the poet wonders:

> What is your substance, whereof are you made,
> That millions of strange shadows on you tend? . . .
> Describe Adonis, and the counterfeit
> Is poorly imitated after you;
> On Helen's cheek all art of beauty set,
> And you in Grecian tires are painted new.

> (53.1–2, 5–8)

The 'shadows' which attend the young man (perhaps his servants and admirers, or representations of him, either pictorial or verbal) give little clue to his substance, and so the poet is left uncertain both of the youth's real character and of how to describe him. How can one represent this man's physical beauty, since neither Adonis nor Helen are adequate images? Indeed, any description of these mythological figures themselves will only be inadequate imitations of the young man's beauty, since it is he himself who embodies the true ideal form. This deployment of both male and female examples shows an awareness of the youth's androgynous beauty, but at the same time indicates that the language of homosexual love – if it is to be more profound than Barnfield's sensuous longing – has to be exfoliated from inside the discourse of heterosexual passion.

The gift of a blank notebook from the poet to the young man (77) offers a private space in which the youth may understand himself and the relationship through his own writing, but no such response to the poet's work is ever delivered, unless sonnet 122 records it. This poem assures the lover that 'thy gift, thy tables, are within my brain/ Full charactered with lasting memory' (122.1–2), and because the contents of the lover's notebook ('tables') are etched on the poet's memory, he has given the book itself away. The poem concludes with the justification that for the poet to keep the book as a memorial of the youth 'were to import forgetfulness in me' (122.14). Whether we imagine this book to contain the youth's writings or the poet's, for the poet to pass them on to a third party seems strangely like a betrayal, however much he may try to turn it into an emblem of faithfulness. In either case, there is no security in such writing. The private space of these lovers' discourse remains something which is never quite shared between them, and never quite opened up to the reader: its meanings have to be fashioned by wresting other people's usages. And there remain so many blank spaces between the poems.

What kind of conclusion do the *Sonnets* reach? There is no narrative closure, nor is there any clear symbolic closure in a culminating image; at no point is sexual consummation figured directly. Instead there are several different forms of surrender, and multiple farewells. In sonnet 87 the poet relinquishes the youth in a poem which returns to the difference of power and status between the two men, reworking the imagery of sonnet 58:

> Farewell, thou art too dear for my possessing,
> And like enough thou know'st thy estimate.
> The charter of thy worth gives thee releasing;
> My bonds in thee are all determinate . . .

(87.1–4)

This desolate poem, which bitterly characterizes the youth as too valuable and the poet himself as worthless ('for that riches where is my deserving?': 87.6), ends with the idea that the poet's possession of the youth was as insubstantial as a dream:

> Thus have I had thee as a dream doth flatter,
> In sleep a king, but waking no such matter.

(87.13–14)

But this renunciation is as temporary and as unavailing as the moments of possession have been, and the poem leads into a group of sonnets which try to excuse the youth's fault, the canker (whatever it may be) which has corrupted his rose.

The last two dozen poems in the collection focus on the youth's sexual involvement with the 'dark lady', who has apparently been the poet's mistress, and these sonnets beat with an intense sexual jealousy which seems directed as much at the loss of the youth as the loss of the woman. At the same time as these poems surrender the youth to the woman, they attempt desperately to reclaim him by denying his autonomy: the identities of the three parties are fused and confused through fierce punning on 'will' (= William/ penis/ vagina/ sexual appetite: 134–6) and a convoluted play with the idea that the youth is, or possesses, the poet's own self (133–4): all these are attempts to write the poet into the sexual union of the young man and the dark lady, instead of standing Antonio-like on the edge of the stage.

The last poem in the group addressed to the youth is in an altogether different key: number 126 celebrates his beauty and his privilege in apparently being free from the ravages of time; but while Nature may detain him awhile from the process of ageing, ultimately she will surrender him to time and decay:

> She may detain, but still not keep her treasure.
> Her audit, though delayed, answered must be,
> And her quietus is to render thee.

> (126.11–12)

The poem had begun 'O thou, my lovely boy . . .', but the truth of that word 'my' has been in doubt throughout the sequence. As we read through this poem the focus shifts from the poet's possession of the boy to Nature's possession; finally Nature will give him up to Time. By the end of the poem the artist who earlier had made so many protestations of his ability to cheat Time by conferring immortality, has withdrawn from the scene. Where we would expect a concluding couplet, there is only silence: the poem ends at line 12, and the 1609 edition marks with brackets the missing lines. What more could be said? Finally the effort to hold this youth – and to hold him in words – is given up.

4

From the Restoration to the Romantics

How tired I am of keeping a mask on my countenance. How tight it sticks – it makes me sore.

The Journal of William Beckford in Portugal and Spain, p. 41

A SUBCULTURE AND ITS OBSERVERS

In the Renaissance texts discussed in the previous chapters, homosexual desire is either expressed within the continuum of public masculine relationships, or located in a privileged space, Barnfield's green world of pastoral delight or the secret folds of time and space within Shakespeare's *Sonnets* – places fashioned by the private imagination. But in the period between the later seventeenth century and the early nineteenth, a marked shift occurred in the way such desire was represented. A homosexual subculture emerged in London and some other cities, providing a new milieu for the social expression of desire, and prompting outraged comments by hostile observers who represented this increasingly visible way of life as a threat to godly British masculinity. The city took on a new configuration, for its geography now included cruising grounds and specialized clubs, the 'molly houses' where men gathered not only to have casual sex but to establish relationships which they celebrated in rituals which parodied those of the world outside. Here were lives which were not aligned with those masculine relationships which society approved, for they transgressed boundaries of class and social orderliness. These desires were no longer invisible by virtue of merging into the language of the orthodox world: instead, they escaped recognition by being hidden away until revealed by the puritanical vigilance of the Society for the Reformation of Manners, which from the 1690s onwards patrolled the city to uncover and publicize behaviour which it considered immoral. A contest for possession of social space was interwoven with a struggle for the power to define sexual behaviour: the men who frequented the molly houses were insisting on having a collectively-determined space in which they could assert their own sexuality, and the map of London now included a network of semi-clandestine places which offered relative security. Meanwhile anxiety about what was happening to masculinity was played out on the public stage, particularly in the comedy of the Restoration and early eighteenth century: here characters who are thought to prefer sex with men increasingly came to be seen as part of a specialized, identifiable group which had its own social spaces and leisure activities, but also threatened the language and *mores* of polite society.

Along with this change in the perception of social space went a change in the kind of world which literature provided, from an ontological to an epistemological space. In other words, Renaissance texts had fashioned an imagined world in which homosexual readers could live, in which their desires could generate speech and narrative, and the male body could be presented as the object of erotic and emotional interest: the text became a safe haven in which a special way of being was made possible; eighteenth-century texts, by contrast, are engaged in exhibiting homosexual men as objects to be read and recognized, thus providing that knowledge which is needed by the heterosexual writer and reader in order to place and punish homosexual desire. There is consequently a crucial shift in the possible relations of reader to text, for no longer does literature give the homosexual reader a resource for living, a medium for understanding his feelings and imagining ways of expressing them; rather, literature has become a cabinet of curiosities, a space in which specimens are classified and exhibited as cautionary examples. There is also a change in the kind of looking which literature enables, from texts which invite and reward the gaze of private erotic pleasure, to texts which submit their objects to the disapproving glare of social appraisal.

This anxiety to seek out and exhibit men who had sex with other men led to a wave of hangings and lynchings. While trials and executions for sodomy were rare in the sixteenth and seventeenth centuries, in the eighteenth and early nineteenth centuries hangings were more common: the rate seems to have fluctuated between one or two per decade in the late eighteenth century and one or two per year in the early nineteenth, with periodic purges and panics. While some sodomites were hanged, other victims of public morality (particularly men whose activity could not legally be deemed 'sodomy', which required evidence of penetration and emission) were exhibited in the pillory where the crowd pelted them with mud, bricks and dead animals. Some men remained locked in the pillory until the crowd had murdered them, as Edmund Burke described to the House of Commons in 1780:

> one of them being short of stature, and remarkably shortnecked, he could not reach the hole made for the admission of the head . . . the officers of justice, nevertheless, forced his head through the hole, and the poor wretch hung rather than walked as the pillory turned round . . . he soon grew black in the face and the blood forced itself out of his nostrils, his eyes, and his ears . . . the mob, nevertheless, attacked him and his fellow criminal with great fury . . . the officers seeing his situation, opened the pillory, and the poor wretch fell down dead on the stand of the instrument. The other man, he understood was so maimed and hurt by what had been thrown at him, that he now lay without hope of recovery. (Quoted from Crompton, *Byron and Greek Love*, p. 32)

Thus was English morality satisfied.

When the pressure to identify and punish was so fierce, the free expression of desire which we find in Renaissance texts was no longer possible. The longing gaze and the passionate devotion described in *Hero and Leander* or Shakespeare's *Sonnets* now had no safe private space to inhabit, nor could they ask to be construed within an unthreatening tradition of eroticized male friendship. Though desire may now have been acted out more freely within the confines of the molly houses, it virtually disappeared from the page. There are hardly any literary descriptions of the male body which are coloured by a homoerotic desire; the pleasures of the desiring gaze and the promises of consummation to follow have vanished. Instead homophobic texts by writers such as Garrick or Smollett require their readers to run their eyes over the clothed male body (a body often excessively, over-delicately clothed) in order to recognize the signs of deviance and danger. What is now shaping the gaze of male on male is an anxiety which seeks to distinguish the normal from the deviant, friends from sodomites. In the new culture of sensibility where men were encouraged to give free rein to their tender emotions (in novels like Henry Mackenzie's *The Man of Feeling* (1771)), it became vital to distinguish the male from the molly, and to mark out the boundaries of acceptable behaviour.

The anxieties which attended the rise of the self-defining homo-sexual culture can be traced in the mythologies promoted by the pamphlet literature. *The Phoenix of Sodom* [1813] describes the activ-ities of the Vere Street coterie and other late eighteenth-century scandals, and even if the details are factually correct they have been selected to suggest that these men are engaged in a parody of godly, polite society. Sunday was the 'grand day of rendezvous'; the meet-ing place included a room furnished as a chapel for marriages; another room had four beds where the nuptials were consummated by the couples in the sight of each other; one group of men dressed as women and carried out rituals relating to childbirth (pp. 22, 10, 28). Clearly readers are to be shocked that a counter-society seems to have grown up, usurping women's roles (and names), and devising ceremonies which mock the social and sacred rituals of the heterosexual world. The public and the private have become confused: here public rituals are parodically staged in private, and private sexual acts performed before onlookers. The pamphlet also notes the involvement of men from different classes, and refutes the common assumption that 'this passion has for its objects effeminate delicate beings only' (p. 13) – a particularly worrying observation since it thus becomes impossible to identify a sodomite by perceiving his outward effeminacy. It was the very visibility of the behaviour which caused offence to Charles Churchill. 'Sodom confronts and stares us in the face' (l. 294) he claimed in his poem *The Times* (1764), offering an example of the blatant sexual invitation to be found in society nowadays: behind a rich man's chair stands a beautiful boy, 'decked with a solitaire/ Which on his bare breast glittering played' (ll. 418–19). The anonymous poem *Sodom's Catastrophe* (1748) de-scribes a grove of trees whose fruits are speciously alluring, but rotten inside:

> So tempting and so fair, the gilded skin
> Where rottenness and dust lie hid within:
> Such are the cheating prospects which are found
> Through all the coasts of this enchanted ground:
> True emblem of those fair, but false delights
> By which the rude unwary Sodomites
> Were overthrown.

(p. 61)

The emblem is confident that the relationship between attractive surface and rotten core is legible. It was a confidence not shared by all who tried to read this new class of men.

In this milieu, consummation cannot be represented as the aim of desire, only as the object of disgust. It cannot be something which is part of the British way of life, only something which foreigners indulge in. And yet some writers did use tales set abroad to suggest homoerotic possiblities which evoke a double frisson of desire and danger, while students of ancient Greek literature and sculpture found that these relics of another culture nourished their own emotions and suggested legitimate alternative forms of social and sexual behaviour. This chapter will explore the literature created in and around the subculture, and the resources which still existed for the expression of homosexual desire when literature had become more anxious and self-conscious about depicting close relations between men.

The homosexual subculture seems to have developed in London in the last decade of the seventeenth century, but prior to that there are indications of homoerotic interests in the writing of the Earl of Rochester from the 1670s. The milieu in and for which Rochester was writing was aristocratic, rakish and predominantly heterosexual, but several of his poems include evocations of the pleasures of sex with boys. One stanza of 'The Disabled Debauchee' describes a contest between the speaker and a woman:

> Nor shall our love-fits, Cloris, be forgot,
> When each the well-looked linkboy strove t'enjoy,
> And the best kiss was the deciding lot
> Whether the boy fucked you, or I the boy.

> (ll. 37–40)

But the outcome of the game is not recorded. In the song 'Love a woman? you're an ass', the argument that the pleasure derived from women is not worth the trouble, and a man is better off drinking with his male friends, culminates with the lines:

> And if busy love entrenches,
> There's a sweet, soft page of mine
> Does the trick worth forty wenches.

> (ll. 14–16)

In the song 'Upon his drinking a bowl' the design of the cup which the speaker calls for includes a homoerotic motif:

> But carve thereon a spreading vine,
> Then add two lovely boys;
> Their limbs in amorous folds entwine,
> The type of future joys.

(ll. 17–20)

The rake's style of life is caught in an anonymous poem from this circle called 'Régime de vivre' which is spoken by a Rochesterian persona. The rake wakes up late to find that his prostitute has left him:

> I storm, and I roar, and I fall in a rage,
> And missing my whore, I bugger my page.

(ll. 11–12)

In these poems, sex with boys is generally imagined only as a hypothetical possibility, rather than as part of a narrative of desire, and the young male body is only sketchily represented. These gestures form part of the rhetoric of an all-male society, offering an easy and unproblematic alternative to (or respite from) sexual involvement with women. In Rochester's writing it is women who generate the writer's emotions – tenderness, lust, contempt, disgust – while the homosexual pleasures remain motifs which help to establish the speaker's libertine credentials and to remind women that they are not indispensable.

One of the products of the Rochester circle, though its authorship is uncertain, is a piece of pornography in dramatic form called *Sodom, or, The Quintessence of Debauchery*, which circulated in manuscript. It depicts a King Bolloximian who has grown tired of sex with women and has decided to turn to buggery. As in Rochester's poems, the homosexual choice is presented as a deliberate turning away from women which is prompted by boredom or a desire to humiliate the woman. Though the stage directions call for frequent displays of male nudity, the text shows no interest in the male body itself as the object of desire, and the characters are reduced to convenient orifices: 'his arse shall for a minute be my spouse', Bolloximian tells Pockinello (I. i. 54). The play focuses on a bored quest for new sensations, and the king is pleased with the stronger physical pleasure which sodomy provides. The other pleasure which the pursuit of sodomy offers is that of transgression, and homosexual sex is envisaged as the acme of excess and deviance, 'the quintessence of debauchery', indeed. The play takes many of its gestures from the ranting speeches of Restoration heroic drama, as when the king declares: 'I'll heaven invade and bugger all the gods' (V. i. 13). Thus the play associates sodomy with blasphemy, a double transgression. In the final scene we learn that the nation has become diseased because of the craze for sodomy, and is being punished for doing 'what love and nature disallows' (V. i. 35). The king and his court are consumed in an apocalyptic ending complete with shrieking demons, fire and brimstone. *Sodom* is generated by a bored search for excess, the desire to discover yet new taboos to break, rather than any interest in love between men, and its frisson depends upon the reader sharing its essentially conservative assumption that sodomy is the ultimate form of transgression against society, nature and God.

Poetry which describes a different homosexual milieu is provided by Aphra Behn, whose work is often interested in the attractiveness of sexual ambiguity in both men and women. In her poem 'On the death of Mr Greenhill, the famous painter' she writes that the artist was 'soft and gentle as a love-sick maid' (l. 22), and 'had all that could adorn a face,/ All that could either sex subdue' (ll. 44–5). This is phrased as a compliment which suggests that the dual sexual attraction was all of a piece with his artistic accomplishment, part of his grace and creativity. A fascinating ambiguity also characterizes the descriptions of John Hoyle, who was apparently Behn's lover for a while. In 'A Ballad on Mr J.H., to Amoret asking why I was so sad' Hoyle is described as intelligent, beautiful and well-dressed, but the accent is particularly on his grace and purity, which are figured through pastoral images:

> His cassock was of green, as trim
> As grass upon a river brim;
> Untouched or sullied with a spot . . .

> (ll. 13–15)

In her poem 'Our Cabal' Hoyle appears with his companion Edward Bedford, thinly disguised as 'Lycidas' and 'Philander'. The female narrator finds Hoyle difficult to read. He is accompanied by women to whom he 'barely returns civility', and

> His tongue no amorous parley makes,
> But with his looks alone he speaks:
> And though he languish, yet he'll hide
> That grateful knowledge with his pride.

(ll. 165–8)

No words from him will reveal any love which Hoyle may have for a woman, no matter how gratifying that knowledge might be to her. At Hoyle's side is Bedford,

> ... who ne'er paid
> A sigh or tear to any maid:
> So innocent and young he is,
> He cannot guess what passion is,
> But all the love he ever knew
> On Lycidas he does bestow,
> Who pays his tenderness again,
> Too amorous for a swain to a swain.
> A softer youth was never seen,
> His beauty maid, but man his mien; ...
> His eyes towards Lycidas still turn,
> As sympathising flowers to the sun,
> Whilst Lycidas whose eyes dispense
> No less a grateful influence
> Improves his beauty, which still fresher grows:
> Who would not under two such suns as those?

(ll. 181–98)

Behn moves beyond the conventions of homoerotic pastoral by writing about identifiable contemporaries who are part of her own social milieu (it is 'our cabal') rather than an exotic subculture; moreover, she is trying to map complex desires which do not make themselves easily accessible to the poet's or reader's understanding. Philander's feeling for Lycidas is not passion but an immature love, and yet 'tenderness' can be a strong word in the Restoration erotic vocabulary, often used for a woman's acceptance of a man's sexual advances. The response of Lycidas to Philander is 'too amorous for a swain to a swain', and yet it is not condemned. The eyes of Philander are turned towards Lycidas, whose own eyes return a nourishing influence. Despite the difference in age, this is evidently a mutually loving relationship. But it clearly excludes the female viewer, who would herself relish a tender look from Lycidas. The poem ends with the narrator suggesting to her friend Cloris that they should try their luck with Lycidas, but the success or otherwise of the women's attempt to break into this homoerotic bond is not recorded. The poem seems unable or unwilling to move beyond its recording of the woman's gaze into a narrative in which she would be competing with homosexual desire. Gentleness and delicate beauty are, for this female observer, attractive masculine traits, and the homoerotic relationships between the men in her circle in no way compromise their masculinity. Behn's gaze is affectionate, if puzzled and perhaps disappointed, and the desire to know is for once free from the desire to punish; but it is still an outsider's view.

There is one text which ostensibly comes from within the homosexual subculture and claims to preserve its authentic voice, the semi-fictional *Love Letters written between a certain late Nobleman and the famous Mr Wilson* (probably first published 1723, reprinted 1745). It is not simply another of the period's epistolary novels, yet the letters which it presents have clearly been edited for publication, and the degree of editorial intervention (or outright invention) is now impossible to determine. It is offered as a collection of genuine documents to a readership interested in homosexual scandal in high society, and it includes sufficient circumstantial detail about the fashionable London world and enough teasing half-allusions to give it plausible connexions with the London of the reader's own experience, connexions which different readers may have found worrying or alluring.

The famous Mr Wilson was the young Edward Wilson, killed in a duel in 1694, whose rapid rise from poverty to conspicuous wealth had occasioned much speculation a generation earlier. The *Love Letters* imply that the source of this mysterious wealth was not gambling, alchemy, necromancy or a secret mistress, as had been suggested, but a prominent nobleman. The twenty short letters are framed by an editorial preface and concluding observations which claim to piece the fragmentary narrative together into a coherent whole, and yet leave many gaps to tease and prompt the reader's imagination.

The preface (pp. 13–14) addresses the reader as a member of polite society who may be surprised, or even 'a little alarmed', at 'a piece of history which has lain so long in the dark, and is now, more by chance than any other means, coming to a fair and open light'. This stress on the unfolding of the story from private spaces to the gaze of 'the politer part of mankind' is a key part of the preface's strategy, and the editor reassures his reader that the letters are authentic, for they 'were found in the cabinet of the deceased, which had passed through some hands before the private drawer, the lodgement of this scene of guilt, was discovered.' The reader is therefore promised the opening out of dark secrets, access to the contents of the previously overlooked secret drawer, and a secure knowledge of what had hitherto been the subject of 'dark guesses and conjectures'. Knowledge, then, is what this text offers, and it is in order to make the reader's knowledge complete that 'the editor has been obliged to connect the broken parts of this story by some additional remarks which have come to his knowledge from several hands, with whom the parties were very familiar'. The editor thinks that the letters testify to their genuineness by their very style: they are open about what they are, for 'the thing speaks itself', and they reveal the nobleman who wrote them to be a man 'of birth, and figure, and many other court-like accomplishments'. And yet what the letters reveal so plainly is also 'a sin which is not familiar to our northern climate', and readers are advised that to savour the elegance of the nobleman's letters they will have to translate the story into the normative terms of their own social milieu 'by applying the passion of these letters to distinct sexes . . . all the weeds will then vanish, or be turned into flowers'. The stylistic felicities can be appreciated undisturbed through this apparently unproblematic translation between genders. The preface moves curiously between assertions of openness and legibility, and evocations of the hidden, for the revelation is incomplete: one letter which relates to a living person is withheld, though 'another opportunity may make that supplement both a necessary and useful key to the whole adventure.' In sum, the preface offers the revelation of dark secrets, and at the same time promises a civilized pleasure which can only be derived by translating the text out of its homosexual milieu. That invitation, however, is disingenuous, for everything about the book

– from its title to its enticing preface, its fragmentary text in a language which has been specifically forged to take account of the dangers of clear interpretation, and its disapproving editorial commentary – marks it out as a book whose purpose is to reveal a clandestine milieu of forbidden pleasures. The world of homosexual passion is, paradoxically, both closed and opened, both completely legible yet an incomplete text, a special world yet one which lies within the fashionable London familiar to the reader. Translation is necessary for one kind of readerly pleasure, yet at the same time impossible without destroying the very reason for the text's existence.

The first letter, from the nobleman to Wilson, shows that Wilson has misinterpreted the nobleman's preliminary advance, for what was offered was not, as he suspected, a duel, but 'a challenge where to give and receive excess of pleasure was to have been the only combat between us'. This letter suggests various interpretations of Wilson's motives for not responding: he may have 'a cold insensibility', or a 'peevish, coy pride' like a woman who has to be courted, or simply be waiting for money. Various rhetorical strategies are already at work here, and one wonders whether these are the terms which an actual correspondent used, or the terms which the compiler of this volume thought appropriate: the letter constructs the young Wilson in feminine terms, as the one who needs to be wooed; it presents homosexual desire as aiming hedonistically at 'excess of pleasure'; and it establishes for us the geography of the subculture, which is evident in the postscript appointing a rendezvous: 'Greenwich Park, be behind Flamstead's House, and I shall see you, tomorrow nine at night, don't fail to come.' Wilson's reply in Letter II explains that the preliminary letter had included 'ambiguous phrases which lay liable to variety of constructions', and reveals that Wilson assumes (or finds it a safer strategy to assume) that the stranger who is propositioning him is 'a fine lady'.

A gap in the narrative entices the reader to imagine for himself the encounter behind Flamstead's House, but Letter III, from the nobleman to 'my Willy', makes an invitation which leaves little to the imagination: 'then come away, the bath is ready, that I may wrestle with it, and pit it, and pat it, and ––––– it; and then for cooler sport devour it with greedy kisses; for Venus and all the poets' wenches are but dirty dowdies to thee'. Once again, the postscript reveals the texture of this milieu: 'Put on the Brussels head and Indian atlas I sent yesterday'. (This refers to a lace headdress and a silk satin dress.) For all the nobleman's contempt of women, dressing his lover in women's clothes is an ingredient in his pursuit of pleasure.

The subsequent letters do not provide a coherent narrative, but instead offer moments which illustrate the pleasures and vicissitudes of such an affair. In Letter IV their mutual acquaintances are puzzled about the source of Wilson's wealth, and the nobleman has to feign ignorance; in VI Wilson describes how he was apprehended by 'a crew of ruffians' while dressed as a lady; in VII the nobleman has heard that Wilson is ill, and consequently suffers 'a thousand dreadful apprehensions'; in VIII he wonders whether Wilson is playing fast and loose with him; in X it is Wilson's turn to be anguished, when he sees the lord at the theatre with 'a new favourite mistress'. The nobleman's reply in Letter XI mixes the language of a lover's endearments with casual disparagement of women:

> Did it fret and tease itself because I have got a wench, but don't let one fear perplex it: when I have thee in my arms, thou shalt see how I despise all the pleasures that changeling sex can give compared to one touch of thine. It's true, I had her dirty maidenhead ... to stop some good-natured reflections I found made on my indifference that way. But thou alone art every and all the delight my greedy soul covets, which is heightened to such an excess that even pains me, to find my dear Willy has such a tenderness for its nown [*sic*] love. Then hasten to my fond heart, that leaps and bounds with impatience to see thee, and devour thee with greedy kisses.

But there is a difference of tone and style between the two correspondents, Wilson maintaining to a certain extent the decorum required by their social distance ('My Lord, it is not to be expressed with how much rapture I received your Lordship's commands to attend you ...': XII) while the nobleman uses a manner which combines a lover's idiolect with straight bribery:

> thou canst be guilty of no crime to me but that of this peevish absence, which I shall chide it for, and beat it, and then eat it up with greedy kisses. I have got the six pretty horses it said it liked before it left the town, and something it shan't know of till it comes. (Letter XIII)

But soon the nobleman erupts in jealousy:

> Is this thy faith? Is this thy return to all my foolish lavish fondness? It seems I have taught you a trade, and harlot-like you intend to be as common and as despicable as those abject wretches . . . What, couldst thou find none but that old nauseous dog to kiss and slobber thee? (Letter XV)

Since the last letter between them (XIX) addresses Wilson as 'my dearest boy' we suppose that the difference was made up, but there is no clear conclusion to the correspondence, which ends with an enigmatic letter from Wilson to a 'Mr L---'.

The concluding editorial observations fill out the story by describing how 'Mrs V--ll--s' tried to discover Wilson's secret, and how the nobleman's casual seduction of 'Cloris' (presumably the mistress of Letters X–XI) led to her death. The duplicity of the nobleman in deceiving Cloris is paralleled by his dissimulation in the face of polite society during his affair with Wilson, while the editor adds the suggestion that Wilson was skilled in the arts of deceit and was led by a merely mercenary interest to counterfeit a passion for the nobleman which he did not actually feel: thus the story is fashioned editorially into a cautionary tale of the multiple duplicities which attend homosexual behaviour. The editor also invites the reader to be surprised that 'so unnatural an appetite' was expressed in so 'tender, passionate and obscene a manner' (p. 35). This retrospective stress on the open sexuality of the language contrasts with the expectation raised in the preface that we are about to encounter a tenderness and passion which will gratify polite taste: after reading the letters we are now helped to the comforting discovery that corrupt passion reveals itself in corrupt language. Whatever the truth may be about the origin and authenticity of the letters themselves, the editorial framework which turns them into a text for public consumption has made them speak to the anxieties of a society in which homosexual relationships are conducted in the midst of the fashionable world, adapting its haunts, its strategies of concealment and its languages of desire. The *Love Letters* exhibit the homosexual milieu as something to be revealed, known, and worried over. The revelation is fragmentary, and the reader's knowledge of this half-hidden world which folds itself within his own milieu remains imperfect and tantalizingly conjectural. But perhaps that tantalizing half-knowledge is itself an important source of pleasure, as both the text and its gaps feed the voyeuristic imagination of the reader, whatever his own sexuality.

FOPS OR MOLLIES? FRIENDS OR LOVERS?

In Restoration comedy the few characters who are given homosexual interests inhabit almost the same social space as the others; they have not yet become a source of anxiety to society, and they can be useful adjuncts to the progatonists in the competitive world of predatory heterosexuality. One such character is Sir Jolly Jumble in Thomas Otway's *The Soldier's Fortune* (1681). This is how Fourbin describes his encounter with Sir Jolly:

> Walking one day upon the Piazza about three of the clock i' th' afternoon . . . I chance to encounter a person of goodly presence, and worthy appearance . . . who perceiving me also equipped as I am with a mien and air which might well inform him I was a person of no inconsiderable quality, came very respectfully up to me, and, after the usual ceremonies between persons of parts and breeding had passed, very humbly enquired of me what is it o' clock . . . The freedom of commerce increasing, after some little inconsiderable questions *pour passer le temps* and so, he was pleased to offer me the courtesy of a glass of wine . . . In short we agreed and went together. As soon as we entered the room, 'I am your most humble servant, sir', says he; 'I am the meanest of your vassals, sir', said I; 'I am very happy in lighting into the acquaintance of so worthy a gentleman as you appear to be, sir', said he again. 'Worthy Sir Jolly', then came I upon him again o' t' other side (for you must know by that time I had groped out his title) 'I kiss your hands from the bottom of my heart, which I shall be always ready to lay at your feet.' . . . he had nothing to say; his sense was transported with admiration of my parts. (I. i. 102–39)

Two social worlds meet here, but pleasurably rather than threateningly. At one level this is the comically ceremonious meeting of two men who are hoping to clinch a business deal, but the audience is offered an undercurrent of innuendo which reshapes this as an encounter in a cruising ground. On stage the implications could be spelt out very easily. When Sir Jolly appears it becomes clear that his profession of go-between or marriage-broker is fuelled by a strong voyeurism:

> Ah my little son of thunder, if thou hadst her in thy arms now between a pair of sheets; and I under the bed to see fair play, boy, gemini, what would become of me? . . . There would be doings, oh Lawd! I under the bed! (II. i. 30–4)

His interest evidently lies more with the man than the woman:

> *Sir Jolly (to Beaugard)*: My hero! my darling! my Ganymede! how dost thou? Strong! wanton! lusty! rampant! hah, ah, ah! She's thine, boy, odd she's thine, plump, soft, smooth, wanton! hah, ah, ah! Ah rogue, ah rogue! here's shoulders, here's shape! there's a foot and leg, here's a leg, here's a leg – Qua a-a-a-a. *(Squeaks like a cat, and tickles Beaugard's legs).* (I. i. 234–9)

Sir Jolly's imagination quickly moves from the woman's body to the man's, and where his imagination leads his hands follow. Sir Jolly may be absurd, but he is not sinister; he is not exclusively homosexual, nor is he effeminate; his sexuality may be jumbled but it is still jolly, and he performs a useful role within the play's stylized version of the audience's own social world.

In early eighteenth-century drama, however, we find effeminate figures held up to ridicule as a result of what seems to be a double fear about masculinity: on the one hand, a specific group of men are fairly openly enjoying sex with other men; on the other, men generally are being encouraged to conduct themselves in a more civilized way, to put aside their rough and violent behaviour and make them fit company for women in their leisure hours. The anxieties expressed about the new homosexual subculture may be related to anxieties about men becoming effeminized as part of the eighteenth-century pursuit of politeness and sensibility. Certainly a recurring theme in the new depiction of homosexual men is their effeminacy, and the usual name for them is 'molly', from the Latin *mollis*, soft.

One such figure is Mr Maiden in Thomas Baker's play *Tunbridge Walks* (1703). Maiden used to be a milliner's apprentice until, he tells us, 'a gentleman took a fancy to me, and left me an estate; but that's no novelty, for abundance of people nowadays take a fancy to a handsome young fellow' (p. 7). Homosexuality and effeminacy are explicitly linked in this characterization. Maiden never desires 'any private love-favours' from women (p. 8), and several innuendos suggest a simultaneous fascination with and recoil from male sexuality: 'if he had drawn his sword, I should have swoonded away' (p. 9); 'there's nothing we beaux take more pride in than a set of genteel footmen' (p. 41); and when Squib and Loveworth drag Maiden off to the tavern he cries out, 'O Lard, I shall be ravished' (p. 31). The song which Maiden arranges to have performed assembles the clichés conveniently:

> If moving softness can subdue,
> See, nymphs, a swain more soft than you:
>   We patch and we paint,
>   We're sick and we faint,
> To the vapours and spleen we pretend;
>   We play with a fan,
>   We squeak and we scream,
> We're women, mere women i' th' end.
>
>   Your airs we defy,
>   Your beauty deny,
> Be as gay and as fine as you can;
>   Ye nymphs have a care,
>   Be more nice and more fair,
> Or your lovers in time we may gain.

(p. 20)

The motivation behind this song is complex. Though sung on stage on behalf of Maiden and his kind, it is evidently produced at another level on behalf of men who are troubled by the new phenomenon. The mollies are translated completely into women of the most vain and frivolous kind, thus distancing homosexual interests as far as possible from the kind of masculinity implicitly shared by playwright and audience. A contempt for women is equally apparent, along with a wish that women themselves should be 'more nice [i.e. refined] and more fair' if they are to attract and hold the attentions of men. Woven into this song is a plea to women by heterosexual men to make themselves more attractive, as if it were feared that men's heterosexual feelings were not strong enough to survive unassisted.

Maiden does not frequent taverns with the boisterous rakes, but takes tea with the ladies, discussing with them the finer points of women's fashion and household management, and even goes about dressed in women's clothes: 'I was dressed up last winter in my Lady Fussock's cherry-colour damask, sat a whole play in the front seat of the box, and was taken for a Dutch woman of quality' (p. 21). Maiden is part of a group which meets at his chambers:

> There's Beau Simper, Beau Rabbitsface, Beau Eithersex, Colonel Coachpole, and Count Drivel that sits with his mouth open, the prettiest company at a bowl of virgin punch – we never make it with rum nor brandy, like your sea-captains, but two quarts of mead to half a pint of white wine, lemon juice, borage and a little perfume; then we never read gazettes . . . like your coffee-house fellows, but play with fans, and mimic the women, scream 'hold up your tails', make curtsies and call one another 'Madam'. (pp. 30–1)

Maiden's milieu combines the over-refinement of delicate drinks with the under-refinement of Count Drivel, and the whole is parodic and parasitic, a culture of mimicry which apes women and has no claim to be part of masculinity. Indeed, Maiden has no claim to be part of polite society at all, for at the end of the play it emerges that the story of an estate left to him by a wealthy male admirer was merely a jest contrived to make Maiden ridiculous. He is returned to his previous life as a member of the working class ('forced to turn mechanic'), and in fact as a con-man: 'I have a brother too', he says, 'so like me nobody can distinguish us, and we used to cheat folks and lay it upon one another' (p. 60). It is a clear sign that Maiden and his kind can be accorded no substantial public presence, no identity of their own: they are mere parody and pretence.

Maiden has a successor, Fribble, in David Garrick's play *Miss in her Teens* (1747), who is similarly an expert on female fashion and recoils from 'masculine beasts' such as rude hackney-coach drivers. Garrick's caricature occasioned a reply by Nathaniel Lancaster called *The Pretty Gentleman* (1747) which opens by ostensibly rebuking Garrick for making fun of men like Fribble, but soon reveals itself to be a satire on effeminacy. The tract begins by tracing the history of the pretty gentlemen (none are recorded until the reign of James I, we are told) and says that they are now determined to polish British manners. Their scheme of reformation is promoted by 'The

Fraternity of Pretty Gentlemen', and 'the grand principle of this fellowship is mutual love, which, it must be confessed, they carry to the highest pitch' (p. 9). This innuendo about the sexual basis of their association is confirmed by an allusion to the 'Theban band', the regiment of male lovers described in the *Symposium*, while another allusion to Plato describes the bond which unites them: 'Such an harmony of temper is preserved amongst them . . . that the spirit of one seems to have passed into the other; or rather, they all breathe the same soul. This is the secret charm that the Platonists talk of, the intellectual faculty which connects one man with another, and ties the knot of virtuous friendship' (pp. 9–10). It is clear how we are expected to understand this 'intellectual faculty' and 'virtuous friendship'.

The pretty gentlemen spend their time in feminine occupations, because they are physically unsuited to masculine pursuits:

> there is something in the drudgery of masculine knowledge by no means adapted to youths of so nice a frame . . . The enfeebled tone of their organs and spirits [with puns on the meanings 'penis' and 'semen'] does therefore naturally dispose them to the softer and more refined studies: furniture, equipage, dress, the tiring room and the toyshop . . . Or, if the mind is bent upon manual exercise, the knotting-bag is ready at hand . . . With equal skill their practised fingers apply the needle and rejoin the lace; with equal facility they convey the gliding shuttle through the opening thread, and form the various knots. Pretty innocents! How virtuously, how usefully are their hours employed! Not in the wrangling squabbles of the bar, or the unmannerly contentions of the senate; not in the robust sports of the field, or in a toilsome application to ungentlemanlike science; but in the pretty fancies of dress, in criticisms upon fashions, in the artful disposition of china jars and other foreign trinkets; in sowing, in knitting garters, in knotting of fringe and every gentle exercise of feminine economy. (pp. 10–12)

The idea that their devotion to feminine pastimes is a substitute for the pursuit of masculine knowledge is important, for the tract suggests that it is the very capacity for thought which is being undermined along with the traditional gender roles. True knowledge – obtained with effort and deployed to the public benefit – is rejected by such people. Rational discourse and the culture which it makes possible are threatened by the way the pretty gentlemen use language merely to chatter:

> There are two kinds of conversation: the one close and continued, the other loose and unconnected. The first was practised amongst us whilst the enemies of elegance prevailed, but now the latter has deservedly gained the ascendant, as it is perfectly suited to the turn and cast of our polite assemblies of every denomination. The gravity of dull knowledge is at last happily exploded: masculine sense and wit are rejected as obsolete and unfashionable talents, and better supplied by the more engaging charms of the contrary qualities. Nothing is now heard but sweet chit-chat and tender prittle-prattle, shreds of sentiments and cuttings of sentences – all soft and charming, elegant and polite. (pp. 15–16)

The power of the mind to pursue connected thinking (figured as a masculine characteristic) and the capacity of language to signify ideas, are alike threatened by the disconnected chatter which the pretty gentlemen have introduced into 'our polite assemblies of every denomination'. In their writing, 'happily freed from the shackles of connecting and restraining rules, the diction roves and wanders, now here, now there, and with a wondrous facility glides so imperceptibly from one flower to another that the most subtle penetrator would be at loss to find where this ends and where that begins' (p. 25). The pretty gentlemen take care never to contradict something another person has said, happy to surrender their own judgement in the name of good breeding. This subculture is damaging society at large by destroying the pursuit and deployment of knowledge, and the very capacity of language to convey ideas and promote sound judgement.

Much is made of the false refinement of the language used by these gentlemen, and Lancaster is at pains to catch the accent: 'Oh! pard'n me, mi dear! I ke'n't possibly be of that apinion!' (p. 14). As in the *Love Letters*, linguistic and moral corruption coalesce, for apparent dissent 'is only a polite artifice that he may flatter your judgement with a finer address'. A shocking transgression of decorum may draw the ultimate rebuke: 'O! fie! ye filthy creter!', yet even that is modulated into a corrupt elegance:

> The epithet 'filthy', as it appears upon paper, may seem somewhat coarse and unclean, but were you to hear how he liquidates

the harshness of the sound, and conceals the impurity of the idea by a sweetened accent, you would grow enamoured of his address, and admire the enchanting beauties of refined elocution. *Oh! fie! ye filt-hy creter!* How easy, how gentle, how humane a chastisement for the highest offence! (pp. 14–15)

The tract concludes by attempting to define the kind of elegance promoted by these pretty gentlemen:

> Elegance is the absence or debilitation of masculine strength and vigour, or rather, the happy metamorphosis, or the gentleman turned lady; that is, female softness adopted into the breast of a male, discovering itself by outward signs and tokens in feminine expressions, accent, voice, air, gesture and looks. Or, as the French more clearly define it, a *je ne sçais quoi.* (p. 33)

Definition is vital, for the society of real men and real women needs to know what it is dealing with, yet definition proves elusive, and the description unravels into a series of alternatives and further explanations, enacting the difficulty of pinning down this creature of change. The definition envisages a femininity adopted into the heart of the male, but not as a secret, for this change will make itself manifest and legible by many outward signs. The resort to *je ne sçais quoi* ('I don't know what') is a comic gesture of resignation, but one which carries a sharp point: the phrase had been used by French neoclassical critics to evoke that indefinable brilliance of imagination and language which characterizes the perfect utterance. It is an apt gesture with which to dismiss these indefinable perverters of language and destroyers of social and sexual definition.

A comparable anxiety over definitions is evident in the sensitivities surrounding male friendship which are exemplified in the adaptation of *The Merchant of Venice* made in 1701 by George Granville under the title of *The Jew of Venice.* The prologue contributed by Bevill Higgons is spoken by the ghosts of Shakespeare and Dryden. After lamenting the debased judgement of audiences who are unmoved by passion, and 'deaf indeed to nature and to love', deserting true drama for French farce, 'Dryden' complains:

> Through perspectives reversed they nature view,
> Which give the passions' images, not true:

> Strephon for Strephon sighs, and Sappho dies
> Shot to the soul by brighter Sappho's eyes:
> No wonder then their wandering passions roam,
> And feel not nature, whom th' have overcome.
> For shame let genial love prevail again,
> You beaux love ladies, and you ladies men.

(sig. A4ʳ)

So society is deserting the natural in pursuit of the unnatural, and not only in its theatrical preferences: men are now in love with other men, and women with women. Granville seems anxious to avoid any suspicion of impropriety in the relationship between Antonio and Bassanio, and drives home a clear and emphatic distinction between friendship and love, consistently excising lines in the original which might have suggested an exclusive and possibly physical union between the two men. As Granville stresses in his preface, the reader 'will observe . . . many Manly and Moral Graces in the Characters and Sentiments', and it is into the extended definition of moral manliness that Granville's play puts most of its energy.

The adaptation opens without Antonio's melancholy: there is no secret here to be read or guessed at. When he offers to help Bassanio, he does not say (as Shakespeare's character does):

> My purse, my person, my extremest means
> Lie all unlock'd to your occasions.

(I. i. 138–9)

but:

> My purse, my person, my extremest means,
> Are all my friend's.

(p. 2)

Granville's erasure of this implication of a shared secrecy may reflect unease about the connotations which secrecy shared between men had now acquired, while the idea that Antonio's person might 'lie all unlocked' to Bassanio's needs must in 1701 have seemed too much like a sexual invitation. To avoid any doubt, Granville makes Antonio define friendship as he rebukes Bassanio for his hesitant way of asking a favour:

> Is this to be a friend? With blushing cheek,
> With downcast eyes and with a faltering tongue,
> We sue to those we doubt: friendship is plain,
> Artless, familiar, confident and free.

> (p. 2)

Friendship is open and unblushing; to be a man of silence and secrecy, or one who avoids the gaze of others and speaks his requests falteringly, would run the risk of being interpreted as a man with something unmanly to hide.

Granville is careful to stress that although Antonio may give his body for his friend, this gift has no erotic significance; instead it is an example of that generosity and benevolence which is characteristic of manly and moral virtue:

> what is a pound of flesh,
> What my whole body, every drop of blood,
> To purchase my friend's quiet!

> (p. 9)

If Antonio's offering of his body for Bassanio is pure benevolence, Shylock's obsession with Antonio's flesh is something more than pure malevolence, as he takes pleasure in contemplating which part of Antonio's body he will cut off:

> Let me see. What think you of your nose,
> Or of an eye--- or of ---- a pound of flesh
> To be cut off, and taken from what part
> Of your body--- I shall think fit to name.

> (p. 8)

The play pauses over the possibility that an unnameable part of Antonio's body – represented in the text only by dashes – might be the object of Shylock's perverse sexual interest, and this innuendo helps to establish Shylock as a threat to the kind of open, manly comradeship exemplified by Antonio and Bassanio.

Manliness does not require displays of affection and emotion to be suppressed, but it does require that they be carefully defined and not left open to misconstruction. When Antonio and Bassanio part for the latter to go to Belmont, Bassanio exclaims:

> One more embrace: to those who know not friendship
> This may appear unmanly tenderness,
> But 'tis the frailty of the bravest minds.

(p. 20)

In the trial scene, Antonio's self-sacrifice is made into a moment of total openness:

> Now, do your office,
> Cut deep enough be sure, and whet thy knife
> With keenest malice; for I would have my heart
> Seen by my friend.

(p. 35)

Antonio's heart evidently harbours no secrets: the openness of this male bond reassures us that it carries no danger. In Shakespeare, Bassanio and Gratiano both say that they would willingly sacrifice their wives so as to redeem Antonio's life. Granville removes this assertion of the primacy of the male bond over the obligations of love and marriage, substituting an offer from Bassanio to die in Antonio's place. There then follows a contest between Antonio and Bassanio as to which of them is to die for the other, so that the issue is not the rivalry of male friendship versus marriage, but rather which of the men is to have the opportunity to make the ultimate demonstration of friendship. Bassanio draws his sword to kill Shylock, and although the Duke is outraged at this violation of the court, he admires Bassanio's virtue more than he blames his passion: thus the passion is clearly virtuous, not excessive or suspect. At the end of the scene Bassanio embraces Antonio, but at the same time celebrates his love for Portia; these are the twin guarantors of his existence:

Once more, let me embrace my friend: welcome to life,
And welcome to my arms, thou best of men:
Thus of my love and of my friend possessed,
With such a double shield upon my breast,
Fate cannot pierce me now, securely blessed.

(p. 38)

The play's conclusion is that love and friendship are complementary, and are to be understood through reciprocal definition.

Granville's play, written at the moment when the homosexual subculture emerges, takes pains to define the relationship between Antonio and Bassanio as friendship, and to define the meaning of friendship as mutual benevolence; it makes the relationship open to the view, avoids places of secrecy, and calls attention to how any display of emotion or offering of the body is a token of moral manliness. In the light of the anxieties voiced in the prologue, it is evident that Granville carefully removed from Shakespeare's text any material which in the new climate could be construed as suggesting covert homosexual bonding.

The anxiety produced in others by the new (or newly visible) group of men who are now identifiable as effeminates and sodomites is evident in Smollett's *Roderick Random* (1748). In chapter 34 the narrator describes the arrival on board his ship of Captain Whiffle. The captain's clothes are more than expensive and fastidious, they are refined to the point of effeminacy: 'His coat, consisting of pink-coloured silk, lined with white, by the elegance of the cut retired backward, as it were, to discover a white satin waistcoat embroidered with gold, unbuttoned at the upper part, to display a brooch set with garnets, that glittered in the breast of his shirt, which was of the finest cambric' (p. 195). Smollett's description focuses on the disclosures which Whiffle's costume makes, the way fabrics open out enticingly to reveal riches underneath, and advertise the pleasures of their texture. His feminine delicacy unfits him for the manly work of a naval officer (he has only 'meagre legs'), and he has 'a mask on his face, and white gloves on his hands, which did not seem to be put on with an intention to be pulled off occasionally, but were fixed with a ring set with a ruby on the little finger of one hand, and by one set with a topaz on that of the other.' The mask and gloves protect his delicate skin, but do not conceal his nature, which they actually make more easily legible. The long description, from which these are only samples, is offered as a lesson in the art of recognition, and when we are told that Whiffle is accompanied by attendants who 'seemed to be of their patron's disposition', the word 'disposition' signals a shared interest which is not simply sartorial. Whiffle's personal surgeon, called Simper, has a cabin next to the captain's, 'that he might be at hand in case of accidents in the night' (p. 199), and no sooner has the reader noticed the innuendo than his inference is confirmed by the verdict of the ordinary sailors, who accused Whiffle 'of maintaining a correspondence with his surgeon, not fit to be named'. This is the culminating line of the episode, completing the reader's lesson in how to recognize the signs of deviant sexuality.

The narrator, however, is a slow learner – though in this respect his *naïveté* is supposedly to his credit – and he is easily duped later in the novel by Earl Strutwell (chapter 51). The earl favours him 'with a particular smile, squeeze of the hand, and a whisper, signifying that he wanted half an hour's conversation with me *tête à tête*' (p. 307). When Random is admitted to the earl's chamber, Strutwell 'frequently squeezed my hand . . . looking at me with a singular complacency in his countenance' (p. 308). Our hero weeps for gratitude at the earl's offers of help in securing a job, and this demonstration of sensibility provokes another demonstration from Strutwell, who 'caught me in his arms, hugged and kissed me with a seemingly paternal affection' (p. 309). Strutwell leads the conversation round to another subject, producing a copy of Petronius' *Satyricon* and testing Random's reaction to his subject matter:

> I own . . . that his taste in love is generally decried, and indeed condemned by our laws; but perhaps that may be more owing to prejudice and misapprehension, than to true reason and deliberation. The best man among the ancients is said to have entertained that passion; one of the wisest of their legislators has permitted the indulgence of it in his commonwealth; the most celebrated poets have not scrupled to avow it at this day; it prevails not only over all the east, but in most parts of Europe; in our own country it gains ground apace, and in all probability will become in a short time a more fashionable vice than simple fornication. (p. 310)

Strutwell then argues that 'the practice of this passion' (interestingly, he has no name for it himself) has the social advantage that it does

1. (*left*) Caravaggio,
    *David with the Head
    of Goliath*

2. (*below*) Crispin Van
    den Broeck *Two
    Young Men*

3. Michelangelo, *Archers Shooting at a Herm*

4. Ingres, *Oedipus explaining the riddle of the Sphinx*

5. (*above*) Joseph Wright
   of Derby, *The
   Gladiator*

6. (*right*) Herbert List,
   Rome, Italy, 1949

7. Frédéric Bazille, *Summer Scene*

8. (*below*) Henry Scott Tuke, *August Blue*

not entail prostitution or illegitimate offspring or disease, and then concludes: 'Nay, I have been told that there is another motive perhaps more powerful than all these, that induces people to cultivate this inclination; namely, the exquisite pleasure attending its success'. Random declares his 'utter detestation and abhorrence' of this by quoting lines from one of Smollett's own satires, at which Strutwell feigns satisfaction. The narrator is soon disabused by a more worldly-wise friend, who tells him that Strutwell is 'notorious for a passion for his own sex', and uses his servants like jackals to run down strangers who are then 'stripped . . . of their cash and everything valuable about them – very often of their chastity' (p. 313). So Strutwell is a fraud: he masquerades as a man of wealth and influence, but has neither; he proffers humanity and sensibility but is no more than a beast of prey. The narrator's education is completed when he is told that the servant who glared at him when he seemed to be favoured by the earl 'was at present the favourite pathic of his lord' (p. 313). This ends the chapter, and completes the revelation of the secrets at which the narrative had previously hinted. Random's lesson in how to recognize predatory homosexuals – which is also a lesson for the reader – is now complete.

But what is particularly interesting about this episode is the speech of justification which Smollett writes for Strutwell. We seem to hear, albeit through a distorting medium, a voice from the eighteenth-century subculture justifying his homosexual desire by invoking a number of values characteristic of the Enlightenment. It was permitted by the Greeks, praised by the poets, and is widely practised abroad; its condemnation by British laws is due more to prejudice than reason. We even hear a benevolent concern for the health of society. But of course Smollett inserts plenty of pointers which prepare the reader to share the narrator's revulsion – the idea that this is a foreign practice which is now gaining ground in England; the description of it as a 'fashionable vice'; and the voluptuary's culminating argument, that 'the gratification of this appetite' produces the most exquisite pleasure. We have here simply the language of vice and appetite, not of desire for the male body, let alone love. This love can, it seems, be given a voice only by its enemies.

But one text which ostensibly denounces sodomy also provides an alternative perspective, and gives the reader an opportunity for homoerotic pleasure even as the act is being condemned. In John Cleland's *Memoirs of a Woman of Pleasure* (1749) – commonly known as *Fanny Hill* – there is an episode in which the narrator, Fanny, finds herself in an inn. Into the room next door come two men, one aged 'towards nineteen, a tall, comely young man', the other a country lad 'not above seventeen, fair, ruddy, completely well made . . . a sweet pretty stripling' (p. 157). With some difficulty Fanny manages to create a spy-hole in the partition which divides the two rooms, and mounts precariously on a chair to see what the young men are doing. At first they are 'romping and pulling one another about, entirely, to my imagination, in frolic and innocent play', but soon they start to kiss and embrace. Then:

> the eldest unbuttoned the other's breeches, and removing the linen barrier, brought out to view a white shaft, middle-sized and scarce fledged; when after handling, and playing with it a little, with other dalliance, all received by the boy without other opposition than certain wayward coynesses, ten times more alluring than repulsive, he got him to turn round with his face from him, to a chair that stood hard by; when knowing, I suppose, his office, the Ganymede now obsequiously leaned his head against the back of it, and projecting his body made a fair mark, still covered with his shirt, as he thus stood in a side view to me but fronting his companion, who presently unmasking his battery produced an engine that certainly deserved to be put to a better use. (p. 158)

Fanny imagines that the elder boy's penis must be too large to permit 'things being pushed to odious extremities', but she is soon proved wrong, reflecting piously that all young men should be similarly disabused of such ignorance, 'that their innocence may not be betrayed into such snares'. She continues to watch the proceedings, 'purely that I might gather more facts', until the pair have finished. In her haste to raise the alarm and have the youths apprehended, Fanny jumps off her chair and trips, falling senseless to the ground. By the time she comes round, the culprits have escaped.

The episode is complex, and invites contradictory modes of reading. Fanny as narrator makes much of her desire for knowledge, claiming to be motivated simply by 'a spirit of curiosity . . . to see who they were' (p. 157), but as she watches she realizes not just 'who they were' but 'what they were' (p. 158), so that the young men become objects of a special form of knowledge, classified as types.

Unlike *Roderick Random*, this text does not assume that the narrator's ignorance and revulsion will be shared by the reader, for the narrator is clearly compromised. Fanny makes considerable efforts to be a voyeur, intruding on the space which the boys had carefully made private, and her viewpoint is both literally and figuratively precarious: she makes a great fuss about condemning the 'miscreants' in 'so criminal a scene', and intends to hand the boys over to the law to be hanged, yet as a prostitute her own moral position is scarcely more secure than her uncomfortable perch on the chair. Moreover, the episode provides much more than Smollett's kind of cautionary knowledge: those innocent young men about whom Fanny is so concerned could actually learn some useful hints on sexual technique from her detailed description, which also offers the homosexual reader the kind of pornographic pleasure provided to a different readership by the scenes of heterosexual intercourse which constitute most of the book – scenes which also gratify the homoerotic glance in their detailed descriptions of the sexually excited male body. After all Fanny's anxiety to discover who or what these young men are, they do not conform to the effeminate stereotypes promoted by Lancaster and Smollett, and her outrage is seen to be excessive. Fanny initially sees the two simply as attractive young guys, and although it is the elder who is penetrating the younger, the difference in age is slight; again, although the country boy is the passive partner (and is called by Fanny 'Ganymede' and 'minion') the implicit class distinction is not extended so far as to make one partner exploited: they show mutual affection and give mutual pleasure. This scene of reciprocal sexual satisfaction between two attractive and vigorous young men has nothing in common with representations of the mollies.

The description sits awkwardly with Fanny's commentary, and is completely at odds with the subsequent remarks of her friend Mrs Cole, who says that whatever may be the case abroad, in Britain 'there was a plague-spot visibly imprinted on all that are tainted with it', who lack 'all the manly virtues of their own sex, ... filled up with only the very worst vices and follies of ours', who ape women's behaviour while simultaneously loathing and condemning them (pp. 159–60). This assertion that homosexual men are instantly recognizable and blatantly effeminate is totally at variance with the scene which we have just read. Both Fanny and Mrs Cole are compromised commentators, as prostitutes 'out of whose mouths this practice tended to take something more precious than bread' (p. 159).

A male reader could take his cue from the way that Fanny's prejudiced and inept voyeurism is punished by her fall, and reject the intrusion of the female gazer into this world of male pleasure; thus he might be drawn himself into this circuit of male/male sexuality, viewing the couple not only with erotic satisfaction but also with a sense of recognition quite different from Fanny's, recognizing himself and his desires in these boys as he could not do with any comfort in most texts from this period.

A LANGUAGE THAT IS FOREIGN

In the hostile circumstances of eighteenth-century England it was almost impossible for writers to create public texts which gave unambiguous expression to homosexual desire. Instead they travelled abroad, either literally or in their imaginations, finding in southern Europe a sexual freedom which England forbad: Walpole in Italy, Beckford in Portugal, Byron in Greece. The writings which draw upon the culture of the ancient Mediterranean, particularly that of Greece, often present an idealized homoeroticism which lays overt emphasis upon aesthetic pleasure and philosophical seriousness; but alongside this rhetoric of beauty and purity there is another language which reminds us constantly of danger, for this mythologized Mediterranean is not only a world of sunlight and statuary, it is also figured through images of the abyss, of darkness and danger, of unspeakable secrets. The English writers who sought out the freedom of the south carried with them the psychological prisonhouse of the north.

The homoerotic mythology fashioned around the Greek world saw that culture's erotic delight in the naked male body as a sign of its proximity to nature and to the pristine origins of human society. Richard Payne Knight's scholarly study of the ancient cult of Priapus, complete with illustrations of phalli, implied that modern civilization (particularly because of Christianity) was a degenerate and oppressive society compared with ancient Greece. Knight's book appeals to an Enlightenment rationalism as well as to an interest in the cult of the phallus, suggesting that a world in which the phallus can be so openly celebrated provides a healthy alternative to the constraints and hypocrisies of Christian England. The influential German critic Johann Joachim Winckelmann, whose writings were translated by Henry Fuseli in 1765, read Greek statuary with an intensely erotic pleasure within his aesthetic gaze, and he is equally enthusiastic about the precision of the sculpture and the perfection of the bodies which it represented. The Greek male body, he says, was fashioned 'by the influence of the mildest and purest sky', trained by nude exercise, untrammelled by restrictive clothing, and free from those modern diseases which disfigure man's beauty (p. 62). The gymnasia in which young men trained naked were privileged spaces not only for the athletes but for their observers, and served as the schools of art and philosophy where a sculptor might study 'the elasticity of the muscles, the ever varying motions of the frame, the outlines of fair forms, or the contour left by the young wrestler on the sand.' Such 'beautiful nakedness' cannot now be found in the models whom modern artists hire for life classes (p. 64). In Winckelmann's myth the admiration of naked male beauty is an admiration for nature's pristine ideal which can no longer be attained in the modern age but can still be glimpsed (and still provide the foundation for art) through the contemplation of Greek statuary. In Greece the artist's and philosopher's gaze was free to dwell on such beauty in the publicly-sanctioned private space. Now such a space exists only when created by the gaze of the art-lover at the fragments which remain, a gaze which provides erotic pleasure, though now only surreptitiously, and which always has to be ready to explain itself as a purely aesthetic interest.

Though the rediscovery of Greek antiquities proceeded apace, there was less interest in Greek thought; the *Symposium*, for example, was little studied in Greek and available only in a poor bowdlerized translation. The version made by Shelley was a remarkably faithful and eloquent rendering which made Plato's dialogue on love between men accessible for the first time in English, even though it was heavily edited for its posthumous publication in 1840. Shelley seems to have had few homoerotic inclinations himself, but in his unfinished *A Discourse on the Manners of the Ancient Greeks relative to the Subject of Love*, intended as a preface to his translation, he made a bold effort to understand the place of homosexual relations in Greek society, and to explain them sympathetically to an English readership whose conventional views on love and sex he detested. According to Shelley's vision, any sexuality should be part of a full, imaginative communion; intercourse should be with someone who is beautiful in body and mind, and should involve the highest human faculties. Shelley argues that because Greek women were not particularly beautiful, and were deprived of access to the political and cultural world outside the home, they were hardly fitted to fulfil the combined sexual, emotional and spiritual role of a man's true partner. But how could such a profoundly satisfying union between men involve a form of sexual intercourse which many have branded unnatural? Shelley argues that 'the act itself is nothing', and objections to it could arise only from the 'arbitrary distinctions of society' or 'the indestructible laws of human nature' (p. 109). As for the first, Shelley asserts that the overriding principle is that no act should give more pain than pleasure. As for the laws of human nature, Shelley argues that sexual intercourse should be with a partner beautiful in body and mind, should be temperate, and should be according to nature (though he does not define this key term). Applying these principles to Greek homosexuality, Shelley says that we do not know exactly what Greek men did with one another, but it could hardly have involved anything which degraded the beloved. It is likely that, just as one may ejaculate during a dream about one's beloved, so the same 'almost involuntary consequences' may occur when a man enjoys 'a state of abandonment in the society of a person of surpassing attractions', without 'the necessity of so operose [laborious] and diabolical a machination as that usually described' – by which he means anal intercourse (p. 110). Shelley's only substantial objection to the sexual practices of the Greeks is that women were excluded from society and thus from the profound union which sex brings about; but even sex between men 'in the grossest sense' could hardly be more unnatural than the young Englishman's usual recourse to diseased prostitutes. Shelley's version of Greek homosexuality, then, is predicated upon a rejection of the degradation of sex and of women which he sees at work in contemporary England, together with an acceptance of some spontaneous physical delight as part of the rapturous emotional union between men.

Shelley's idealization of Greek relationships between men – which is also part of his vision of an ideal modern sexuality – is seen again in his notes on classical sculpture, particularly on a statue of Bacchus and Ampelus, which shows the two youths naked, Bacchus with his arm around the younger boy's shoulder, and the two gazing into each other's eyes. Shelley stresses their delicate forms, their gentleness and grace, and sees the beauty of the two youths as something untouched by the corruptions of the world. The terms in which the body of Bacchus is described link the appreciation of male beauty to the hearing of Platonic harmonies:

The flowing fulness and roundness of the breast and belly, whose lines fading into each other are continued with a gentle motion as it were to the utmost extremity of his limbs. Like some fine strain of harmony which flows round the soul and enfolds it and leaves it in the soft astonishment of a satisfaction, like the pleasure of love with one whom we most love, which having taken away desire, leaves pleasure, sweet pleasure. (pp. 21–3)

In Shelley's reading the intense bond between these two youths is all the more pleasurable and harmonious for being without desire. Yet across this ideal picture falls a shadow, for when inviting the reader to recall an image of schoolboy intimacy, Shelley adds a parenthesis which reminds us of the oppressive policing of masculine desire and friendship in England:

Just as you may have seen (yet how seldom from their dissevering and tyrannical institutions do you see) a younger and an elder boy at school walking in some remote grassy spot of their playground with that tender friendship towards each other which has so much of love. (p. 21)

The Greek example is redolent of an erotic pleasure in the male form leading the viewer naturally into a satisfaction which fuses the emotional and the spiritual; the English equivalent is imagined as a relationship which is banished to an irrecoverable schoolboy past, shadowed by the adult world's anxious dissevering of love from friendship and of boy from boy.

In thus speaking a language that is foreign (to use Freud's phrase once more), writers fashioned alternatives to the prurient puritanism of England. But the texts which result from this reveal both literary and psychological stresses. Byron confided his passion for the Cambridge chorister John Edleston to some of his friends, but in the poems which were addressed to or inspired by him (the 'Thyrza' lyrics) Byron thought it wise to change his gender. Some of the poems in which Byron explored strange passions in exotic locations have homoerotic undercurrents. In his eastern Mediterranean tale *Lara* (1814), Byron implicates the reader in imagining a dangerous homosexual relationship before moving us back into a less threatening version of exotic passion. There is some secret about Lara which no one knows except his devoted page boy. There was 'something more beneath/ Than glance could well reveal, or accent breathe .../... some deep feeling it were vain to trace/ At moments lighten'd o'er his livid face' (Canto I, ll. 77–84). Lara and his page speak a foreign language which no one else knows, and in a moment of passion Lara utters words which the page recognizes 'were not such as Lara should avow,/ Nor he interpret' (Canto I, ll. 238–9). The poem emphasizes Lara's inscrutability, and the secrecy which enfolds the two men, linked as they are by a language which is inaudible or indecipherable to others: they seem 'to share between themselves some separate fate,/ Whose darkness none beside should penetrate' (Canto II, ll. 452–3). The eroticism in the page's devotion to his master is made clear in the description of the boy's beauty, the passionate gazes which he fixes on Lara, and his abstraction from everything else 'that lures the eye, and fills the heart' (Canto I, ll. 528–53). The page's light form and 'darkly delicate' brow might (the poem suggests) lead the reader to suppose that this is a girl in disguise, but Byron dispels that suspicion, for there is 'something in his gaze,/ More wild and high than woman's eye betrays' (ll. 578–9). We are therefore encouraged to admire the page's beauty as the beauty of a young man, and to imagine that the boy's devotion has a homoerotic character. By the time Byron eventually reveals that the page is indeed a girl, the poem has made us complicit in recognizing these elements as signs of homosexual secrecy, and the concluding revelation cannot wholly efface the reader's unsettling experience of having created a homosexual world which has no foundation save his own suspicions about secrecy between men – and perhaps the gossip which he has heard about Byron's relationships.

Neither Byron nor Beckford were comfortable under the moralizing scrutiny to which English society subjected them. William Beckford found it prudent to leave England after his association with the adolescent William Courtenay came to the notice of the boy's family. Beckford was especially attracted to young boys; both his diaries and his novel *Vathek* (1786) celebrate their beauty, but these evocations are interwoven with images of danger. In *Vathek* (pp. 24–7) the Caliph Vathek is obsessed with the treasure of the pre-Adamite sultans (perhaps an image for the unattainable riches of an innocent sexuality untainted by the Fall) which have been promised to him by the sinister Giaour. The latter had come to the Caliph's attention by interpreting some indecipherable inscriptions which had been tantalizing him (perhaps an image for an unattainable clarity of understanding about sexuality, suggesting a desire for an imposs-ibly open and legible homosexual text). The route to the treasure lies through a chasm ('a black streak that divided the plain'), at the bottom of which stands a door of ebony which may be unlocked with a golden key. To persuade the Giaour to allow him entry, Vathek selects fifty beautiful boys for sacrifice. We watch the 'lovely inno-cents' as they play, 'mutually imparting a thousand caresses'. Pre-paring for some games, the boys 'were soon stripped, and presented to the admiration of the spectators the suppleness and grace of their delicate limbs'. As prizes the boys receive items of Vathek's cloth-ing, who 'undressed himself by degrees'. One by one, the boys are pushed by Vathek over the edge of the chasm to be devoured by the Giaour, but as the last boy is dispatched, chasm, door and Giaour vanish, and Vathek, cheated of the promised riches, is left alone on the plain to face the wrath of the boys' parents. This incident weaves together innocence and damnation: there is no mistaking the novel's erotic interest in the boyish bodies, an interest repeated later in the descriptions of the beautiful thirteen-year-old Gulchenrouz, with his pouting 'vermilion little lips' (pp. 65, 68). The book fulfils Beckford's fantasy of a perpetual childhood of innocent physical play, and when the fifty missing boys meet Gulchenrouz, they 'vied with each other in kissing his serene forehead and beautiful eye-lids' (p. 97). At the end of the novel, Gulchenrouz passes 'whole ages in . . . the pure happiness of childhood' (p. 120), while a differ-ent fate awaits Vathek, who 'for the sake of . . . forbidden power, had sullied himself with a thousand crimes'; he becomes 'a prey to grief without end' (p. 120). Though Vathek's desires are overtly mercenary and heterosexual, there is a persistent strain of imagery which tells another story: the emphasis on transgression and taboo, and Vathek's renunciation of the upper world of light for the dark-ness and forbidden treasure of the secret lower regions, suggest forbidden sexual pleasures. The dark chasm with its door awaiting the golden key invites interpretation as a symbol of sodomy (with-out making that reading inevitable), but it has a second significance, implying the abyss of social disgrace – and even execution – which awaits the man who acts upon his desires for pubescent boys.

Beckford wrote three 'episodes' for inclusion in *Vathek*, though these were not published with the main text. In 'The story of the two princes, Alasi and Firouz' Alasi is not attracted by marriage or the pleasures of the harem; he creates for himself a retreat in the middle of the forest, into which bursts the young Prince Firouz, 'an

angelic figure', 'an incomparable pearl' (pp. 114–5). Alasi is so struck
by the sound of Firouz's voice and the glances from his eyes that
his reason is confounded and his words fragment into stammering
and silence (p. 116). Firouz demands to be loved uniquely, insisting
that Alasi reject his fiancée. The revelation that Firouz is a girl
arrives late enough for the reader to have experienced the frisson
of a story of homosexual attraction and possessiveness, a relationship made possible by the privilege of rank and the security of the
enclosed spaces of the pleasure-ground which Alasi has created.
(There is a comparable trick in the passionate encounter between
the Abbot and the young monk Rosario in the monastery garden in
chapter two of Matthew Lewis's *The Monk* (1796): when Rosario is
revealed to be Matilda, an extreme form of transgression is replaced
by one which sits more comfortably within the conventions of exotic
fiction, so that the reader has had the pleasure of imagining the
worst without the embarrassment of being committed to any narrative consequences.) In 'The story of Princess Zulkais and Prince
Kalilah' the forbidden love is incest, but the stern lecture which the
thirteen-year-old Kalilah receives from his father about his indiffer-
ence to manly pursuits and his tendency to 'wilt like a narcissus'
and be 'perverted' by his sister, suggests that the story of this delicate
youth can be read as an easy code for a forbidden homosexual relationship. Once again images of destruction traverse the evocations
of childhood pleasure, as the nurse tries to save Zulkais from 'the
black abyss into which your impetuous inclinations will unfailingly
hurl you', while Kalilah feels that he is falling into 'a gulf which had
no bottom' (pp. 125–9).

Beckford's journal of his visit to Portugal and Spain records his
infatuation with several boys – the initially gauche thirteen-year-
old Dom Pedro who comes to reciprocate Beckford's affection; the
seventeen-year-old chorister Gregorio Franchi who later became
Beckford's intimate friend and agent; and the delectable Mohammed,
the twelve-year-old brother of the ambassador from Tripoli. Though
aware of the dangers of a 'scrape' (p. 41), Beckford finds that Portuguese manners allow him considerable freedom with boys, and
there are many pages which record the pleasure of dancing with
them or skipping through the gardens, with Beckford enjoying 'all
the fancies and levities of a child' himself (p. 41). He imagines
reclining on a beach by moonlight with 'some love-sick languid
youth', enjoying 'exquisite though childish sensations' (pp. 46–7).
He plays with the boys' hair, and exchanges kisses, but much as he

may like to cast himself in the role of a child, his behaviour evidently trod the boundaries of the illicit: after speaking about Dom Pedro to one of the Portuguese nobles, Beckford realizes that he has said too much: 'I could not help saying a thousand things which ought never to have been uttered. *Faire sans dire* [do without saying] is an excellent maxim' (p. 238). When Beckford writes about Franchi, the diary often breaks into fragmented syntax or words which are then deleted: after writing 'I loaded Franchi with childish caresses' a line is heavily deleted (p. 164); later we find: 'Franchi – caresses [erased words] fondness' (p. 279). Beckford's insistence on his own childlike delight in play does not obscure the fact that some of these caresses are of a kind which cannot be openly recorded. A warning is encoded in a dream (pp. 246–7) in which Beckford sees his own eldest child lying strangled on the steps which lead down into the vault which holds his mother's dead body: a chilling image of the murder of childlike innocence, and the destruction of his own family, on his descent into the 'dark abode'.

Beckford's diary is full of evocations of the private spaces – particularly the half-wild gardens, and the apartments softened with exotic hangings and filled with what he calls the effeminate music of the harpsichord – where Portuguese custom allowed him to make free with the company of boys. Yet both the joyous privacies of Portugal and the lurid chambers of *Vathek* are temporary retreats, playgrounds of the mind in which the adult can neither put aside his sexuality and become a child, nor safely draw the child into his own adult sexuality. The shadow of the hangman is never wholly absent. When Beckford returned to his English residence at Fonthill, he had a huge wall built round the extensive estate, to protect both himself and the wildlife which he loved from his boorish and predatory neighbours. Into his scrapbooks he pasted newspaper accounts of sodomy trials, creating his own archive, a private text appropriated from the hostile literature of 'Enlightenment' England.

In Goethe's *Elective Affinities* (1809) one of the characters remarks that while women wish to stand alone without other women, 'with men it is otherwise. A man desires another man: if there were no other man he would create him: a woman could live an eternity without its occurring to her to bring forth her own kind' (Part 2, ch. 7). This aphorism recalls that powerful dream (which we noted in some of Shakespeare's characters) of excluding women from the work of procreation, and establishing a form of generation which is wholly male. A striking analysis of the dangers of this aspiration is provided by Mary Shelley's *Frankenstein* (1818). The story of how Frankenstein manufactures a living creature from parts of dead bodies is set within the framework of another story, for the book opens and closes with letters from an explorer, Robert Walton, who is trying to find a passage through the frozen seas to the north of Russia. Walton has also been engaged in another quest, however, the quest for a male friend, for as he tells his sister: 'I desire the company of a man who could sympathise with me; whose eyes would reply to mine' (p. 17). When he meets Frankenstein on the ice – exhausted from the pursuit of his creature – Walton restores him to animation, almost recreating him in a proleptic echo of Frankenstein's own act of creation. Walton begins to love Frankenstein as a brother while recognizing that he is merely the shadow of his former self: 'yet have I found a man who, before his spirit had been broken by misery, I should have been happy to have possessed as the brother of my heart' (p. 26). And so we approach the story of Frankenstein's act of all-male creativity via a preliminary narrative of unavailing male creativity and disappointed male desire.

Frankenstein shares with Walton the awful story which he has told to no one else: thus the story of a perverted creativity which he is trying to reverse poignantly forms the basis of a friendship which will bear no fruit. Frankenstein had arrived at university to study science, but his only preparation had been a fascination with the alchemical works of Cornelius Agrippa without knowing how utterly outmoded such thinking had become. His intellectual world was therefore unique, an unrivalled command of modern chemistry and biology coupled with that longing for the power to transform the base into the golden, and to discover the secret of life, which had inspired the Renaissance magus. Frankenstein's world is now a dark and solitary one, composed of secret researches and the furtive nocturnal plundering of graveyards.

Frankenstein had taken care to select for his creature limbs and features which were beautiful in themselves and in the right proportion, yet the resulting body is monstrous: not only is it huge (eight feet tall), its potential beauty is marred by the clearly visible arteries and muscles beneath the skin, and the lifelessness in the pale, watery eyes. We are offered a reading of a naked male body which dwells on its creator's desire to produce beauty, but those very features which reward the reader's erotic glance in other texts – the clear skin, the strong muscles, the lively eyes – are here turned into signs of monstrosity. Frankenstein describes the creature as 'it' when it is first awakened, but switches to 'his' when describing its lack of beauty, as if the body has to be gendered in order to be read.

The shadow of this monstrous male creature falls across all Frankenstein's most intimate relationships. The much-deferred wedding of Frankenstein and Elizabeth results only in her being killed by the creature on their wedding night. Frankenstein's relationship to the creature seems to be a dark parody of his relationship with Henry Clerval, his close friend from childhood. Rushing away in horror from his first sight of the living creature, Frankenstein unexpectedly meets Clerval, and it is Clerval who nurses him through the illness which is brought on by Frankenstein's revulsion from his creation. Later, Frankenstein is haunted by visions in which he sees sometimes the eyes of the creature, sometimes the eyes of Clerval (p. 176). The creature also makes impossible any real relationship between Frankenstein and Walton, for as Walton says towards the close of the narrative:

> Must I then lose this admirable being! I have longed for a friend; I have sought one who would sympathise with and love me. Behold, on these desert seas I have found such a one; but, I fear, I have gained him only to know his value and lose him. (p. 204)

Though this novel is no simple allegory, it does seem to speak of the dark side which attends male bonding and all-male creativity. Frankenstein pursues his creature across the wildest places on earth in what seems a nightmarish parody of the exotic quest for the beloved. A concern for male friendship and for the beauty of the male body are also translated into grimly perverse forms. It is a travesty of Joseph Wright's painting (Plate 5), in which a pool of light envelops the statue of the nude gladiator and touches the faces of the men who study it, creating a safe, shared space for the gaze of pleasure and of knowledge. In the literature of this period love between men rarely finds safe spaces to inhabit, and is all too often seen as a disruptive force which perverts the bonds of sociability. The male gaze reads other men in order to discriminate and then to incriminate, seeking in the face of the other not the promise of love but the marks of monstrosity.

5

The Victorian Period

Our interest's on the dangerous edge of things . . .
We watch while these in equilibrium keep
The giddy line midway: one step aside,
They're classed and done with.

Browning, 'Bishop Blougram's Apology'.

ON THE DANGEROUS EDGE

The Victorian period placed a high value on intense bonds between men, which were first fashioned at school and then contributed to the nineteenth-century projects of commercial and industrial growth, the expansion of empire, and the recall of the nation to Christianity. By contrast with this strongly affective and efficient masculinity, however, there were doubts about the virility of men who were attracted to the decorative and the foreign, whether in elaborate fashion or in the splendid ritual of the Anglo-Catholic movement. Forms of art which valued richness of style and surface above moral purpose attracted criticisms of decadence and depravity. Some canonical literature (including Shakespeare's *Sonnets* and Plato's dialogues) fell under the suspicion of promoting unhealthy kinds of feeling, while several contemporary writers were seen to have crossed the boundary into unacceptable versions of male relationships: *The Times* was disturbed by *In Memoriam*, Hopkins recoiled from Whitman's poetry, and the trials of Oscar Wilde in 1895 presented the Victorian public with a way of life which it had previously not known of, or had seen but not labelled. Now the precise implications of kinds of friendship, styles of dress, or turns of phrase in letters and poems, were debated in court: definitions became crucial.

The present chapter explores the languages which were available in the nineteenth century for the expression of male friendship and love, the blurring of the two, the disguising of the one as the other, and the opportunities for homoerotic expression which were offered by the vocabularies of comradeship, religious devotion, aesthetic pleasure, and the recurrent lure of ancient Greece. To begin with, it is necessary to sample the language of male friendship, and to register some of its tensions, before moving on to the various expressions of passionate and erotic feeling.

One staple version of Victorian masculinity is represented by *Tom Brown's Schooldays* (1857), Thomas Hughes's story of Rugby school under the reforming headmaster Thomas Arnold. It depicts the emergence of an ethos of Christian manliness at the school in the 1830s, exemplified through the transformation of Tom Brown. Brown comes from a family which typifies immemorial England, deeply attached to the English countryside, and dogged fighters for their rights and for victims of injustice. But at Rugby Brown drifts into a habit of neglecting his lessons and getting into scrapes, leading Dr Arnold to worry that if Brown does not 'gain character and manliness' he could become a corrupting influence. The headmaster resolves to test his intuition that Brown is essentially good-natured by entrusting to his care a new boy, George Arthur, a pale and delicate lad whose father is dead and who has no brothers to teach him manliness. Without the protection of someone like Brown, Arthur's time at public school would inevitably be miserable. But as Brown reluctantly takes Arthur under his wing, and teaches him the arts of survival, he begins to learn more important lessons from Arthur himself.

The tide turns when Arthur kneels down at his bedside to say his prayers, provoking derision from the rest of the dormitory and a slipper thrown by 'a big brutal fellow'. Brown retaliates by hurling a boot at Arthur's attacker, and the next day begins to say his prayers openly himself, setting an example which other boys gradually follow. On another occasion he finds Arthur crying, and puts his arm round his neck to comfort him in an impeccably manly gesture. Arthur is reading the Bible, and crying because he recalls the times when his father used to read with him. Brown had thought that Arthur would be 'softened and less manly' for thinking of home, but he learns true Christian manliness from the story of Arthur's father, a clergyman who had 'battled like a man' with 'a pure wholesome Christian love' for his parishioners. Later Brown is drawn into a fight with Slogger Williams in defence of Arthur. The latter had been translating a passage of Homer in class when he was overcome with emotion at what he was reading and burst into tears;

when Williams is asked to take over, it becomes apparent that he has not prepared the passage, and he is punished. After the lesson, Brown has to rescue Arthur from Williams's revenge and takes on the Slogger in an heroic encounter which goes down in school legend. The lines which had so upset the boy were from Helen's lament for Hector, where she recalls how he had protected her from insult in the hostile world of Troy. Hughes invites us to see Arthur's response as a mark of civilized sensitivity, not unmanly weakness, and it is Brown's friendship with Arthur which draws him away from his previously rough and thoughtless behaviour without making him in any way effeminate. He learns true muscular Christianity, and even starts preparing his own Greek translations without a crib.

The friendship with Arthur awakens in Brown a manly tenderness, a sense of duty, and a willingness to fight only when necessary. The friendship is carefully characterized by Hughes as free from the dangers of some schoolboy relationships, particularly those between older and younger boys. At one point a boy tells Brown and his chum East that they are required to go and fag for an older boy who is his protector. Unlike Arthur, this 'young gentleman' is 'one of the miserable little pretty white-handed curly-headed boys, petted and pampered by some of the big fellows, who wrote their verses for them, taught them to drink and use bad language, and did all they could to spoil them for everything in this world and the next'. Hughes adds a footnote to this sentence:

A kind and wise critic, an old Rugbeian, notes here in the margin: 'The small friend system was not so utterly bad from 1841–1847.' Before that, too, there were many noble friendships between big and little boys, but I can't strike out the passage; many boys will know why it is left in. (p. 182)

Brown and East deal with the effeminate boy roughly but not unfairly, and send him back to his protector; by contrast, the pretty boy curses and threatens them with a retribution which he is too feeble to inflict himself – a combination of weakness and blasphemy which is clearly the antithesis of Tom Brown's increasingly exemplary Christian manliness. This admonitory vignette of the white-handed boy destined for corruption underlines by contrast Arthur's true sensitivity and Brown's capacity for noble friendship: Brown is ready to take his place in the fictional world of the Victorian adult male.

Many Victorian novels represent the bond between men as the primary locus of security and loyalty, and the passionate language which is often used might suggest homosexual feeling were it not that these relationships are so obviously commonplace and safe. From among many possible examples, Wilkie Collins's *Armadale* (1864–6) may serve to illustrate how strong can be the language used for the devotion between men without there being any suggestion of sexual interest.

The story centres on two young men, both called Allan Armadale, who are kept apart because of a feud between their fathers. One of them rejects his family and adopts the name of Ozias Midwinter, and by chance (though much of what happens in *Armadale* seems fated rather than either casual or willed) comes across the other Allan Armadale. The two become devoted friends, with the thoughtless and carefree Armadale unaware of the brooding Midwinter's true identity. Right from the start Armadale 'had taken a violent fancy' to Midwinter (p. 49), and the passion was reciprocated: Midwinter tells their mutual friend, the Reverend Decimus Brock, that he has changed under a good influence:

'What was it?'
'My love for Allan Armadale.'
He cast a doubting, almost a timid, look at Mr. Brock as he gave that answer . . .
'Have I no right to speak of him in that way?' he asked, keeping his face hidden from the rector. 'Have I not known him long enough; have I not done enough for him yet? Remember what my experience of other men had been, when I first saw his hand held out to me; when I first heard his voice speaking to me in my sick room . . . *His* hand put my pillow straight, and patted me on the shoulder . . . ask your own heart if the miserable wretch whom Allan Armadale has treated as his equal and his friend, has said too much in saying that he loves him? I do love him! It *will* come out of me – I can't keep it back. I love the very ground he treads on! I would give my life – yes, the life that is precious to me now, because his kindness has made it a happy one – I tell you I would give my life—'
The next words died away on his lips; the hysterical passion

rose, and conquered him. He stretched out one of his hands with a wild gesture of entreaty to Mr. Brock; his head sank on the window-sill, and he burst into tears. (p. 85)

Later, when Midwinter believes that his presence with Armadale is endangering his friend, he receives a letter from Mr Brock which reassures him, and exclaims: 'If the thought of leaving him breaks my heart, the thought of leaving him is wrong!', and 'he pressed the rector's letter, in his wild passionate way to his lips, as he looked at Allan through the vista of the trees' (p. 248). The timidity which precedes Midwinter's revelation, the hysterical passion which interrupts his speech, the tears, the kissing of the letter – all these might easily be a woman's behaviour, and yet nowhere is Midwinter presented as unmanly. Rather, he is strong, practical and independent, perhaps too imaginative and brooding, yet his foreboding vision turns out to be more justified than Armadale's thoughtless optimism. The hesitancy and the passion which attend Midwinter's expression of love are attributable not to any guilty emotions but to the social impropriety of an impoverished nomad claiming friendship with a member of the landed gentry.

The two men set up house together, Armadale as landowner, Midwinter as his steward, but the arrival of two eligible women threatens to divide them; indeed, one chapter is headed 'She comes between them'. The chief threat to their happiness and their friendship is the fulfilment of the ominous dream which Armadale has had when asleep on the hulk of the ship on which (unknown to him) Midwinter's father had killed Armadale's father. The accomplishment of the dream is associated with the mysterious figure of a woman, and much of the energy of the plot is directed towards discovering this woman's identity and thwarting her plans. Armadale and Midwinter have to avoid repeating the murderous bond which united their fathers, and also avoid being driven into mutual suspicion and mistrust by the woman's machinations. The greatest fear is that the primary security of the male bond will be broken by the woman, a foreigner who comes from the families' murderous past. The book ends with the two friends together in a liminal scene: they have escaped death at the hands of the woman, who had become Midwinter's wife; she has killed herself; and it is now the eve of Armadale's wedding. Temporarily the two men are free of women, and reunited as a self-sufficient male couple, and it is there that Collins closes his novel rather than with Armadale's wedding: the eternity frozen by the novel's final scene is the eternity of a contented male couple.

In Bram Stoker's *Dracula*, published in 1897 after the trials of Oscar Wilde had forced an awareness of homosexual behaviour upon the public consciousness, the dividing line between homosocial bonding and homosexual desire would seem to be clear, yet these distinctions are subjected to a curious form of undoing. When the young solicitor Jonathan Harker arrives in Transylvania to attend to the needs of his employer's client Count Dracula, he has done his research and knows as much as he can about the territory into which he is moving. As he is the story's narrator at this point, we share his epistemological confidence. But attaining secure knowledge becomes increasingly problematic. The locals pretend not to understand Harker and his errand, and refuse to explain to him their evident fear; later on, the men who are engaged in the struggle against Dracula enlist as much modern medical knowledge and technology as they can muster, along with the fruits of research in ancient lore. To know Dracula in just one shape is hardly to know him at all, so different is his life by day and by night. The book's concern with the difficulty of knowing the full story of Dracula's activities and of understanding his pleasures obviously had a special resonance in the wake of the Wilde affair, with its disclosures of undreamt-of encounters behind a respectable façade. This is not to suggest that vampirism should be read as a metaphor for sexual relations between men, but the intimate male relations which the book describes would inevitably have been occasions of anxiety for some readers.

The threat to Harker from Dracula hovers on the edge of being homosexual without this ever being as explicit as it is in the earlier tale by Eric, Count Stenbock, 'The True Story of a Vampire' (1894). There the vampire's victim is a twelve-year-old boy; the two kiss on the lips, and the vampire calls him 'My darling, . . . my beloved! my life'; they meet at midnight, with the boy dressed only in a nightshirt. *Dracula* is more disturbing in that it interweaves desires which we might try to differentiate as homosexual, homosocial and heterosexual. Harker shudders at a touch from Dracula (p. 28). Areas of the castle are forbidden to Harker, who nevertheless transgresses this taboo, and pays the price for it. When falling asleep in a forbidden room, he is approached by three female vampires, whose advance he awaits with erotic anticipation: 'I closed my eyes in a languorous ecstacy and waited – waited with beating heart' (p. 54).

But Dracula intervenes furiously, pulling the women away and exclaiming: 'How dare you touch him, any of you? how dare you cast eyes on him when I had forbidden it? . . . This man belongs to me!' The women reply with the accusation 'you yourself never loved', to which the count rejoins: 'Yes, I too can love; you yourselves can tell it from the past. Is it not so? Well, now I promise you that when I am done with him you shall kiss him at your will' (p. 55). The suggestion that the count has been sexually interested in these women in the past does not deflect but rather strengthens the implication that it is a sexual interest which he now takes in the recumbent Harker. After the count throws the women a half-smothered child to keep them satisfied, Harker faints in horror, and what Dracula then does to Harker is unknown, for it disappears into the silence which falls when the chapter ends, since there is no omniscient narrator to fill in the gaps in Harker's knowledge. When Harker awakes he is in his own bed, and deduces that Dracula must have carried him there and undressed him. Later Dracula is seen wearing Harker's clothes (p. 62).

The activities of Dracula hover on the verge of the homosexual, though his primary interest is in Lucy; the activities of the five men who band together to destroy him and protect her hover also on this dangerous edge. The lawyer Harker joins with the director of a lunatic asylum Dr John Seward, Seward's old tutor from Holland Dr Van Helsing, the Honourable Arthur Holmwood, and the American man of action Quincey P. Morris: a cross-section of masculine achievements, bringing together Victorian law, medicine and aristocratic respectability with the Dutchman's esoteric knowledge and the American's frontier spirit. As Lucy weakens from her loss of blood, Van Helsing tries repeated transfusions, the first from her fiancé Arthur, whom he recognizes as a prize specimen of masculinity:

> When first the Professor's eye had lit upon him he had been angry at any interruption at such a time; but now, as he took in his stalwart proportions and recognized the strong young manhood which seemed to emanate from him, his eyes gleamed. (p. 159)

This is the excitement of the homosocial medic, rather than the homoerotic vampire, but there is enough of an echo between the two for the reader to register discomfort, and to hope that Stoker's boundaries are well fenced. The bond between the men becomes more intimate as a second transfusion is needed, with Seward as donor, then a third, with Morris contributing his blood. In Lucy's body the blood of the three men is mingled, and it is their blood on which Dracula feeds. Lucy is therefore the medium through which the heroes meet in blood-brotherhood; but she is simultaneously the medium through which Dracula consumes the men's life-blood. When Dracula is finally dispatched it is at the cost of Morris's life, but a year later a child is born to Harker and his wife Mina, whom they call by the names of 'all our little band of men' (p. 485), as if all the men had had a share in his creation. Van Helsing may have been successful in containing the vampire within the bounds which he marked out with the consecrated host, but the passions which draw men together were not so easy to define and contain.

FORMS FOR DESIRE

Alongside such representations of intense male friendship, there developed various literary modes in which homoerotic desire could be figured. The poet William Cory referred to 'fragments and symbols of the bliss unknown' (*Ionica* [1891] p. 83), and much of this writing was indeed fragmentary, presenting episodes of precious friendship or moments of erotic vision rather than extended narratives; and yet the bliss so described was hardly unknown, however prudent it may have been to simulate ignorance: a vocabulary was fashioned which permitted the articulation of desires even if their consummation was withheld and the emphasis placed instead on looking, longing and loss.

Much of the literature of homosexual desire in the nineteenth century focused on boys rather than adults. Volumes of verse romanticized the bloom of youth as glimpsed on the public school playing fields or in the bathing places (see Plates 7 and 8). The adult's awareness of the innocence of youth and its transience helped to license an appreciation of boyish beauty and to suggest that it was inaccessible. To watch boys swimming naked in pools and streams or in the sea was to observe merely a natural beauty in a natural setting, but such observation also guarded itself against reproach by translating the scene into a picture, making the boys' beauty a pure, aesthetic pleasure. In Frederick William Rolfe's 'Ballade of Boys Bathing' (Reade, *Sexual Heretics*, pp. 226–7; first printed in *The*

Art Review, 1890) the observer focuses on the colour of the boys, 'white boys, ruddy, and tanned, and bare' against the blue water, and ends with a promise to paint the scene with 'tinctures rare'. S.S. Sale, in a sonnet printed in 1890 in *The Artist* (a journal which often included homoerotic images and verses), watches some grimy boys who in their play suddenly strip and plunge into the river:

> Changed by a miracle, they rise as though
> The youth of Greece burst on this later day,
> As on their lithe young bodies many a ray
> Of sunlight dallies with its blushing glow.

> (Reade, p. 228)

In the eyes of the cultured onlooker, the Victorian world is transformed into an idealized Greek world, as such 'naked purity' brings to life the ashes from a classical urn and recalls Narcissus and Daphnis, two archetypes of homosexual desire. Once this translation has been effected, the poet can admit that the scene makes his 'pulses throb and burn'.

Alan Stanley's poem 'August Blue' (1894; Reade, pp. 347–8) was occasioned by Henry Scott Tuke's painting of boys bathing (see Plate 8). It begins by evoking the colours of the sea, the sky and the boat – silver, white, grey, red, gold and amber – and then enlivens the scene with passionate excitement as the sun holds a goblet of 'fervid wine' and the young day glows with fire. Only once aesthetic delight in colour has been infused with passion does Stanley turn to describe the boys, directly addressing the lad who is about to dive:

> Stripped for the sea your tender form
> Seems all of ivory white,
> Through which the blue veins wander warm
> O'er throat and bosom slight,
> And as you stand, so slim, upright
> The glad waves grow and yearn
> To clasp you circling in their might,
> To kiss with lips that burn.

We imagine the sensual pleasure which the boy receives from the embraces of his lover the sea, a motif which recalls Marlowe's Leander embraced by Neptune:

Say, does it thrill you through and through
With ardent love, the sea? . . .
While the mad waves clasp you fervently
Possessing every limb.

The poet's address to the boy receives no answer, but the desired response is implicit in the boy's surrender to the water, our proxy. The final stanza invites us to 'Gaze on him, slender, fair, and tall' while the sea 'deigns to creep and cling, and crawl, / His worshipper to be.' The reader began the poem as a connoisseur, became a lover, and ends as a worshipper.

The poem makes clear the process of reading such images which permits a homoerotic glance to take possession of the warm flesh represented by the cool paintwork. This aesthetic prizes colour and texture rather than the other elements which we might usually value in painting, such as form or composition, or the evocation of generic, historical and social connexions, so that it becomes easy for the gaze of aesthetic appraisal to move from the surface of the canvas to appropriate the surfaces of the body which the paint represents. The body is freed from a social or historical context, idealized and mythologized, and so made available for possession. This possession is accomplished by the eye, but the rapture of the eye in surveying the boy's flesh is a substitute for (or a preliminary to) a physical possession which cannot be directly represented.

Nevertheless, certain geographical and quasi-historical frameworks made homoerotic possession imaginable within public spaces. In the case of Greece and Italy, the free display of nakedness in the sunlight, and the open and demonstrative affection between men, seemed to offer both an unembarrassed display of male beauty and a freer mode of comradeship than England permitted. Travellers sampled the Mediterranean's opportunities, poets recreated them in their imagined worlds. Mention of Greece also carried an awareness – implicit or explicit – of the licence provided to sexual relations between men by classical literature and social custom. In some cases a contrast was drawn between the freedom of the Greeks and the repression and hypocrisy of Christian England, a specific form of that more general comparison between the Hellenic and Hebraic cultures which featured in the writings of Matthew Arnold.

The most explicit defence of homosexuality and attack on English attitudes came in the anonymous and covertly-printed poem *Don*

Leon (1866). This purports to be written by Byron, and mixes supposedly autobiographical accounts of his youth and his adventures in Greece and Turkey with satirical attacks on the English laws against sodomy. 'Byron' describes his infatuation at Cambridge with the chorister Edleston:

> Oh! how I loved to press his cheek to mine;
> How fondly would my arms his waist entwine!
> Another feeling borrowed friendship's name,
> And took its mantle to conceal my shame.
> Another feeling! Oh! 'tis hard to trace
> The line where love usurps tame friendship's place.
> Friendship's the chrysalis, which seems to die,
> But throws its coil to give love wing to fly.

> (pp. 8–9)

The narrator goes on to argue that nature has given these feelings, and that reason suggests that there is nothing wrong with the expression of mutual love. He cites precedents in Plato, Horace and other classical writers, and in Shakespeare, 'Dame Nature's child' (pp. 10–12). Schoolboys find mutual comfort and pleasure in the sexual expression of their affection, which is better for them than seeking satisfaction from prostitutes, with all the social and medical ills which that entails. For the author of *Don Leon* England is both savage and hypocritical, and 'Byron' finds freedom only in the countries of the Mediterranean. A voice whispers in his ear:

> Go, lay thee down beneath the shady plain,
> Where Phaedrus heard grave Plato's voice complain.
> Another Phaedrus may perchance go by,
> And thy fond dreams become reality.

> (p. 19)

In a Greek house the narrator meets a boy of pleasingly androgynous appearance, who becomes his page. The narrator's love for the boy is expressed first in terms of rapturous gazing, but then in physical possession:

> How oft at morn, when troubled by the heat,
> The covering fell disordered at his feet,

I've gazed unsated at his naked charms,
And clasped him waking to my longing arms.

(p. 22)

The narrator taught him to swim, and 'brought him gently to the sunny beach,/ And wiped the briny moisture from his breech' (p. 23).

As well as offering this ostensibly autobiographical material, *Don Leon* argues against the savage punishment meted out by the English judiciary for sexual relations between men, pointing out that sodomy is common amongst soldiers and sailors, while schoolmasters enjoy whipping boys on their bare buttocks. The verse is supported by extensive notes which weave together a history of homosexual behaviour from classical, medieval and Renaissance literature and history, and from early nineteenth-century press reports of court cases. *Don Leon* is an uneven poem, but its appeal to nature and reason, Plato and Shakespeare, social good and individual liberty, makes it read like a belated document from Enlightenment and Romantic culture, even while its notes are documenting the plight faced by homosexual men in the nineteenth-century police court.

While the contemporary Mediterranean offered practical opportunities for the satisfaction of homosexual desires, ancient Greece provided the mythology which represented such desires as part of the mainstream of European culture. The translation of the *Symposium* by Benjamin Jowett in 1871 made this text widely available, but it was particularly Walter Pater who linked Greek culture with the cultivation of aesthetic and sensual pleasure, with more than a hint of homoerotic pleasure. In his essay 'Lacedaemon' (1893) he imagines a Platonist from Athens visiting Sparta and encountering an unfamiliar version of the Hellenic ideal of masculinity. Whereas Athens permitted 'Platonic loungers after truth or what not' to observe the boys as they exercised naked in the gymnasium, Sparta did not; but instead of the personal homoerotic glance Sparta subjected the boys to 'the imperative, inevitable gaze of his fellows, broad, searching, minute' (pp. 198–9). The Spartan lad was educated through a tough régime which produced an austere form of manly beauty: 'no warm baths allowed; a daily plunge in their river required. Yes! The beauty of these most beautiful of all people was a male beauty, far remote from feminine tenderness; had the expression of a certain *ascêsis* in it; was like un-sweetened wine. In comparison with it, beauty of another type might seem to be wanting in edge or accent' (p. 200). This form of masculinity stands in contrast to the androgynous figures celebrated by some of Pater's contemporaries (such as the Oxford connoisseurs who collected Magdalen College choirboys), and is more in tune with the heroic martial nudity of Louis David's painting *Leonidas at Thermopylae* (1814). Sparta produced a comradeship between men which was that of lover and beloved, and which came to full fruition on the battlefield. What then, says Pater, was the point of all this rigorous training of the body? 'An intelligent young Spartan might have replied: "To the end that I myself may be a perfect work of art, issuing thus into the eyes of all Greece."' (p. 209). It is interesting that, having delineated a society which demanded conformity to its own purposes, and the subordination of the individual to the collective ethos, Pater should conclude with an individualistic and aesthetic version of the Spartan ideal, and offer us an image of a Greek male who, precisely because he has turned himself into a work of art, can stand unashamed under the gaze of any outsider.

It was his presentation of the cult of the self, the pursuit of pleasure and sensation, and the elevation of the Hellenic world over the Christian, which gave Pater's work a special frisson for Victorian readers. In the conclusion to *The Renaissance* (1873) he identified as a characteristic of modern thought the idea that not only are all things in flux, but all principles are inconstant too. In a world without eternal principles, the individual mind inhabits 'its own dream of a world', and is itself continually refashioned; many impressions and sensations come our way, and these form part of what Pater calls 'that strange perpetual weaving and unweaving of ourselves'. Within this world of flux, moments of perfection offer themselves to the attentive observer, providing intellectual, aesthetic and physical pleasure:

> Every moment some form grows perfect in hand or face; some tone on the hills or the sea is choicer than the rest; some mood of passion or insight or intellectual excitement is irresistibly real and attractive to us, – for that moment only ... While all melts under our feet, we may well grasp at any exquisite passion, or any contribution to knowledge that seems by a lifted horizon to set the spirit free for a moment, or any stirring of the senses, strange dyes,

strange colours, and curious odours, or work of the artist's hands, or the face of one's friend . . . With this sense of the splendour of our experience and of its awful brevity, gathering all we are into one desperate effort to see and touch, we shall hardly have time to make theories about the things we see and touch . . . The theory or idea or system which requires of us the sacrifice of any part of this experience, in consideration of some interest into which we cannot enter, or some abstract theory we have not identified with ourselves, or of what is only conventional, has no real claim upon us. (pp. 152–3)

Even when detached from the homoerotic elements in Pater's writing, this passage has crucial consequences for the understanding of homosexual desire. It enjoins the individual to set aside inherited systems of morality; to concentrate on the appreciation of transitory perfection; to appreciate that perfection through the senses, notably sight and touch; to relish the strange; and to regard passion and bodily beauty as being just as much the objects of sensuous possession as are works of art. 'Exquisite' and 'strange' are key words, and the cultivation of exquisite sensations and recherché pleasures was to be a hallmark of the decadent literature of the later nineteenth century. A philosophy such as Pater's opened the way for the pursuit of physical sensation without reference to a socially-determined moral framework, and allowed a homoerotic delight in male beauty to be presented as aesthetic appreciation.

But we need to be cautious here: words such as 'strange', 'odd', 'curious' or 'queer' had a wide semantic range: in Dickens they commonly refer to psychological quirks and social secrets which have nothing to do with homosexuality; in Pater they signal a relish for the outré which may include homoerotic pleasure, but is not confined to that; while after the trials of Oscar Wilde they more readily suggest homosexual pleasures. So we need to recognize that many Victorian evocations of secrecy and strangeness have nothing to do with homosexuality, and are often signs of male anxiety about women's secrets (as in *Lady Audley's Secret* or *Bleak House*) or (particularly in Dickens) spring from a concern about the almost unfathomable workings of capitalism. The dark places of the Victorian imagination did come, towards the end of the nineteenth century, to include homosexual relationships amongst their possibilities, but writers (such as Henry James) could exploit the indeterminacy of such a vocabulary for their own ends.

A sub-Paterian interweaving of the religious, the aesthetic and the erotic marks the story 'The Priest and the Acolyte' by John Francis Bloxam, published anonymously in the Oxford magazine *The Chameleon* which appeared for just one number in December 1894 and also contained paradoxes by Wilde and poems by Lord Alfred Douglas. The story illustrates the difficulties of translating the Greek model of love between an adult male and a boy into Victorian culture, and it is not surprising that it was cited at Wilde's trial as an egregiously offensive work. A young priest falls in love with his fourteen-year-old acolyte, Wilfred. The tale opens with the priest sitting in the confessional, weary of hearing the same familiar sins and wishing that people would be more original in their vices. Then his new acolyte makes his confession, and through the grating the priest recognizes his 'long soft curls' and 'large moist blue eyes' (p. 350). The priest's sudden love for the acolyte displaces his religious devotion:

> he knew that henceforth the entire devotion of his religion, the whole ecstatic fervour of his prayers, would be connected with, nay, inspired by, one object alone. With the same reverence and humility as he would have felt in touching the consecrated elements he laid his hands on the curl-crowned head, he touched the small pale face, and, raising it slightly, he bent forward and gently touched the smooth white brow with his lips. (p. 350)

The boy responds by kissing him on the lips. Wilfred is not only beautiful, he is a work of art: himself the orphan son of an artist, he comes to the priest at night in a setting reminiscent of a Victorian genre painting, for as the priest breaks off his prayers he discovers the boy outside his window, standing in the moonlight 'with his bare feet on the moon-blanched turf, dressed only in his long white night-shirt' (p. 352). The priest brings the boy in, holds him close and kisses him, in the first of many night-time meetings. Eventually the local people report the pair to the rector, who interrupts them one night as the boy is sitting on the priest's lap. Bloxam's description of the lovers' embraces goes no further than kisses, but the congregation and the rector evidently suspect the worst. The priest and the boy decide to die together, and after a final confession the priest celebrates a requiem mass for the repose of their souls. Into the chalice he pours a phial of poison instead of the usual wine, and administers this to Wilfred with the words (once sacred, now made blasphemous), 'The Blood of our Lord Jesus Christ, which was shed for thee, preserve thy body and soul unto everlasting life' (p. 359). Then he drains the chalice himself, and priest and acolyte die together on the altar steps.

This use of religious ritual for the consummation of their love is the last of several appropriations and displacements of Christian language. The confessional is the site of the priest's meeting with the boy; the mass becomes the regular celebration of their love; and as the priest tries to pray, the sight of the crucifix and its 'cold figure with the weary, weary face' is replaced by a vision of 'the flushed face of a lovely boy' (p. 351). The priest also rejects the moral codes of Christianity, asking the rector: 'what right have you, or anyone, to tell me that such and such a thing is sinful for me?' (p. 357). He argues vehemently against the force of convention which obliterates individuality and difference, and even sees himself and Wilfred as the martyrs of some new reformation: 'In God's eyes we are martyrs, and we shall not shrink even from death in this struggle against the idolatrous worship of convention' (p. 358).

The turning of religion into a source of aesthetic pleasure is apparent throughout this story. The beauty of the services thrilled the priest, and prayer itself became a source of 'pleasure, excitement, almost a fierce delight of sin' (p. 357). There are some sins, he says, which are 'more beautiful than anything else in the world' (p. 356). The death of the lovers is an exquisite performance and a ravishing sight. As Wilfred prepared for the mass, 'over his night-shirt the child arrayed himself in his little scarlet cassock and tiny lace cotta. He covered his naked feet with the scarlet sanctuary shoes' (p. 359). The chalice which administers the poison is of gold, set with precious stones. The closing tableau offers a scene of pathos and beauty: 'On the steps of the altar was stretched the long, ascetic frame of the young priest, robed in the sacred vestments; close beside him, with his curly head pillowed on the gorgeous embroideries that covered his breast, lay the beautiful boy in scarlet and lace' (p. 360). The boy's beauty has an innocence which attracts the priest, but he is also allured by the idea that the pursuit of beauty entails the pursuit of vice, and his passion for Wilfred becomes that unusual sin which his jaded palate was seeking at the opening of the story. Religion is reduced to repressive convention on the one hand, and fetishistic ritual on the other, while ideas such as innocence and purity, sin and vice, lose their meaning and become ways of enhancing the frisson of pleasure.

A tension between the Greek and Christian worlds, and between homoerotic attraction and ascetic renunciation, is seen in the poetry of Digby Mackworth Dolben (1849–67), himself a devotee of religious ritual, and the object of the erotic devotion of Gerard Manley Hopkins (an unrequited love which has left traces of its deeply troubling effect in Hopkins's poetry). Dolben's poetry was written while he was a schoolboy at Eton, in love with another boy called 'Marchie' Gosselin; Dolben was also a tertiary Benedictine, enjoying the danger of hovering on the brink of conversion to Rome. Dolben uses religious language about his love for Gosselin. In the poem 'On river banks my love was born' he recalls the encounter in which the beloved 'drew/ My whole soul to him' (ll. 11–12), and Dolben knew – in language which could have come from a hymnal – that he

> . . . was born to be my king,
> And I was only born to sing,
> With faded lips, and feeble lays,
> His love and beauty all my days.

>   (ll. 13–16)

Passing angels 'whispered to me: "LOVED AT LAST"' (l. 82). The poet gives his beloved a flower which he crushes against his breast, leaving a stain. As they wander together through an idealized land, the poet comes to understand 'Hidden meanings, hidden duties,/ Hidden loves, and hidden beauties' (ll. 63–4). These loves are not only hidden from the reader, they are lost to the poet, who now laments this lover and the golden days and enchanted landscape which they once enjoyed. In some of Dolben's poems the expression of his love for Christ takes on a distinctly homoerotic tone. In 'Brevi tempore magnum perfecit opus' ['the great work was perfected in a short time'] the seventeen-year-old youth devotes himself to Christ. Christ has 'set upon those virgin lips the signet of His Love' and as the boy experienced 'the stirring of the passions and the movement of the blood', he 'clung with deepening tenderness about the wounded Feet, / And nestled in the Master's Breast with rapture new and sweet' (ll. 19, 22–4). Although this inherits a tradition of reverence for the wounded or dead body of Jesus, its erotic language reminds us that much of the pederastic writing of the nineteenth century delights in imagining boys wounded or dead.

An idealized Greece is the other principal influence upon Dolben's homoerotic imagination. In 'A Poem without a Name II' Dolben begins with a clear invitation to sexual possession, imagining the day

> When your kind eyes shall bid me say,
> Take, Marchie, not of mine, but me,
> And be mine only Poetry.

(ll. 4–6)

Dolben waits 'with Eros glowing at my side' (l. 55), and goes on to a vision of Greece in which his beloved stands on a headland while the waves 'in wild desire' toss about his feet, and in another scene 'my Hylas' (Hylas was the boy whom Heracles loved) lies tantalizingly beyond the waters' reach, 'coronalled with curly gold' (l. 71). Consummation is deferred here, but it is imagined more directly in 'Coré' (the Greek for 'girl'). The speaker of the poem is a young woman who laments her lost lover, and the gender of the speaker allows Dolben to be unusually explicit in his presentation of sexual desire for a man. The speaker's longing 'filled my veins with all desire' (l. 9), until 'unveiled he came to me,/ With the passion of the sea' (ll. 58–62). Then after a description of the beauty of his hair and eyes comes an evocation of the passionate intercourse which this lover from the sea promises:

> Full desire, and faint delight,
> Words that leap, and lips that bite,
> With the panther lithe and light.

(ll. 91–3)

Through this version of Greece, Dolben has created a space for his erotic imagination to be given relatively free rein.

One of the special interests of this poetry is that it is written not by an older man longing for the unrepeatable pederastic pleasures of the ancient world, but by a schoolboy who has fully absorbed the message of sexualized Hellenism. A trio of poems on the theme of vocation spell out the attractions of this available but forbidden love. To surrender to it might be to offend against a Christian vocation, but in 'Vocation B.C.' the young shepherd is called to serve Apollo. Dolben is clearly trying to imagine conditions in which a longing for homoerotic fulfilment might not be proscribed, and could even be construed as a calling. In 'B.C.' the shepherd boy worships Apollo as 'the God of beauty' who has lifted him into 'a purer, higher, nobler, life' (l. 23), and his rapturous contemplation of the god's statue leads him to desire the sight of Apollo's own form, 'in all the glory of immortal youth' (l. 40). There is no guilt here, for Apollo is specifically invoked as the conqueror 'over sin and shame and death' (l. 43). But Dolben cannot quite commit himself to this Hellenic idyll, and the poem ends by imagining that the god who bent over the boy, and whose lips kissed his pale cheek, was Jesus rather than Apollo, for the poet knows 'Who is the God of Love' (l. 108). The awkwardness of this transition from Greek to Christian worlds exemplifies the problem which Dolben has in trying to hold together these two ways of thinking.

This tension is overt in 'From "Vocation"', which is mostly a monologue by the monk Jerome shut in his cloister. He longs to have been able to wander through ancient Greece, which his imagination presents as a land of erotic opportunities. The voices which he hears are singing 'those ancient victories of Love'(l. 12), and the dearest legend of all is that of Apollo and his love for Hyacinthus. Jerome imagines mingling with the crowd listening to some philosopher, and he admires the 'young cheeks that glowed' (l. 21). Revolting against his life in the cloister, Jerome longs for Athens, 'home of life and love', and that 'free, joyous life' and the 'warm, glowing love' which are now barred to him. He too invokes Apollo, wishing to be possessed sexually by him: 'Come to me as thou cam'st to Semele' seems to import a reference to Semele's sexual relationship not with Apollo but with Zeus, who eventually consumed her in a flash of lightning. Though Dolben's mythology may be muddled, Jerome's longing for ecstatic consummation is clear. The poem ends with Jerome's dissatisfied monologue being answered by a hymn sung by Brother Francis.

A final renunciation of Dolben's love for another man because of religion is enacted in 'A Letter', which explains why he is turning away from his lover to embrace Christ. Using an image which evokes that quintessential homoerotic space, the bathing pool, he says that his 'love-current' once ran:

> marred with slime and choked with weed,
> (Long lost the silver ripple-song,
> Long past the sprouting water-mead,)

(ll. 11–13)

This was 'utterly,/ With all its waves of passion, set/ To you' (ll. 15–17). Yet all this love was poured into 'broken cisterns'. Now the name of Jesus has 'burned away the former shame' (l. 24), and this divine lover brings him 'The Face of loveliness unmarred,/ The Consummation of desire' (ll. 64–5). The eroticism of this spiritual consummation is continued in the ecstatic recollection that 'how the waters were made sweet,/ That night, – Thou knowest, – only Thou' (ll. 73–4), 'Thou' here being Christ. The turn away from homosexual union is figured as a homosexual union.

TENNYSON AND HALLAM

The feelings which Alfred Tennyson had for Arthur Henry Hallam are not easy to interpret, but for present purposes it is unnecessary to make biographical conjectures about Tennyson's emotions and sexual desires. What is beyond dispute is that no one in Tennyson's life made such a profound impression on him as Hallam, and no event affected him as traumatically as Hallam's death. Tennyson repeatedly uses the word 'love' for his feelings towards Hallam, and the poetry which was inspired by Hallam's death is not only passionate but full of expressions which are ordinarily associated with sexual desire and with marriage; at some points Tennyson seems to transgress accepted boundaries of decorum, as the recognized vocabulary of ordinary Victorian male friendship proves inadequate for this extraordinary passion.

Tennyson and Hallam met in 1829 when they were both undergraduates at Cambridge. Hallam was by all accounts a charismatic figure, charming and intelligent; no less a judge than Gladstone thought him the most talented man he had ever known. The friendship between Tennyson and Hallam flourished, nurtured partly by a shared interest in poetry. When Hallam became engaged to Tennyson's sister Emily, the bond between the two men was in one respect strengthened and formalized, though Hallam's commitment to Emily was also a sign that his feelings for Tennyson were limited, and they had probably never been as intense on his side as on Tennyson's. But in 1833, when on holiday in Vienna, Hallam suffered an apoplectic attack and died. He was twenty-two.

There seems to have been one place in particular which was associated in Tennyson's mind with his love for Hallam, the valley of Cauteretz in the Pyrenees, which they had visited in 1830. As Robert

Bernard Martin observes in his biography, something profound happened to Tennyson in this valley: 'recurrently sounding through the poetry written after the Pyrenean trip is the word "valley", always connected with love, usually with youth, and frequently with Arthur Hallam ... Was it there that Tennyson recognized fully for the first time how much another person meant to him?'. In any case it became 'the most potent spot poetically that Tennyson ever knew' (p. 120). Revisiting the place in 1861 he wrote the lines 'In the Valley of Cauteretz' recalling that there 'I walked with one I loved two and thirty years ago'; in this spot Hallam was made present to him once again, for 'The voice of the dead was a living voice to me' (ll. 4, 10). In his sonnet 'Check every outflash' (1831) Tennyson describes a valley which has physical resemblances to Cauteretz and is mythologized as a 'haunted place ... dark and holy' (l. 8). The poem opens with an injunction to curb speech:

> Check every outflash, every ruder sally
>   Of thought and speech; speak low, and give up wholly
>   Thy spirit to mild-minded Melancholy;
> This is the place.

(ll. 1–4)

It ends with the recollection that here 'in this valley first I told my love' (l. 14). There is an important but obscure connexion between the restraint of speech now – in the poem's present tense as poet and reader approach the valley – and the breaking of restraint in the past. Are we invited to imagine that the telling led to acceptance, making the spot holy for that reason? The valley's holiness is figured in images traditionally associated with erotic love, and the vocabulary is taken in particular from Milton's descriptions of the paradise shared by Adam and Eve: the 'crispèd' waters, the nightingale, the woodbine; even the midges indulge in a 'wanton gambol' (cp. *Paradise Lost* IV. 237, 345, 602, 629, IX. 216). Or did the telling lead to rebuttal, so making the spot a site of melancholy? Is the opening injunction to restrain speech partly a retrospective rebuke to the poet himself for having spoken words which should have been left unsaid, words which made the valley dark? There seems to be an irresolvable secrecy here. The poem resists being enlisted in biographical speculation, but some things are clear: the valley is the site of the disclosure of the poet's love ('I told my love' is the period's conventional phrase for a declaration of passion, as well as echoing the disguised Viola's half-disclosure to Orsino in *Twelfth Night* II. iv. 111); and Tennyson decided not to reprint it after its initial periodical publication in 1831 and 1833. Did that last line seem too blatant, too much of a self-exposure, after Hallam's death, and after the intensity of Tennyson's feelings for Hallam had been made public through *In Memoriam*?

In the early 1830s Tennyson also wrote a series of poems in which the speaker or protagonist is a woman who experiences unrequited desire for a male lover. 'Mariana' (1830) expresses the longing of a woman for a man who is unattainable; shut up in her moated grange she repeatedly laments 'He cometh not . . . he will not come'. In 'The Lady of Shalott' (1832) the lady is also shut away, fashioning a work of art (a tapestry) by looking at the reflexion of the outside world in a mirror. When she dares to look directly at Sir Lancelot as he rides by, 'The mirror cracked from side to side' (l. 115), the making of art is abandoned, and the lady sets off after him, only to meet her death. The sexual attraction of Lancelot is underscored by the observation that 'from his blazoned baldric slung/ A mighty silver bugle hung' (ll. 87–8). The story of Mariana is renewed in 'Mariana in the South' (1832), which originated during Tennyson's visit to the Pyrenees with Hallam, and was revised in 1842 to include lines 61–84 which may be a reaction to Hallam's death: they imagine the abandoned lover receiving a response from 'an image' (recalling perhaps the veiled image of Hallam from *In Memoriam*). 'Fatima' (1832) presents another woman longing for her lover: she has enjoyed just one kiss from him, and vividly imagines the ecstasy of sexual union with him. The poem was untitled until 1842, so in its original form, voiced by an ungendered speaker, it could be read as an expression of homosexual desire, and even with its final title a male reader can easily associate himself with the longing which the poem expresses:

> From my swift blood that went and came
> A thousand little shafts of flame
> Were shivered in my narrow frame . . .
>
> Before he mounts the hill, I know
> He cometh quickly: from below
> Sweet gales, as from deep gardens, blow
> Before him, striking on my brow.

> In my dry brain my spirit soon,
> Down-deepening from swoon to swoon,
> Faints like a dazzled morning moon . . .
> The skies swoop down in their desire . . .
> My heart, pierced through with fierce delight,
> Bursts into blossom in his sight.
>
> My whole soul waiting silently
> All naked in a sultry sky . . .
> I *will* possess him or will die.

(ll. 16–39)

The speaker's desire collapses three time schemes, fusing together the memory of a past kiss, the intense longing in this unbearably extended present, and the temporary eternity of orgasm with the much-desired lover. 'Oenone' (1832) was drafted in the Pyrenees, and opens with an evocation of a vale in Ida. The lines describing Paris make him clearly the object of sexual desire:

> white-breasted like a star
> Fronting the dawn he moved; a leopard skin
> Drooped from his shoulder, but his sunny hair
> Clustered about his temples like a God's:

(ll. 56–9)

Oenone laments that the man she loves has chosen Aphrodite instead of Pallas – has chosen love for a woman instead of wisdom. Was there (as Robert Bernard Martin suggests) an attempt here to confront Hallam's choice of Emily? One wonders whether the rhyme of 'Emily' and 'Semele' was wholly fortuitous when one reads the poem called 'Semele' (1833) in which Tennyson gives voice to the excited desire of a woman who has asked to be ravished by Zeus not under a veiling form, but in his own proper shape. Whether or not Tennyson wrote these poems as ways of exploring a love for Hallam which included sexual desire, there is no doubt that they provide an imagined space in which poet and reader can own those lyrical utterances and unconsummated narratives which enact desire for a man who is indifferent to, or who has even rebuffed and forsaken, the speaker.

The major response which Tennyson made to Hallam's death was *In Memoriam*, which was built up over an extended period from groups of lyrics and eventually published anonymously in 1850. The work was not composed in the order which it now has, and the individual sections are often semi-autonomous, like fluid sonnets. Indeed, Shakespeare's *Sonnets* were an influence upon *In Memoriam*, and the different ways in which Tennyson's contemporaries viewed this precedent illustrate Victorian sensitivities on the question of Shakespeare's poems and on the proper language for emotional relations between men (see *Poems*, ed. Ricks, ii, 313–14). Benjamin Jowett commented that Tennyson used to think Shakespeare 'greater in his sonnets than in his plays', but that he held this view only 'in his weaker moments' when influenced by 'the great sorrow of his own mind'. Jowett continued:

> It would not have been manly or natural to have lived in it always. But in that peculiar phase of mind he found the sonnets a deeper expression of the never to be forgotten love which he felt . . . The love of the sonnets which he so strikingly expressed was a sort of sympathy with Hellenism.

Though Jowett's chief point is that Tennyson's critical judgement was affected by his grief, by the end of the century the association of unnatural and unmanly behaviour with Greek sympathies had become such an unmistakable signal of homosexual interests that Tennyson's son (called Hallam Tennyson) cut the first and last sentences in that quotation when preparing his life of his father. Arthur Hallam had also admired the *Sonnets*, though his father was suspicious of the feelings which they expressed, which he found

> of such an enthusiastic character, and so extravagant in the phrases that the author uses . . . Notwithstanding the frequent beauties of these sonnets, the pleasure of their perusal is greatly diminished by these circumstances; and it is impossible not to wish that Shakespeare had never written them. There is a weakness and folly in all excessive and mis-placed affection.

Some of this language convicting Shakespeare of unmanly weakness and excessive emotion occurs again in the anonymous review of *In Memoriam* printed in *The Times* (possibly written by the father of Gerard Manley Hopkins). Unlike Dryden's memorial poem for Oldham – one of Dryden's 'most manly and dignified utterances' – Tennyson's poem is marred by 'the enormous exaggeration of the grief'. The 'wailings' of this poem strike the reviewer as having gone beyond the boundaries of masculine feeling. The reviewer then questions the nature of the feelings articulated in this poem:

> A second defect, which has painfully come out as often as we take up the volume, is the tone of – may we say so? – amatory tenderness. Surely this is a strange manner of address to a man, even though he be dead:-
>
>> "So, dearest, now thy brows are cold,
>> "I see thee what thou art, and know
>> "Thy likeness to the wise below,
>> "Thy kindred with the great of old.
>>
>> "But there is more than I can see,
>> "And what I see I leave unsaid,
>> "Nor speak it, knowing death has made
>> "His darkness beautiful with thee." [74, ll. 5–12]
>
> Very sweet and plaintive these verses are; but who would not give them a feminine application? Shakespeare may be considered the founder of this style in English. In classical and Oriental poetry it is unpleasantly familiar. His mysterious sonnets present the startling peculiarity of transferring every epithet of womanly endearment to a masculine friend ... We really think that floating remembrances of Shakespeare's sonnets have beguiled Mr. Tennyson.

Explicitly the reviewer accuses Tennyson only of using exaggerated expressions and being unduly influenced by Shakespeare, but by evoking the 'unpleasantly familiar' homosexual contents of classical and oriental poetry, and by finding Shakespeare's mode of address to the young man in the *Sonnets* a 'startling peculiarity', the implication is clear enough that the feelings articulated by *In Memoriam* can only be interpreted as erotic. The reviewer is also troubled by the obscurity of Tennyson's language in places. He concedes that 'the emotions of the heart and of the fancy have their own dialect', but observes that 'in passages of emotional tenderness and taste there is a reflective light to be thrown from the reader's experience of corresponding sensations': in other words, Tennyson's poem does not evoke in the reader equivalent feelings about the loss of a male friend. Again the poem is convicted of expressing feelings outside the normal experience of male Victorian readers. The reviewer has difficulty following Tennyson's meaning when the poem takes flight into mystical realms, and seems especially troubled by passages which present a vision of Hallam's beauty transfigured in death: one example which is quoted as a case of Tennyson's obscurity reads: 'Come, beauteous in thine after form,/ And like a finer light on light' (91, ll. 15–16; 'on' is a misquotation for 'in'). Though the criticism is overtly directed at a conceptual and linguistic obscurity, the reviewer's anxiety seems to be generated partly by the offence inherent in making a male friend's beauty the subject of such a sublime vision.

Throughout *In Memoriam* Tennyson uses the word 'love' for his feelings about Hallam. Like Shakespeare's *Sonnets*, Tennyson's poem subjects this word to an intense re-imagining, working out a newly-felt definition of love. Tennyson admits that his love and his words are alike inadequate:

> I cannot love thee as I ought,
>   For love reflects the thing beloved;
>   My words are only words, and moved
> Upon the topmost froth of thought.

(52, ll. 1–4)

but he is consoled by 'The Spirit of true love' (presumably Hallam himself translated now into some higher and purified form) and by the reassurance that 'Thou canst not move me from thy side' (52, l. 7). The Spirit continues with a lovely, quasi-biblical consolation: 'Abide: thy wealth is gather'd in,/ When Time hath sundered shell from pearl' (52, ll. 15–16). The tenses in those lines are strange: the sentence does not quite say 'thy wealth is now gathered in, because Time has sundered . . .', which would imply a gathering up which is completed; nor does it say 'thy wealth will be gathered in when Time has eventually sundered . . .', which would promise a future completion. Instead, the grammar fuses the two time schemes into an illogical but powerfully indeterminate statement which reassures the poet that his wealth (his moral nature, his love for Hallam, and Hallam himself) is safely gathered in beyond harm, while implying that the action of Time is still continuing. The importance of this minor obscurity (so characteristic of the poem, as *The Times* complained) is that the precise imprecision manages to depict a love which is outside of the normal processes of time as represented in logical language, and to suggest a fusion of the poet's self, his love, and Hallam himself.

Tennyson freely uses those words 'dear' and 'dearest' which surprised *The Times*: 'So, dearest, now thy brows are cold' (74, l. 5); 'Ah dear, but come thou back to me' (90, l. 21); 'Oh, wast thou with me, dearest, then' (122, l. 1). Perhaps because of the review, Tennyson was defensive about this, and remarked: 'If anybody thinks I ever called him "dearest" in his life they are much mistaken, for I never even called him "dear"' (*Poems*, ed. Ricks, ii, 441–2). But in saying this, Tennyson is only claiming to a friend that in life, in the actual words which he spoke to Hallam, he observed the proprieties: his comment does not address the question of the proprieties of poetic expression, or the kinds of feeling which such words convey.

Characteristic of the way Tennyson represents his love for Hallam is his deployment of metaphors and similes which unambiguously evoke heterosexual passion, sometimes casting himself as the male partner, sometimes as the female. In section 7 Tennyson describes (with a clearly autobiographical 'I' at this point) how he stands outside the house where Hallam used to live:

> Dark house, by which once more I stand
>   Here in the long unlovely street,
>   Doors, where my heart was used to beat
> So quickly, waiting for a hand,
>
> A hand that can be clasped no more –
>   Behold me, for I cannot sleep,
>   And like a guilty thing I creep
> At earliest morning to the door.

> (7, ll. 1–8)

The next section introduces a comparison with 'A happy lover who has come/ To look on her that loves him well', but finds the girl gone; immediately 'all the place is dark, and all/ The chambers emptied of delight' (8, ll. 1–2, 7–8). Tennyson offers this as an exact analogy for his own case, and the lines on his plight replicate the language of the forsaken lover:

> So find I every pleasant spot
>   In which we two were wont to meet,
>   The field, the chamber and the street,
> For all is dark where thou art not.

(8, ll. 9–12)

Tennyson even takes the comparison further, likening his poetry, which Hallam cared for, to a flower which the forsaken lover finds as he wanders, and cherishes because his girl had tended it.

More explicit is the language of marriage which Tennyson uses for his relationship with Hallam, or rather, for the relation in which he now thinks of himself as standing to his lost friend. When leading up to his poignant epigram ''Tis better to have loved and lost/ Than never to have loved at all' (27, ll. 15–16), Tennyson says that he does not envy 'the heart that never plighted troth' (27, l. 10), clearly implying that his own heart has plighted troth with Hallam, and using a phrase which normally referred to the exchange of lovers' vows preceding marriage. He compares himself to a bereaved fiancée condemned to perpetual maidenhood (6, ll. 25–44), and to a girl who loves a man 'whose rank exceeds her own' (60, ll. 2–3); he is anxious that he will 'be thy mate no more' (41, l. 20); and he represents himself as widowed in the phrase 'Till all my widowed race be run' (9, l. 18; again at 17, l. 20). He is married to Sorrow ('no casual mistress, but a wife,/ My bosom-friend and half of life' (59, ll. 2–3)), where Hallam seems to have been partly metamorphosed into this personification of Sorrow, enabling him to be thought of not only as the poet's 'bosom-friend' but as his wife, 'lovely like a bride' (59, l. 6). In the next sentence Tennyson writes of his 'centred passion' (is that 'erotic passion' or 'suffering'?) and 'the creature of my love', and continues:

> And set thee forth, for thou art mine,
>   With so much hope for years to come,
>   That, howsoe'er I know thee, some
> Could hardly tell what name were thine.

(59, ll. 13–16)

By this stage it is thoroughly unclear as to whom 'thee' refers to – Sorrow, or Hallam, or the poet's passion? Is it the sorrow, or the love, or the loved one which eludes naming? The obscurities of Tennyson's thought and style function here as positive fluidities which help him to evade convention and to say things which would be crass or shocking if translated back into some literal paraphrase. The most striking example of marital imagery occurs in section 13:

> Tears of the widower, when he sees
>   A late-lost form that sleep reveals,
>   And moves his doubtful arms, and .feels
> Her place is empty, fall like these;
>
> Which weep a loss for ever new,
>   A void where heart on heart reposed;
>   And, where warm hands have prest and closed,
> Silence, till I be silent too.

(13, ll. 1–8)

Though the next line describes Hallam as 'comrade', this unexceptionable word in no way undoes the obvious physical intimacy in that evocation of the widower putting his hand out to find the bed empty, a scene which inevitably makes more physical the otherwise potentially abstract image of Tennyson and Hallam reposing 'heart on heart', and prevents us from seeing merely manly comradeship in the phrase 'warm hands have prest and closed'.

It is, indeed, the extraordinary physicality of Tennyson's language about Hallam which makes this poem stumble at the boundary between the safe and the unsafe. Examples of the poem's recurring evocation of the two men's clasped hands have already been quoted, and there are more, notably in the lines which imagine Hallam's body buried at sea, recoiling from the thought that the 'hands so often clasped in mine,/ Should toss with tangle and with shells' (10, ll. 19–20). Then, imagining Hallam's body being prepared for burial, Tennyson thinks of breathing life into Hallam's lips:

> I, falling on his faithful heart,
>   Would breathing through his lips impart
> The life that almost dies in me;

(18, ll. 14–16)

An erotic charge is scarcely concealed in some of these evocations of physical contact:

> Descend, and touch, and enter; hear
> The wish too strong for words to name;
> That in this blindness of the frame
> My Ghost may feel that thine is near.
>
> (93, ll. 13–16)

What is this wish too strong to be named? It must be more than the wish enunciated in line 16, which is simply that his spirit should feel Hallam's spirit near him: 'enter' speaks of something more than nearness. Section 122 makes another plea for Hallam's presence, beginning with the epithet 'dearest', and saying:

> If thou wert with me, and the grave
> Divide us not, be with me now,
> And enter in at breast and brow,
> Till all my blood, a fuller wave,
>
> Be quicken'd with a livelier breath . . .
>
> (122, ll. 9–13)

This may well be thought of as a purely spiritual consummation, but the images which Tennyson chooses for it easily suggest the sharpness of physical ecstasy – 'flash of joy', 'lightnings', 'breaks out' – and invite us to return and reread the images 'rose up', 'burst' and 'bare' in the opening stanza on the poet's spiritual protest (122, ll. 1–4).

The alterations which Tennyson made to this poem, as he compiled and revised it in a series of notebooks over seventeen years, often disclose a nervousness and uncertainty at precisely those points when he is trying to find words for his intense love for Hallam, and is trespassing on the dangerous ground of erotic consummation. In his drafts Tennyson conceives of his love for Hallam as entailing a secret: in the section which recalls a lost time of intimate communion, the line which in the printed text reads 'I wander, often falling lame' (23, l. 6) was originally 'The secret oft I falter lame' (thus Shatto and Shaw; Ricks reads a different punctuation); and when the poem imagines Hallam looking into Tennyson's heart, the line 'See with clear eye some hidden shame' (51, l. 7) originally read 'See with clear sight my secret shame' in one manuscript, while in another the last three words have been heavily deleted and are now illegible. The poem as printed avoids any suggestion of secret feelings. Tennyson also became sensitive to the extravagance of his evocation of Hallam's beauty: lines deleted from drafts of section 130 include:

> I know the beauty which thou wast,
> Thy single sweetness in the Past,
> Yet art thou oft as God to me.

Other hesitations concern the use of marital language. In the stanza:

> Two partners of a married life –
> I looked on these and thought of thee
> In vastness and in mystery,
> And of my spirit as of a wife.
>
> (97, ll. 5–8)

the last line is audacious enough in this printed form, but in one manuscript draft it had read 'And of my soul as of thy wife', while in another manuscript a stray line follows – 'Long married souls, dear friend, are we' (*In Memoriam*, ed. Shatto and Shaw, p. 114). In both manuscripts there follows a stanza which did not survive into the published text:

> They madly drank each other's breath
> With breast to breast in early years.
> They met with passion and with tears,
> Their every parting was a death.

Whatever Tennyson's reasons for cancelling this stanza, it is striking that when originally developing the comparison of himself and Hallam with a married couple, he thought it entirely appropriate to imagine that marriage as physically passionate. When Tennyson thought of some future state in which he would again enjoy Hallam's love, he printed his vision thus:

> And love will last as pure and whole
> As when he loved me here in Time,

> And at the spiritual prime
> Rewaken with the dawning soul.

> (43, ll. 13–16)

but in the privacy of his notebooks Tennyson imagined this differently:

> And therefore that our love was true
> Would live thro' all & pure & whole
> Within the bosom of the soul
> Lie, lapt till dawn, like golden dew.

> (Shatto and Shaw, p. 71)

In its original form, Tennyson's vision was of two lovers lying together until dawn.

The hesitations which we glimpse in the manuscripts are traces of a recoil from words which say too much, but they also reveal a struggle to control the time – to imagine the kind of time – in which the relationship with Hallam might be located. The lines quoted earlier from section 52 exemplify Tennyson's need to keep time fluid, to undo the finality of Hallam's death and to fashion some form of present union with him instead of trusting to an almost unbelievable afterlife. The tenses shift and blur. Similarly some of the manuscript drafts reveal difficulties over the imagined time scheme. The cancelled stanza beginning 'They madly drank . . . ' envisages passionate encounters and partings repeated over some years as part of a long-term mutual love, yet the relationship realized here so sharply does not correspond with the time and feeling actually shared by Tennyson and Hallam: it functions as a parallel biography, an alternative history. The vision of the lovers enfolded together till dawn also inhabits a strange kind of time, for it moves through three incompatible time schemes: 'was', 'would live', 'lie' – past, conditional, present. The draft sketches an unrealized, unrealizable time, whose syntax cannot be connected to the syntax of the main poem. *In Memoriam* sometimes revisits specific times past, and places where Hallam used to live – the dark house or the college rooms – but even more poignant than these are the poem's attempts to create times and places of erotic consummation which could never have been, paradises never found. The hesitations in the drafts are more than indecisions over matters of poetic decorum: they are Tennyson's belated creations of a union which never quite became imaginable. In the margins of the elegy for Hallam are these fragmentary elegies for a poet bereaved of that which he had never possessed.

Tennyson's strange ways of imagining union with Hallam found one still stranger expression. According to the diary of Sydney Waterlow, Edmund Gosse 'professed to have heard Tennyson tell how he had been to re-visit old scenes & had been moved by familiar sights & associations. "And what do you think I saw", he said in his booming voice; "I saw two boys copulating on Arthur Hallam's grave".' Whether this was Gosse's imagination, or Tennyson's, or sober truth, the anecdote seems to unfold the unrealized primal scene of Tennyson's imagination.

WALT WHITMAN AND THE LOVE OF COMRADES

The most distinctive, and for some English readers the most disturbing voice among those poets who expressed desire for other men, was the American Walt Whitman. His collection *Leaves of Grass* was first published in 1855, and then expanded and revised repeatedly up to his death in 1892. In England he became a challenge and a resource for those writers who were exploring their own feelings about men. Gerard Manley Hopkins wrote to Robert Bridges: 'I always knew in my heart Walt Whitman's mind to be more like my own than any other man's living. As he is a very great scoundrel this is not a pleasant confession. And this also makes me the more desirous to read him, and the more determined that I will not' (Robert Bernard Martin, *Gerard Manley Hopkins*, p. 350). Others found Whitman a more welcome revelation. Bram Stoker sent an enthusiastic confessional letter to Whitman (see *Dracula*, pp. 487–97), while for John Addington Symonds *Leaves of Grass* was 'a sort of Bible' (*Memoirs*, p. 189). Edward Carpenter, D.H. Lawrence and Ivor Gurney all wrote poems in Whitman's style.

　Whitman himself was concerned to fashion a language which would enunciate his emotional and erotic feelings, and his aspirations for a democratic society based upon male bonding, but this language had to carry his own stamp and not be moulded by contemporary conventions. To start with, Whitman made his own person the object of the reader's attention, but only on his own unusual terms. The first edition of *Leaves of Grass* was published without the author's name on the title page, but carried a portrait of Whitman striking the pose of an American working man, his shirt open, his hat aslant, his gaze offering the reader a quizzical challenge. A fascination with his own body, a strong auto-eroticism, is an important element in his homosexual sensibility. In the opening poem, which in later editions was entitled 'Song of Myself', Whitman represents his own body as a landscape alive with sexual excitement, an intimate geography laid open to give and receive pleasure:

> If I worship one thing more than another
>   it shall be the spread of my own
>   body, or any part of it . . .
> Firm masculine colter it shall be you!
> Whatever goes to the tilth of me it shall be you! . . .
> Breast that presses against other breasts it shall be you! . . .
> Root of wash'd sweet-flag! timorous pond-snipe! nest of
>   guarded duplicate eggs! it shall be you!
> Mix'd tussled hay of head, beard, brawn, it shall be you!
> Trickling sap of maple, fibre of manly wheat,
>   it shall be you! . . .
> You sweaty brooks and dews it shall be you!
> Winds whose soft-tickling genitals rub
>   against me it shall be you!
> Broad muscular fields, branches of live oak,
>   loving lounger in my winding paths, it shall be you!
> Hands I have taken, face I have kiss'd, mortal
>   I have ever touch'd, it shall be you.

(ll. 527–43)

The eroticized landscape which Whitman unfolds here is something more complex than just a series of metaphors for his own body. While some images do have a particular reference (the penis and testicles visualized as a 'timorous pond-snipe' guarding a nest of eggs), others seem to offer specific connotations only to veer away: 'tussled hay' delivers both tactile and visual precision as an image for the head and the beard, but when the line moves on to place 'brawn' in apparently the same grammatical sequence, the metaphor disappears. Whitman's grammar is often loose, and the discontinuities create scope for the reader's imagination. Images without precise referents, such as 'fibre of manly wheat' or 'winding paths', also stimulate the reader's imagination without confining it, and in such cases we see how erotic is the kind of reading which Whitman invites, since the reader is left free to trace whatever winding paths he wishes over the poet's body. Whitman's images often elude the classic distinction between metaphor and metonymy: one thing is not quite a metaphor for something else which is distinct and separate from it; nor are things connected metonymically, with one item being part of a larger whole. Ambiguity about exactly what is being named, and exactly what kind of connexions are being made between people and between bodies is crucial, not only to protect Whitman from scandal but, more positively, to urge the reader into rethinking these connexions for himself, imagining new ways of seeing the body, the landscape, and emotional bonds between men.

Whitman's ecstatic communion with this sexualized landscape is written in such a way as to include sexual union with other male bodies, their breasts, genitals and muscular fields, though much is left implicit and meanings are achieved through carefully unspecific and deniable connexions. The line which celebrates his own penis as a 'firm masculine colter' (a colter is a blade) is followed by a line in which his body waits to be tilled as if by the blade of a spade or plough – implicitly, then, by another man's colter. Everything depends upon the juxtaposition of the two lines, a connexion which evades exact logic and hands over to the reader the responsibility for making this interpretation. Whitman is reworking the traditional heterosexual image of the woman being tilled by the man's plough (cp. Shakespeare, *Sonnets* 3.6; *Measure for Measure* I. iv. 39–44), and this is one example among many of Whitman's fashioning of a persona which may be primarily male but can occasionally include the female in a discontinuous doubling or blurring of gender. When Whitman describes sexual pleasure, his syntax avoids being specific about who the partners are and what they are doing:

> Blind loving wrestling touch, sheath'd hooded
>   sharp-tooth'd touch!
> Did it make you ache so, leaving me?
>
> Parting track'd by arriving, perpetual payment of
>   perpetual loan,
> Rich showering rain, and recompense richer afterward.

Sprouts take and accumulate, stand by
    the curb prolific and vital,
Landscapes projected masculine, full-sized and golden.

(ll. 642–7)

Aptly registering the heady confusions of sexual union, nouns and noun phrases are linked in apposition, or just find themselves side by side, or drift ecstatically without verbs, careless of cause and effect in an extended present. But for all his indeterminate syntax and imagery, there are clear indications that both bodies are male, and sometimes this is made quite overt, as in this suppressed passage from *Leaves of Grass*:

Thruster holding me tight and that I hold tight!
We hurt each other as the bridegroom and
    the bride hurt each other.

(*1855*, p. 44)

The poet's lover, the 'thruster', is unambiguously male, and Whitman circumspectly removed these lines after the first edition.

Whitman's poetry co-opts the reader, so that in following him from the startlingly exact to the suggestively imprecise we take part in fashioning an erotic interplay between men, and our reading itself becomes such an interplay. The reader's role is brought to the fore in section 11 of 'Song of Myself', beginning 'Twenty-eight young men bathe by the shore' (l. 199). The men are observed by a woman hiding behind the blinds at her window, who in her mind is splashing in the water along with the naked youths, even though she never leaves the security of her house. The voyeur disappears as we read on, and her longing and explicitly female glance is replaced by the unmediated involvement of the reader in the scene, as the water plays over the men's bodies:

Little streams pass'd all over their bodies.

An unseen hand also pass'd over their bodies,
It descended tremblingly from their temples and ribs.

The young men float on their backs,
    their white bellies bulge to the sun,

they do not ask who seizes fast to them,
They do not know who puffs and declines with
    pendant and bending arch,
They do not think whom they souse with spray.

(ll. 211–16)

The woman at the window is a figure in her own right, characterized as handsome and lonely and richly dressed, but she is also a
point of entry into the scene for the reader, providing a viewer with
whom the reader can associate. The woman's gaze is furtive and
secret, and thus the male reader is made aware that his own entry
into the scene is not uncompromised. The 'unseen hand' which
passes over the men's bodies can be that of the female voyeur or
that of the male reader. The description of the men's play which
culminates in the participants being soused with spray invites a
sexual reading but does not insist on it. As Michael Moon has noted,
Whitman was fascinated by liminal places – beaches, shorelines, the
edges of pools – where men may move between different kinds of
existence, and where a man may stand in one world and observe
another; the poetry, too, likes to shape in-between worlds for the
reader to inhabit, where we may move between viewpoints, and
where one image may turn into another, one experience into another,
one gender into another, without any need to insist upon literal
clarity and single meanings.

   In 'The Sleepers' the speaker of the poem, who moves from sleeper
to sleeper imagining and temporarily participating in their dreams,
has a fluid identity which seems to shift between genders, but there
is no doubting the special excitement which is evoked in the account of sex with a male lover ('his flesh was sweaty and panting';
ll. 47–59), and in a subsequent vision:

I see a beautiful gigantic swimmer swimming
    naked through the eddies of the sea,
His brown hair lies close and even to his head, he strikes out
    with courageous arms, he urges himself with his legs,
I see his white body . . .

(ll. 70–2)

The 'I' here easily accommodates itself to a male reader's homoerotic
gaze. Once Whitman's reader has been educated as an interpreter

(and co-creator) of erotic pleasures between men, those passages which seem principally to invite an appreciation of masculine strength and beauty cannot refuse the caress of the unseen hand.

Whitman's most overt exploration of relationships with men is presented in the collection 'Calamus', first added to *Leaves of Grass* in the edition of 1860. Calamus is a rush growing around ponds, and Whitman explained that he wanted to evoke 'the biggest and hardiest kind of spears of grass – and their fresh, acquatic, pungent bouquet' (*Complete Poems*, p. 799). The word comes from the Greek *kalamos*, meaning not only a reed but also a pen, a pipe and an arrow: the word thus combines a clearly phallic image with metaphors for poetic creativity, and also locates the point of origin for this sexuality and creativity in the natural pools used as bathing places which were sites of homoerotic pleasure for many in a period when men habitually swam naked.

Whitman's poetry often shapes the landscape as a site of erotic longing and satisfaction. The opening poem in 'Calamus' has Whitman offering a turning away from the ways of the outside world into new paths:

> In paths untrodden,
> In the growth by margins of pond-waters,
> Escaped from the life that exhibits itself . . .

> (ll. 1–3)

This new life (and new poetry) does not exhibit itself but 'contains all the rest' (l. 11). He promises to sing songs of 'manly attachment' and 'athletic love' (ll. 12, 14) and 'To tell the secret of my nights and days, / To celebrate the need of comrades' (ll. 17–18). There is in this poetry a doubleness about enclosure and exposure, as Whitman resists one kind of exhibition – the displaying of himself in the public world, on other people's terms – only to reveal intimate places. Whitman's spaces are the natural enclosures of wild America, and the relationships which are imagined in these spaces are strikingly different from those entertained in English verses about boys bathing. Whitman's poetry characteristically celebrates achieved love between adults, rather than a longing for the transient beauty of unattainable boys. The muscular strength of the working body attracts him, rather than the lustrous surface of the boyish form at play. His poetry is more tactile than visual, his lovers are not translated into works of art, and no invisible boundary separates a gazer from the erotic object: Whitman does not frame the body so as to preserve it for the eye and keep it from the touch. The English bathing pool is a boys' space which adults cannot enter except in their imagination – or if they do it is with the clumsiness of the observer in Hopkins's 'Epithalamion', who is so struck with the boys' 'downdolphinry and bellbright bodies' that he strips to join them, but in his haste takes off his clothes before undoing his boots; similarly maladroit is Hopkins's attempt to allegorize the scene as representing 'Spousal Love' before the fragment is abandoned. Whitman shares his spaces, moves easily through these liminal areas instead of standing isolated on the edge of other people's happiness. In 'These I singing in spring' the poet wades into the pond where he 'last saw him that tenderly loves me, and returns again never to separate from me' (l. 19) and gathers calamus as 'the token of comrades' (l. 20). In 'When I heard at the close of the day' thoughts about his lover occur to him while swimming; then the lover arrives, and the two men sleep together: 'his arm lay lightly around my breast – and that night I was happy' (l. 13). Throughout this poem the imagery defines this as a thoroughly natural love, and their shared private space is enfolded within the natural world.

If the reader is to share Whitman's privacy, he must learn to co-operate in a new kind of reading. In 'Scented herbage of my breast' Whitman addresses the 'slender leaves' and 'blossoms of my blood', saying: 'I permit you to tell in your own way of the heart that is under you', but immediately confesses, 'O I do not know what you mean there underneath yourselves, you are not happiness, / You are often more bitter than I can bear' (ll. 7–9). The poet himself draws back, uncertain of his feelings now that he comes to the point of disclosing them in poetry; aware of their complexity, he reminds us that his images cannot be confined to a single, clear meaning. This telling of feelings in their own way turns out to be far from straightforward, and in a significant ambiguity he summons up the act of disclosure in a word which promises its opposite – 'unbare':

> Do not remain down there so ashamed,
>   herbage of my breast!
> Come I am determin'd to unbare this broad breast of mine,
>   I have long enough stifled and choked;
> Emblematic and capricious blades I leave you,

now you serve me not,
I will say what I have to say by itself,
I will sound myself and comrades only,
    I will never again utter a call only their call . . .

(ll. 20–4)

This 'unbaring' of Whitman is a revelation of obscurity, or at least
of complexity. In this language the boundaries of the self and the
lover, the human and the natural, are often blurred, and the poetry
suggests that we may take part in several different metonymies,
linked as comrades and linked to the natural landscape.

Reading Whitman requires a readiness to rest in ambiguity and
indefinition, and at several points Whitman addresses the question
of how a reader is to proceed. One poem begins with a warning
that without the reader's answering understanding, the poetry will
not achieve its purpose:

Whoever you are holding me now in hand,
Without one thing all will be useless,
I give you fair warning before you attempt me further,
I am not what you supposed, but far different.
Who is he that would become my follower?
Who would sign himself a candidate for my affections?

(ll. 1–6)

The 'me' who is held by the reader is at once Walt Whitman the
man, Walt Whitman the poet, and the book *Leaves of Grass*. Because
the text has included heterosexual gestures and situations, the
implied reader could be male or female, and 'comrade' can stretch
inclusively to denote a woman. But for the man reading becomes a
homoerotic pleasure:

Here to put your lips upon mine I permit you,
With the comrade's long-dwelling kiss
    or the new husband's kiss,
For I am the new husband and I am the comrade.

(ll. 19–21)

In this relationship between the reader and 'Whitman', the distinction between the homosocial and the homosexual seems to evaporate: the reader may bring the comrade's kiss *or* the husband's kiss, while the poet is both comrade *and* husband: the distinction made in one line seems to be undone in the next, and both kinds of kiss are of lips on lips, and the comrade's 'long-dwelling kiss' is hardly less intimate and erotic than the husband's. Whitman's vocabulary centres on the word 'comrade', but his usage often elides any distinction between friends, comrades and lovers: in the poem 'These I singing in spring', he offers his poems to 'lovers' (l. 1), depicts himself embraced by 'dear friends' (l. 12) and proclaims the calamus as 'the token of comrades' (l. 20). But while much is achieved through significant ambiguities, there are also signs that the poetry has to conceal love. In 'Earth, my likeness' we are told that

> . . . an athlete is enamour'd of me, and I of him,
> But toward him there is something fierce and
>   terrible in me eligible to burst forth,
> I dare not tell it in words, not even in these songs.

> (ll. 5–7)

Some of Whitman's paths are trodden in silence.

JOHN ADDINGTON SYMONDS

John Addington Symonds (1840–93) was one of Whitman's most enthusiastic English readers. Indeed, though Symonds was a prolific scholar, critic and poet, it is as a reader of an emerging homoerotic canon that he is of special interest, for his moral and aesthetic confusion about his own sexuality was explored through a strong imaginative engagement with literary texts which provided him with images and roles. His posthumously published memoirs are prefaced with some lines from *Leaves of Grass* in which Whitman describes the difficulty of knowing another man's life – or, indeed, one's own – which the poet approaches by means of 'a few diffused faint clues and indirections' (*Memoirs*, p. 31). All his life Symonds sought clues in other men's works which might give him some guidance in the confused, often guilty, frequently unsatisfying indirections of his sexual life. As a child Symonds would have a recurring reverie just before falling asleep in which he imagined himself crouched on the floor amid naked sailors (p. 62). As he grew up and absorbed classical literature with an intense sensibility, his yearnings began to be shaped by the ideals of Greek beauty and manliness which were offered to him in the pages of his classical texts and in antique sculpture. But another early influence was Shakespeare's presentation of the ideal male in *Venus and Adonis*:

> It gave form, ideality and beauty to my previous erotic visions. Those adult males, the shaggy and brawny sailors, without entirely disappearing, began to be superseded in my fancy by an adolescent Adonis ... In some confused way I identified myself with Adonis; but at the same time I yearned after him as an adorable object of passionate love. Venus only served to intensify the situation ... I did not want her ... she only expressed my own relation to the desirable male. She brought into relief the overwhelming attraction of masculine adolescence and its proud inaccessibility. Her hot wooing taught me what it was to woo with sexual ardour. I dreamed of falling back like her upon the grass, and folding the quick-panting lad in my embrace. (pp. 62–3)

In Shakespeare's text the homoerotic gaze is accommodated by the descriptions of Adonis's beauty, and of his body as an object of desire; no doubt Renaissance readers had appropriated the text in a similar fashion.

It was primarily through Greek texts, however, that Symonds's homosexual sensibility was fashioned. A reading of Plato's *Phaedrus* and *Symposium* at the age of seventeen came as a revelation, paving the way for his first love: 'I discovered the true *liber amoris* [book of love] at last ... It was just as though the voice of my own soul spoke to me through Plato, as though, in some antenatal experience I had led the life of philosophical Greek lover' (p. 99). But Symonds's response to Greek precedents proved to be contradictory, and a continuing source of unease. On the positive side, his discovery of Greek love enabled him to understand his feelings, encouraged him to cherish ideals of male love and masculine beauty, and provided him with vocabularies for his first relationships. A few weeks after discovering Plato, Symonds discovered Willie Dyer, a choirboy at Bristol cathedral. Symonds was moved more by an aesthetic interest in the service and the building than by piety: 'My soul was lodged in Hellas; and the Christian in me stirred only, like a torpid snake, sunned by the genial warmth of art' (p. 103). He regarded his relationship with Dyer (consummated only in two kisses) as fulfilling the Greek ideal 'of a passionate yet pure love between friend and friend', and an anemone plucked from the spot in the woods where he first kissed Dyer was preserved between the pages of Symonds's copy of Theocritus, marking the place where the poet speaks of the golden age when boys returned one's love.

Later in life Symonds, now married, fell in love with a sixth-former at Clifton College whom he calls 'Norman'. His reflections on the relationship continually use Greek phrases and concepts. Norman's beauty is described in lines from Theocritus, and he has 'the sort of face which seemed made to be cast in bronze' (p. 193). When Symonds confides to his diary his delight in Norman's body, he repeatedly compares him with a Greek statue:

> Oh, the strain of those delicate slight limbs and finely moulded breasts – the melting of that stately throat into the exquisite slim shoulders – as of the Genius of the Vatican – the *sterna th' hôs agalmatos kallista* [most beautiful breast, like that of a statue] . . . features as of some bronze statue, sharp and clear – the chiselled mouth . . . The body is but silent, a dumb eloquent animated work of art made by the divine artificer . . . Shy and modest, tender in the beauty-bloom of ladhood, is his part of sex *kuprin pothousan êdê* [already longing for love] – fragrant to the searching touch, yet shrinking . . . If I could only paint him, as he lay there white upon the whiteness of the bed, and where he was not white, glowing to amber hues, and deepening into darkness of black eyes and hair – dawn of divinest twilight – only one rose upon his flesh, and that the open, passionate, full-perfumed mouth, the chalice of soul-nourishing dew. Norman is all in all and wholly *melichlôros* [pale as honey]. (pp. 209–10)

It seems essential to Symonds's imaginative possession of Norman that the boy should fulfil the promises made by Greek statuary, and be himself a Greek god; the word *agalma* specifically means the statue of a god as an object of worship. Symonds also takes a quasi-painterly possession of the body, though in a text not intended for publication he does not need to maintain the fiction of the chaste eye, and delightedly fuses the different senses ('fragrant to the . . . touch'; 'pale as honey'). But it is striking that this aestheticizing prose is being used not to articulate a distant longing, but to recollect a night of sensual consummation:

I stripped him naked, and fed sight, touch and mouth on these things. Will my lips ever forget their place upon his breast, or on the tender satin of his flank, or on the snowy whiteness of his belly? . . . Will my arms forget the strain of his small fragile waist, my thighs the pressure of his yielding thighs . . . (p. 209).

Symonds, however, insists that at no time 'did any one of those things take place between us which people think inseparable from love of this sort. I was content with contemplation, contact, kissing' (p. 211). Even so, he 'dreaded what that might lead to, if the spiritual and intellectual relation between us remained imperfect' (p. 208).

For Symonds's Hellenism caused him problems as well as offering him satisfactions. His reading of Plato provided him with an ideal of spiritual and intellectual companionship which Willie Dyer and Norman could not altogether fulfil; intercourse would have violated both Platonic ideals and his own lingering fastidiousness, and yet Greek poetry and philosophy and art were telling him of the naturalness of physical love. Another chorister, Alfred Brooke, attracted him at Oxford, but when Brooke gave him an inviting glance, Symonds could barely raise his head from the desk where Plato lay; later when Brooke came into Symonds's bedroom to offer himself, he was sent away without even a kiss (pp. 124–5). Much later Symonds wrote to Jowett about the dangers of allowing young men to read Plato. Those already attracted to men find that 'what they had been blindly groping after was once an admitted possibility', but for a man to have these feelings encouraged is 'maddening, because it is stimulating to the imagination; wholly out of accord with the world he has to live in; too deeply in accord with his own impossible desires' (pp. 100–2).

In his privately printed essay *A Problem in Greek Ethics* (1883), Symonds courageously made a scholarly appraisal of the role of *paiderastia* in Greek society. He carefully distinguished 'two separate forms of masculine passion . . . a noble and a base, a spiritual and a sensual. To the distinction between them the Greek conscience was acutely sensitive' (pp. 9–10). The noble form Symonds describes as chivalrous, comparing it with the courtly love of medieval romance. At Athens *paiderastia* 'was closely associated with liberty, manly sports, severe studies, enthusiasm, self-sacrifice, self-control, and deeds of daring', and had nothing to do with effeminacy. But even this representation of Greek practices would be repugnant to Victorian morality, so he pleads that 'we cannot . . . criticise Greek

morality by our own canons of conduct' (p. 40). He later crossed
out that observation when revising his copy of the pamphlet. The
Greeks seemed to Symonds to have achieved a union of the sensuous
and the spiritual which contrasted acutely with the separation of
the two in Victorian Christianity:

> The interpenetration of spiritual and corporeal elements in a
> complete personality . . . marks Greek religion and Greek art . . . the
> spirit burning through the flesh and moulding it to individual
> forms; the flesh providing a fit dwelling for the spirit which
> controlled and fashioned it . . . it followed as a necessity that their
> highest emotional aspirations, their purest personal service, should
> be devoted to clear and radiant incarnations of the spirit in a
> living person. Over their souls had never passed the withering
> blast of Oriental asceticism or the dessicating breath of Jewish
> morality. (p. 71)

That last sentence was also crossed out in Symonds's copy, no
doubt because it made too direct a challenge to contemporary morality for it to be made public. In the contrast between that bitter
sentence and the rest of the paragraph's heady evocation of Greek
wholeness, we hear Symonds's almost tragic recognition that he
is a man shut out by his own times from what others have found
most life-enhancing.

E.M. Forster's motto, 'Only connect . . .' comes to mind, but for
Symonds the connexions which he made across the centuries seem
only to have made him more conscious of the impossibility of realizing his intellectual, aesthetic and sexual aspirations. In the
Memoirs he recalls the feverish state in which he would stare at the
men and boys bathing naked in the Serpentine, and become in his
daydreams a participant in classical myths:

> Yes, this afternoon I held Lycidas upon the down of beds of
> dreaming . . . From his closed eyelids I kissed the bloom of dreams,
> and from his parted lips I drank the balm of slumber. I was
> Hypnos gazing on Endymion in the cave of Latmos . . .
>
> Four young men are bathing in the pond by the embankment.
> I pass; the engine screams and hurries me away. But the engine
> has no power to take my soul. That stays, and is the pond in
> which the bathers swim, the air in which they shout, the grass on

which they run and dress themselves, the hand that touches them unfelt, the lips that kiss them and they know it not. (p. 167)

This passage painfully shows how difficult he found it to connect Greek ideals and Victorian realities. Symonds does not fully inhabit any of these worlds. He is not in the cave of Latmos; he is physically in the train but his attention is with the bathers; he cannot join the bathers except in his 'soul'; and the soul which Plato prized as the bringer of wisdom has become merely the imaginary location in which the voyeur touches the bathers, secure in the knowledge that they cannot respond.

The reference to the 'hand that touches them unfelt' recalls Whitman, and may be a direct echo, for around the time of that passage (c.1867) Symonds discovered *Leaves of Grass*. From Whitman he absorbed the ideal of comradeship which helped him to achieve 'a sense of the dignity and beauty and glory of simple healthy men' (p. 189), and to enjoy and respect soldiers picked up in London, gondoliers in Venice, farm workers in the Alps. Some of these encounters were fully sexual, but Symonds retained an anxiety about physical consummation, and even wrote to Whitman in 1890 asking him to be explicit as to whether his love of comrades included physical sex (*Letters*, iii, 481–4). Whitman vigorously denied it, but the vehemence of his reply probably says less about Whitman's ideals or practices than about his anger at being asked to explain in someone else's terms a philosophy which he had already defined, with such careful imprecision, in his own language.

Symonds's book on Whitman and his discussion of Whitman in *A Problem in Modern Ethics* (1891) hover around two related issues: the congruence of Whitman's ideals with Greek ideals, and the relationship of comradeship to sexual desire. According to Symonds, Whitman's notion of comradeship recalls the masculine love celebrated in the *Phaedrus* and the *Symposium*. Cleanliness and chastity he finds inseparable from Whitman's ideal of virility. Whitman never suggests that comradeship might occasion physical desire, and yet he never explicitly condemns such desires. Symonds worries away anxiously at this problem, before concluding that Whitman's ideal of 'adhesiveness' is meant to have 'no interblending' with sexual love, and that *Calamus* suggests how abnormal instincts may be raised to a higher plane. Altogether, while Symonds's reading of Whitman may have brought him private encouragement and reassurance, his public accounts of Whitman's work register the unresolved tensions and anxieties which haunted him, ever a prey to mythologies which his society tolerated as symbols but punished as practices.

Two motifs characterize the evocation of homoerotic desire in Symonds's imaginative writing: the presentation of sexual pleasure as aesthetic pleasure, and its containment by death. The essay which gives its title to the collection *In the Key of Blue* (1893) is ostensibly a discussion of how to describe colour in words, particularly how to register the appearance of blue in proximity to other colours. But the essay is limited to observing the male body in association with shades of blue: 'whether the flesh-tints of the man be pale or sun-burned, his complexion dark or fair, blue is equally in sympathy with the model' (p. 4). In pursuit of this apparently aesthetic and linguistic inquiry, Symonds takes his nineteen-year-old Venetian gondolier Augusto 'to pose him in a variety of lights with a variety of hues in combination'. The first study is of Augusto in blue against the black of the night sky, but the verses which record the pictorial effects soon diverge into erotic description:

> The ivory pallor of your face
> Gleamed from those glowing azures back
> Against the golden gaslight; grapes
> Of dusky curls your brows embrace . . .

(p. 6)

The second study, of blue and white, enthuses over 'the ivory of your brows', while Augusto's eyes are 'starry orbs of lustrous jet': here Symonds the scholar of Renaissance literature is deploying the tropes of Elizabethan love poetry. His picture of Augusto also stresses his working-class masculinity when he is seen in a labourers' café dancing 'voluptuously . . . cheek unto cheek' with a male comrade. We contemplate Augusto's lip 'wherefrom Love's self a bee might sip' (p. 10), with echoes of Barnfield. Then a 'symphony of blues and gold' (p. 10) has the pair lounging on the grass amongst shrubs with yellow flowers. Blue with green does not involve Augusto, but presents two dyers, stripped to the waist, with 'nude breasts, and arms of might,/ The pride of youth and manhood white' (p. 12). Then Augusto is posed against a sail of imperial purple, with verbal echoes of Shakespeare's description of Cleopatra's barge. The contexts of these observations have formed an anthology of Symonds's personal erotic preferences: the boyish body, the labouring man, unselfconscious comradeship, along with Renaissance tropes of the body as a cluster of jewels, reclining in – and offering itself as – a bower of bliss. Finally the two men are seen in their shared room, where Symonds looks at Augusto's nude form stretched out on the couch:

> A flawless form of simple strength,
> Sleep-seeking, breathing, ivory-white,
> Upon the couch in candle-light.

(p. 15)

As 'all the blues dissolve', so does Symonds's aesthetic project.

The other way in which Symonds licenses his erotic gaze is by killing the object which it contemplates. The poem 'Eudiades', set in ancient Greece, celebrates the love of the manly athlete Melanthias for the boy Eudiades, and offers the usual descriptions of boyish beauty. Two emphases come to dominate the poem, purity and death. While Eudiades retains his boyish innocence Melanthias is content to sleep chastely with him, but as time passes Melanthias feels increasingly restless and frustrated, while the boy too begins to feel sexual desire. Eventually Eudiades offers Melanthias 'the pleasure none may touch and live/ Thenceforth unshamed' (p. 124). For Symonds intercourse would be not only shameful but even a kind of death: 'fear not to shed my blood;/ For I will die to do thee any good', says the boy. Sexual consummation would be the death of innocence, but would also, it seems, entail some sado-masochistic pleasure. Symonds makes the two lovers decide to eschew sex, and then has them die in slavery in the stone quarries of Syracuse. In part this obsession with death (which is shared by other Uranian writers) is a way of distancing the boys from the grasp of Time or other lovers, arresting their growth (or decay) into adulthood and achieving a form of consummation and possession; but there is also a sadistic streak in this obsession which sometimes colours the aesthetic pleasure.

In 'Midnight at Baiae' the narrator makes his way through a deserted Roman villa, observing the painting and statuary (an anthology of homosexual icons), and noting a cup carved with Maenads drinking the blood of Pentheus; the cup contains blood-dark wine, untasted. Finally the observer sees a sumptuous couch on which reclines the ultimate luxury item:

...I saw a naked form supine.
It was a youth from foot to forehead laid
In slumber. Very white and smooth and fine
Were all his limbs; and on his breast there played
The lambent smiles of lamplight. But a pool
Of blood beneath upon the pavement stayed.
There, where blue cups of lotos-lilies cool
With reeds into mosaic-wreathes were blent,
The black blood grew and curdled...
Spell-bound I crept, and closer gazed at him:
And lo! from side to side his throat was gashed
With some keen blade; and every goodly limb,
With marks of crispèd fingers marred and lashed,
Told the fierce strain of tyrannous lust that here
Life's crystal vase of youth divine had dashed.

(p. 145)

As the observer reads this scene, his gaze registers a decadent pleasure and becomes complicit in the sadistic erotic narrative which it deduces – or constructs. The marks of violence on the youth's limbs are read as signs of someone's sexual pleasure, and other possible explanations are not considered. The youth's blood is seen as part of the decoration on the mosaic floor; his body has been broken like a vase in the pursuit of satisfaction. The naked boy has become part of a gallery in which looking leads to consumption, and sexual possession has become synonymous with death.

OSCAR WILDE

The three trials of Oscar Wilde in 1895 forced the public to acknowledge the previously secret – or only half-recognized – world of sexual relations between men, and raised the question of how one could distinguish 'sodomites' from other men, or close friendship from 'gross indecency'. The law punished sodomy by execution until 1861, when the penalty was changed to life imprisonment; in 1885 the Criminal Law Amendment Act, in a clause moved by Henry Labouchère, criminalized acts of gross indecency between men, not amounting to sodomy, and prescribed a maximum sentence of two years' imprisonment with hard labour. Since 1828 the law had required evidence of the emission of semen before sodomy could be proved, so prosecutions under that heading had become infrequent, but the 1885 act made illegal all forms of sexual contact between men, even in private, and it was this extension of the law under which Wilde was prosecuted. He was involved in three trials. The first was the prosecution for criminal libel which he brought against the Marquis of Queensberry, who had accused him of 'posing as a somdomite' [*sic*]. When the case collapsed and Queensberry was acquitted, Wilde was himself arrested, and along with Alfred Wood faced 25 counts of gross indecency, procuring and conspiracy. The third trial was a retrial on these charges which became necessary when the first jury failed to agree.

The usual legal arguments over the interpretation of evidence extended in Wilde's case to the interpretation of literary texts, and in the first trial, when the point at issue was whether Wilde had defined himself by posing as a sodomite, Queensberry's counsel sought to define Wilde by making him explain his relation to the poses struck in various literary texts including Bloxam's 'The Priest and the Acolyte', Lord Alfred Douglas's poem 'Two Loves', and letters which Wilde had written to Douglas. Counsel tried to get Wilde to agree that 'The Priest and the Acolyte' was 'improper' and 'blasphemous', but Wilde would only say that 'it violated every artistic canon of beauty' (*Trials*, pp. 121–2). The lawyers attempted to demonstrate that the feelings expressed in his letters were improper, while Wilde maintained that one letter in particular – in which he had told Douglas, 'it is a marvel that those red rose-leaf lips of yours should have been made no less for music of song than for madness of kisses', and 'Hyacinthus, whom Apollo loved so madly, was you in Greek days' – was a prose sonnet. Wilde was struggling for the right to use his own artistic and critical language without having it translated into terms prescribed by others. Another text by Wilde which came under particular scrutiny was *The Picture of Dorian Gray*, as counsel sought to establish whether the relationships between men which it presented exemplified 'a proper or an improper feeling' (*Trials*, p. 127).

The Picture of Dorian Gray was first printed in *Lippincott's Monthly Magazine* in 1890, and revised and expanded for publication in book form in 1891. It opens with the painter Basil Hallward talking to Lord Henry Wooton about the portrait of a beautiful young man which he has almost completed. Basil wants to keep its sitter, Dorian Gray, away from Lord Henry, whom he regards as a potentially corrupting influence, but he inadvertently discloses the boy's name, and soon Dorian himself arrives in the studio. Dorian wishes that the face in the portrait could age while he retains his youthful beauty. The wish comes true, and as the picture changes, it registers not only Dorian's advancing years but his increasing moral degeneracy, until he finally stabs it, and in doing so kills himself. The face in the picture reverts to being that of the exquisite boy, while the dead body of Dorian becomes aged and loathsome, recognizable only from its jewellery.

Secrecy and the fear of disclosure are recurring motifs in this tale, and the story itself does not always disclose its secrets to the reader. Repeated hints that these concealments involve homosexual behaviour are counteracted (without being actually refuted) by instances where the secrecy involves some other guilt or crime; and yet there is always the possibility that these named transgressions may be metaphors for unnamable sexual activities. Lord Henry remarks that marriage makes a life of deception necessary (p. 10); but what are the secrets which he has to conceal from his wife? His remark that women are sphinxes without secrets (p. 152) implies that men, on the contrary, do have secrets to hide; but of what kind? Basil initially refuses to exhibit the portrait publicly, fearing that he has put too much of himself into it, and that it would consequently reveal too much. But what the picture ultimately reveals is not Basil's love for Dorian, but Dorian's descent into vice, a vice whose precise nature remains undisclosed. Dorian himself cannot be read, for his features retain a purity which is increasingly at odds with his behaviour (p. 99), so contradicting the nineteenth-century idea that secret sins such as masturbation and sex between men produce a deformed physical specimen whose moral degeneracy is legible in the face. When Basil confronts Dorian about his way of life, and the corrupting effect which he has had on others, he recounts Lord Staveley's remark that Dorian was 'a man whom no pure-minded girl should be allowed to know'. Basil had asked Staveley what he meant: 'He told me. He told me right out before everybody. It was horrible!'. But what Staveley said is withheld from the reader, and we are kept guessing as Basil moves on from pure-minded girls to young men:

Why is your friendship so fatal to young men? There was that wretched boy in the Guards who committed suicide. You were his great friend. There was Sir Henry Ashton, who had to leave

England, with a tarnished name. You and he were inseparable. What about Adrian Singleton, and his dreadful end? What about Lord Kent's only son, and his career? (p. 117)

What about them? Fragmentary hints about some of these stories emerge from Dorian's reply: one involves injudicious marriage, and another fraud, but others are associated more vaguely with 'vices' and 'debauchery'. No explanation is offered in the case of the boy in the Guards, leaving the reader free to make his own guess about how a gentleman might be involved in a scandal with a guardsman. The text implies that Dorian's life involves homosexual affairs, but this is never spelt out. He is said to frequent 'dreadful places' near the docks, often spending nights in an 'ill-famed tavern' there under an assumed name, and to have been seen 'brawling with foreign sailors' (pp. 99–100, 109–10). Dorian and Lord Henry share a house in Algiers (p. 110). His former associate Alan Campbell is black-mailed into disposing of Basil's body after Dorian has murdered him, because Dorian writes a few words on a piece of paper and shows them to Campbell; this text, which evidently reminds Campbell of some unspeakable act whose disclosure would ruin him, remains illegible to the reader of the story. We fill in the gaps, becoming skilled interpreters of teasing signs, alluring ambiguities and discreet silences – reading Wilde's text in a way which partially replicates the way he would have read those signs within his own social milieu which seemed to promise something more than aesthetic pleasure and intellectual satisfaction.

On a larger scale, the narrative of *Dorian Gray* is teasingly discontinuous, and in place of an uninterrupted narrative line Wilde bridges the gap between the initial stages of Dorian's corruption and his ultimate degeneracy with a chapter (11) which describes his pursuit of aesthetic pleasures. While Dorian's activities are hidden from the reader, they are recorded emblematically by the portrait, but Dorian himself is displaced from narrative and fashions for himself an artificial present from a bricolage of historical artifacts. Dorian has fallen under the influence of a book to which Lord Henry had introduced him (partly modelled on J.K. Huysmans's *A Rebours*), in which a young Parisian 'spent his life trying to realize in the nineteenth century all the passions and modes of thought that belonged to every century except his own ... loving for their mere artificiality those renunciations that men have unwisely called virtue, as much as those natural rebellions that wise men still call sin'

(p. 97). Passions and convictions are relished as artifacts for the collector, saintliness and sin alike become emptied of their moral character. As Lord Henry had remarked, 'sin is the only real colour-element left in modern life' (p. 28). Roman Catholic ritual has a 'subtle fascination' for him (p. 103), delighting him aesthetically. Dorian's collection of gems, fabrics, music and perfumes has a sensuous appeal, but many of these artifacts once had an additional historical and cultic significance; now their historic origins have been turned into mere anecdotes whose oddity may be savoured, and these regal jewels and ecclesiastical vestments have become the fetishes of a new cult, the cult of surface and texture and sensation. He uses them not to explore an autonomous past but as a 'means of forgetfulness' to escape from his own fear; though another artifact, the portrait locked away in the attic, is steadily recording the inner history from which he recoils. Violence and death are made into objects of pleasurable contemplation, as Dorian reads and rereads the chapters in the corrupting book which recount the fantastic inter-twining of death and desire in the Italian Renaissance (pp. 113–14). In this passage and elsewhere in Chapter 11 there are indications that homosexual pleasures form part of Dorian's collection of sen-sations: there are allusions to Alexander the Great, St Sebastian, Tiberius on Capri, James I and his favourites, Edward II and Gaveston. One cardinal, the 'child and minion of Sixtus IV . . . gilded a boy that he might serve at the feast as Ganymede'; and there was the pope 'into whose torpid veins the blood of three lads was infused' (p. 114). Perhaps Dorian has collected men along with these other treasures.

It is particularly through works of art that Wilde explores the possibly homoerotic relations between the three principal male char-acters. Basil takes possession of Dorian by turning him into a paint-ing, which he regards as all too blatant a disclosure of his feelings about the boy. He views Dorian's beauty as providing for his period that ideal form which was supplied for late antiquity by the figure of Antinous, the boy loved by the Emperor Hadrian (p. 14). At first, Basil had painted Dorian in classical guise in a series of homoerotic icons – as Antinous, as Adonis, as Narcissus. Lord Henry tries unsuccessfully to buy the picture, and instead collects photographs of Dorian (comically said to number twenty-six or seven in the 1890 text, seventeen or eighteen in 1891). The fact that they are photo-graphic images rather than paintings or drawings is itself suggest-ive at a period when Baron Wilhelm von Gloeden's photographs of nude Sicilian boys were delighting collectors. Of course, there is no suggestion that these photographs of Dorian are in themselves improper, but in a text which is so careful of detail, and so skilled in hinting at the illicit while simultaneously offering respectable meanings, this archive of photographs carries a trace of innuendo. When Lord Henry discovers Dorian's tragic family story it forms 'an interesting background' for his contemplation of him: 'It posed the lad' (p. 33). In Lord Henry's eyes Dorian is a work of art, or at least might be made into one: he 'could be fashioned into a marvellous type . . . Grace was his, and the white purity of boyhood, and beauty such as old Greek marbles kept for us' (pp. 33–4). Dorian becomes, morally, Lord Henry's own creation, and he observes him as if he were his work of art (pp. 48–9). Dorian's own encounter with his portrait is both homoerotic and autoerotic. It marks his entrance into the homoerotic sensibilities of the milieu represented by Basil and Lord Henry, for his sight of the completed painting is a revelation to him of his own beauty, and at the same time a disclosure of how his beauty appears to other men. Dorian declares that he is in love with the picture, and later 'in boyish mockery of Narcissus, he had kissed, or feigned to kiss, those painted lips . . . Morning after morning he had sat before the portrait wondering at its beauty, almost enamoured of it' (pp. 27, 83). Dorian sees himself as an erotically charged artifact, and suspects that Basil loves him no more than he loves any other favourite sculpture; Basil, he thinks, will love him only so long as he retains his beauty, and will cease to admire him at the sign of the first wrinkle. When that moment comes, Dorian says, he will kill himself (p. 26). Stirred by Lord Henry's rhapsodic lecture on the exquisiteness and transience of youth, Dorian is absorbing the contemporary cult of adolescent beauty and the accompanying awareness of its impermanence. What Dorian achieves when the portrait ages instead of him, is that very preservation of youth which pederastic poetry had yearned for, and the novel's final scene offers a grotesque parody of two of that poetry's favourite *topoi*: translated into a painting, the desirable youth is for ever young, but for ever unattainable, while the dead body on which our view rests is not that of a naked boy but a richly clothed man, aged beyond recognition by enacting his vicious desires.

The suggestive reticence of *Dorian Gray*, its way of implying homoerotic desires and homosexual activities without being explicit, is partly a result of the process of revision between the manuscript and the text printed in *Lippincott's* in 1890, and again between that magazine version and the text issued as a book in 1891. To sample some of Wilde's changes is to observe him making the relations between the three principal male characters – Basil, Lord Henry, and Dorian – less erotic. In the first chapter Wilde removed details of physical contact between Basil and Lord Henry. In 1890 Lord Henry lays his hand on Basil's shoulder as they discuss the pleasures of secrecy (p. 175), and as Basil tells Lord Henry that he has revealed too much of himself in the portrait he takes hold of the other man's hand; both gestures are removed in 1891. Wilde also reworked Basil's account of his relationship with Dorian. Whereas in the manuscript Basil is stirred by Dorian's 'beauty', in 1890 this becomes his 'personality' (p. 178). Basil's admission in 1890 to Lord Henry that he 'worships' Dorian is removed for the 1891 edition (p. 179). Also deleted is Basil's remark in 1890 that as he was painting the portrait, Dorian leaned across to look at it, and 'his lips just touched my hand. The world becomes young to me when I hold his hand' (p. 180). In 1890 Dorian and Basil 'walk home together from the club arm in arm' (p. 181) but in 1891 they do not. The manuscript implies a sado-masochistic dimension to the relationship of Basil and Dorian; in a phrase omitted from the printed texts Lord Henry rebukes Basil for making 'yourself the slave of your slave' (p. 180), while in a passage cancelled in the manuscript Basil says that he has given away his soul to one

who seems to take a real delight in giving me pain. I seem quite adjusted to it. I can imagine myself doing it. But not to him, not to him. Once or twice we have been away together. Then I have had him all to myself. I am horribly jealous of him, of course. (p. 181)

When Basil learns of Dorian's engagement to Sybil Vane, he turns pale and his eyes fill with tears, but only in the 1890 text (pp. 206, 210). Another deletion removes a possible trace of the homosexual underworld, for in the typescript Wilde wrote and then excised a sentence about Dorian walking through a sleazy area of London: 'A man with curious eyes had suddenly peered into his face and then dogged him with stealthy footsteps, passing and repassing him many times' (p. 215). All these alterations move the story away from its delineations of a sexual content to the emotional and physical contacts between the male characters; and the sense of inhabiting an all-male world is diluted in the 1891 text by the addition of chapters reporting Dorian and Lord Henry in conversation with aristocratic ladies, and describing Sybil Vane and her family (chs 3, 5, 15–18). It is not surprising that counsel at the first trial preferred to quote from the magazine version of the story.

Counsel also put it to Wilde that he had 'written an article to show that Shakespeare's sonnets were suggestive of unnatural vice', to which Wilde replied: 'On the contrary I have written an article to show that they are not. I objected to such a perversion being put upon Shakespeare' (*Trials*, p. 130). The work referred to is *The Portrait of Mr W.H.* (1889), though just what it might be said to 'show' about Shakespeare is debatable. The narrator of this story hears from his friend Erskine that his friend Cyril Graham had become convinced that he had discovered the identity of the 'Mr W.H.' to whom the *Sonnets* are apparently dedicated: he was Willie Hughes, a boy actor. Erskine had been persuaded by Graham's interpretation, but felt that some clinching documentary evidence was needed before the case could be presented to the world. The evidence turned up in the shape of a portrait of Hughes resting his hand on a copy of the *Sonnets*. Unfortunately, Erskine discovered that it was a forgery which Graham had commissioned. To 'prove' that his theory was correct regardless of this attempt to gild the lily, Graham killed himself. His death did not have the desired effect of persuading Erskine that the theory was true; but neither does Erskine's story have the effect he expects on *The Portrait*'s unnamed narrator, who is thoroughly convinced by the theory. After much research the narrator sends his own version of the thesis to Erskine, but immediately loses belief in it; Erskine, however, becomes convinced all over again.

This tale might appropriately have been set as required reading for the juries in the Wilde trials (and for any reader of *Dorian Gray*), as it is an object lesson in how stories are generated out of fragments and silences, and in how people become convinced by their own fictions. A narrative is invented of Hughes's probable career in Germany, and the very absence of his name from the list of players in the First Folio becomes evidence of his importance. The story of Willie Hughes comes to displace Shakespeare's own text, which is cut up and reassembled in support of the interpreter's theory. That all this is a fabrication does not stop it having a powerful hold upon its deviser's imagination, whether Graham's or the narrator's – or, indeed, Wilde's, who became engrossed by his own story and extensively rewrote it after publication.

When it comes to the presentation of relations between men, *The Portrait of Mr W.H.* is an elliptical and disingenuous text. It approaches the question of Hughes's importance to Shakespeare by signalling this as a mystery awaiting solution: who was this young man who 'was addressed by him in terms of such passionate adoration that we can but wonder at the strange worship, and are almost afraid to turn the key that unlocks the mystery of the poet's heart?' (pp. 1155–6). The theory gives the young man a name, but it gives no name to the relationship. The teasing phrases 'strange worship' and 'almost afraid' promise a danger which the text will be bold enough to confront, but it is not. The word 'strange' is almost enough in this context to signal homosexual passion without further explanation, but the text begins to take back what it had seemed to unfold. It emphasizes the importance of Hughes to the creation of Shakespeare's art, the plays as well as the *Sonnets*, rather than to his emotional or sexual life. (This incidentally constitutes an ironic reversal of the role which Lord Alfred Douglas had in distracting Wilde from his writing, according to the letter which Wilde wrote to Douglas in prison, and which was later published as *De Profundis*.) The text also plays a disingenuous game with Neo-Platonism. Having insisted that the *Sonnets* are not addressed by Shakespeare to 'his Ideal Self, or Ideal Manhood, or the Spirit of Beauty, or the Reason, or the Divine Logos, or the Catholic Church' (p. 1155), but to a particular young man, *The Portrait* goes back on this to place the friendship between Shakespeare and Hughes in the context of Renaissance philosophy. The *Sonnets* come to exemplify Neo-Platonism's 'mystic transference of the expressions of the physical world to a sphere that was spiritual, that was removed from gross bodily appetite, and in which the soul was Lord' (p. 1175). This is offered as a refutation of the suspicion that the *Sonnets* contained 'something dangerous, something unlawful even' (p. 1176), but one would actually have to engage in ingenious contortions of interpretation to find Neo-Platonism in the *Sonnets*. Wilde is trying to present Shakespeare and the other writers who are enlisted at this point (Michelangelo, Bacon, Winckelmann) as admirers of 'intellectual beauty', with no homosexual interests. But although this passage (which Wilde added to the original text) is presented without the evident tendentiousness and sleight of hand which characterizes much of the narrator's argument, it is still a fiction. This tale of idealized friendship cannot be squared with the suggestions of strangeness and danger, or with the way Hughes is cast in a palpably homosexual role as the actor whom Marlowe 'lures' away to play Gaveston in *Edward II*.

'It is the spectator, and not life, that art really mirrors', wrote Wilde in one of the aphorisms prefixed to *Dorian Gray* (p. 3). Wilde's contorted reading of the *Sonnets* mirrors his desire to fashion a language and a tradition for homosexual love which transcends the discourse of the police court. But it became yet another of Wilde's performances whose words and silences alike revealed to the spectators a world which they had preferred not to see.

6

The Modern Period

Now he comes back to me in memories, like an angel, with the light in his yellow hair, and I think of him at Cambridge last August when we lived together four weeks in Pembroke College in rooms where the previous occupant's name, Paradise, was written above the door.

Siegfried Sassoon, *Diaries 1915–1918* (1983) p. 45

During the twentieth century the ways in which sexual relations between men were understood changed almost beyond recognition. In the early years, theorists published accounts of what was variously called 'homosexuality' or 'inversion'. The German lawyer Carl Heinrich Ulrichs argued in the later nineteenth century that homosexuals were to be thought of as female spirits in male bodies, an intermediate sex. At the turn of the century, Havelock Ellis in his *Sexual Inversion* demonstrated the widespread historical occurrence of homosexual behaviour, and urged that it should be regarded as an abnormality or sport of nature rather than a disease or a degenerate condition. Edward Carpenter, in his long Whitmanesque poem *Towards Democracy* (1883–1905) developed a socialist vision of a community based upon love between men, and his idealization of working-class men added a new element to literature's repertoire of homosexual motifs; meanwhile his anthology *Ioläus* (1902) assembled literary examples of passionate friendship from ancient times to the present, forming a homoerotic canon. The present chapter focuses first on the writings of two novelists of the early twentieth century, Lawrence and Forster, the latter timidly homosexual, the former passionately devoted to the ideal of male comradeship which included a strong homoerotic element. The discussion then turns to the literature produced in the two world wars, when languages of companionship and of desire were often interwoven.

D.H. LAWRENCE AND 'ANOTHER KIND OF LOVE'

The place of homoerotic desire within Lawrence's life and writing is complex, and a full discussion would require a book to itself, since it is integral to his understanding of masculinity. Throughout his life Lawrence expressed a need for intimate male friends; a woman could only provide part of the emotional and spiritual satisfaction which he sought, and this he characteristically generalized into a universal male need. So any relationship between men and women in Lawrence's fiction is liable to have been imagined within this context, and his evocation of what women wish for and respond to in men is in part coloured by his own homoeroticism – which is not to say that it is therefore necessarily unconvincing as a representation of a woman's heterosexual desire. In a letter from 1913 he reflected that women may not leave enough scope to a man's imagination:

I should like to know why nearly every man that approaches greatness tends to homosexuality, whether he admits it or not: so that he loves the *body* of a man better than the body of a woman – as I believe the Greeks did . . . I believe a man projects his own image on another man, like on a mirror. But from a woman he wants himself re-born, re-constructed. So he can always get satisfaction from a man, but it is the hardest thing in life to get ones soul and body satisfied from a woman, so that one is free from oneself. And one is kept by all tradition and instinct from loving men, or a man – for it means just extinction of all the purposive influences. (*Letters*, ii, 115)

Later he was to define this union between men in Whitmanesque terms: in *Calamus* Lawrence found what he called 'a real solution – the new adjustment . . . the real implicit reliance of one man on another: as sacred a unison as marriage: only it must be deeper, more ultimate than emotion and personality, cool separateness and yet the ultimate reliance' (*Letters*, iii, 478; cp. ii, 153). This male unison which he longed for would have been institutionalized in the ideal community which he planned, called 'Rananim'.

However, Lawrence also expressed revulsion at the physical manifestation of homosexual desire, for instance in a letter to David Garnett in 1915 about meeting some members of the Bloomsbury group:

I simply can't bear it. It is so wrong, it is unbearable. It makes a
form of inward corruption which truly makes me scarce able to
live. Why is there this horrible sense of frowstiness, so repulsive,
as if it came from deep inward dirt – a sort of sewer – deep in
men like K[eynes] . . . suddenly a door opened and K[eynes] was
there, blinking from sleep, standing in his pyjamas. And as he
stood there gradually a knowledge passed into me, which has
been like a little madness to me ever since. And it was carried
along with the most dreadful sense of repulsiveness – something
like carrion – a vulture gives me the same feeling. I begin to feel
mad as I think of it – insane . . . It makes me dream of beetles.
(*Letters*, ii, 320–1)

The intensity here suggests that some self-hatred is fuelling this
diatribe, for the mere sight of John Maynard Keynes in his pyjamas
would hardly seem to warrant such a reaction. The revelation from
which Lawrence recoils was surely a disclosure of something in
himself. Similarly negative and overheated, apparently, was the tract
on homosexuality called *Goats and Compasses* which Lawrence was
writing early in 1916, and which was later destroyed (*Letters*, ii, 558).

The need to see homosexual desire as destructive also surfaces
occasionally in Lawrence's fiction. The male couple Loerke and
Leitner in *Women in Love* (written 1916, published 1921) who 'had
travelled and lived together in the last degree of intimacy, had now
reached the stage of loathing' (p. 422). The short story 'The Prussian
Officer' (1914) also turns homosexual desire into hatred, though the
sexual nature of the captain's obsession with his young orderly is
left implicit. The officer's fascination with his servant focuses on the
latter's physical assurance, the warmth of his body, the confidence
and freedom with which he moves his 'handsome limbs' (p. 5) in
contrast to the officer's own tense suppression of feeling. The captain
is unmarried, has occasional and unsatisfying affairs with women,
or visits prostitutes, whereas the orderly has a sweetheart for whom
he writes poems. To transform the situation from the routine military
relationship of commander and subordinate, to effect a passionate
link between them, the Prussian officer turns not to affection but
to cruelty, forcing the orderly into an emotional bond based on
resentment and hatred. The officer's eyes hold the youth's eyes in a
gaze which extorts an acknowledgement of a rapport between them,
but it is a rapport based on fear, and the gaze which forged the link
had been prompted by the officer's instant anger at an overturned

wine-bottle. That the officer's obsession with the youth is sexual is indicated by his rage at any reminder of the lad's girlfriend, and by his sarcastic use of 'Schöner' ['handsome'] to address him. Through the story Lawrence runs a thread of vocabulary which implies sexual desire while allowing other meanings: the officer is 'penetrated' by the youth's presence; he tells himself that the lad is *'perverse'* (Lawrence's italics); the orderly tries to keep himself emotionally 'intact'; and the word which is repeatedly used to describe the officer's obsession is 'passion' (pp. 4, 6, 5). The soldier's thighs carry the marks of the officer's passion – the bruises he has received from vicious kicks. The wood where the orderly finally kills the officer is presented as an erotic site 'where great trunks of trees, stripped and glistening, lay stretched like naked, brown-skinned bodies' (p. 13), and the killing is itself an intensely physical struggle, with the officer on the ground and the orderly kneeling over him, experiencing the pleasure of having the officer's rough chin in his hands as he bends the head back to break his neck, with 'all the force of his blood exulting' (p. 15). The killing is a displaced version of the erotic paroxysm which the officer had desired, the response of a heterosexual youth whose emotional privacy has been violated. This translation of desire into hatred, and of erotic consummation into death, concludes with the two bodies lying side by side in the mortuary, the officer's body rigid, but the orderly's still showing such traces of youthful vigour that it seems on the point of being roused into life again. Although the cruelty in 'The Prussian Officer' is associated with a particular military cadre in pre-war Germany, the story inescapably represents homosexual desire as a form of madness which resents the young man's physical and emotional self-assurance, and can only make contact with the other man through intrusion, hatred and destruction.

On the other hand, Lawrence's creative engagement with his own homoerotic interests also led him to more positive ways of re-imagining masculinity. The only one of his male relationships which is likely to have been physically consummated was with the farmer William Hocking in 1916, while Lawrence and his wife Frieda were staying in Cornwall. The Lawrence who was always searching in other civilizations – Etruscans, North American Indians, Australians – for some vital principle of life which was missing from England, found an attractive otherness in Hocking: 'There is something manly and independent about him – and something truly *Celtic* and unknown – something non-christian, non-European, but strangely beautiful and fair in spirit, unselfish' (*Letters*, ii, 664). This was also the period in Lawrence's life when he was demanding an intense relationship from John Middleton Murry. Frieda certainly recognized the homosexual element in Lawrence, and after his death she wrote to Murry: 'he wanted so desperately for you to understand him. I think the homosexuality in him was a short phase out of misery – I fought him and won – and that he wanted a deeper thing from you' (*Memoirs and Correspondence*, p. 328; cp. 274).

The sexual element in Lawrence's need for male friendship may have found physical expression only during a short phase in his life, but an intense and partly homoerotic fascination with the male body runs through Lawrence's fictional exploration of male friendship, and can be traced biographically to his adolescence. Compton Mackenzie recalled him saying: 'I believe that the nearest I've ever come to perfect love was with a young coal-miner when I was about sixteen' (*My Life and Times*, p. 168). However garbled this recollection may be (and there is no other evidence of any close friendship with a coal-miner) it does point to the importance of close male relationships in Lawrence's youth. One of these was with the farmer's son Alan Chambers (perhaps the boy meant in Lawrence's remark to Mackenzie), the original of Edgar in *Sons and Lovers* (1913), whose friendship provides relief for Paul Morel at times when his relationship with Edgar's sister Miriam is under stress. As Lawrence worked alongside Chambers in the fields in 1908 he was conscious of the difference between their physiques, and in an observation which seems to combine autoerotic and homoerotic interests he admiringly noted how his own muscles had been developed through the use of dumb-bells, and observed that his skin was 'soft, and dull with a fine pubescent bloom, not shiny like my friend's' (*Letters*, i, 65). This description comes in a letter to Blanche Jennings in which he rebuts her suggestion that he has no male friends: 'I am very fond of my friend, and he of me. Sometimes, often, he is as gentle as a woman towards me . . . I could show you two men who claim me as their heart's best brother'. The second of these two men was George Henry Neville, a year younger than Lawrence but sexually more mature, whose *A Memoir of D.H. Lawrence* includes some important testimony, even though the degree to which it is free from retrospective myth-making is open to debate.

Two episodes stand out. In the first (pp. 77–81), Neville finds Lawrence at the kitchen table copying Maurice Grieffenhagen's painting *An Idyll*. (This shows a girl being embraced by a strong half-naked youth dressed in skins.) Neville comments on how unconvincingly scraggy the youth appears in Lawrence's drawing, teases Lawrence with having studied himself in the mirror as a model, and then in order to show him 'what a man's back is really like' Neville strips naked in front of Lawrence and starts flexing his muscles. Instead of taking Neville as a model and continuing his drawing, Lawrence just sits and stares at him with 'an expression of perfectly rapt adoration' and finally gasps, 'you're positively a pocket Hercules'. When Lawrence does take up his pencil again, it is only as an excuse to continue gazing. As Carl Baron points out in his edition of Neville's *Memoir* (pp. 174–80), this episode has reverberations in Lawrence's fiction. In *The White Peacock* (1911) the gamekeeper recalls how his wife had made drawings of Greek statues for which he had posed as the model in their bedroom; he had been 'her Croton, her Hercules' (p. 150). Here the sketching takes place within the context of the couple's sexual privacy. While 'Hercules' signals an association with Lawrence's scene with Neville, 'Croton' reveals another significant element in Lawrence's memory. Carl Baron has traced a link to the article on the Olympic games in the Lawrence family's encyclopaedia, where an illustration of a nude discus-thrower accompanies the story of a wrestling contest between a youth and a man from the city of Croton, both of them 'in their nude beauty, glistening with golden oil'. Later Lawrence was to write a nude male wrestling scene for *Women in Love* under the classical title 'Gladiatorial'. What this chain of connexions signals is that the primal scene with Neville held erotic connotations for Lawrence which he explored fictionally in different ways, sometimes using it to define male/male relationships, sometimes transposing it into male/female ones. Lawrence's fiction includes scenes in which a woman gazes at a man's naked back as he washes it: this happens in all three versions of *Lady Chatterley's Lover*, while in 'Daughters of the Vicar' the woman washes the man's back herself. In each case the episode is revelatory, and the opportunity of seeing the man's bare back evokes an awareness of him as an individual, and as a possible lover. These incidents are not disguised homoerotic encounters, or at least not simply that: the gaze which Lawrence fixed on Neville helped his writer's imagination to envisage how a woman might be stirred by the sight of the male body. One should also note, however, that this scene in which a man has his back washed derives from the normal routine in mining families which would have been part of Lawrence's own daily experience of his father, and Lawrence's admiration for the physique of an older man may in part be a filial romance, with his complex feelings about his own father shaping the way in which he imagines adult masculinity.

Another significant episode in Neville's memoir recounts the first occasion on which he persuaded Lawrence to go bathing with him in Moorgreen reservoir (pp. 94–7). While swimming across the reservoir Neville contracted cramp, and Lawrence, watching from the shallows, became convinced that he would drown and stood 'frozen with the horror of it'. Neville recalls that when he got back to the shore, 'slowly, oh, so slowly, his eyes came round to mine and with the dawn of recognition his head sank to my breast and his arm went round my neck as I clasped him close to me'. He comforted Lawrence as one comforts a child, holding him and crooning to him as a way of 'assuring the fluttering heart that it is enfolded in the arms of Love'. Later Lawrence drew on this memory for a bathing scene in *The White Peacock*, in the chapter called 'A Poem of Friendship'.

The narrator of the novel is Cyril Beardsall, a figure who in many respects resembles Lawrence himself. While out walking, Cyril sees a nest in which two tiny larks are huddling together, and he himself longs 'for someone to nestle against' (p. 220). In the subsequent episode Cyril goes swimming with George Saxton, who is modelled on Alan Chambers. As they dry themselves afterwards, Cyril is so engrossed in looking at George's 'handsome physique' that he stops rubbing himself with the towel and just gazes:

> He saw that I had forgotten to continue my rubbing, and laughing he took hold of me and began to rub me briskly, as if I were a child, or rather, a woman he loved and did not fear. I left myself quite limply in his hands, and, to get a better grip of me, he put his arm round me and pressed me against him, and the sweetness of the touch of our naked bodies one against the other was superb. It satisfied in some measure the vague, indecipherable yearning of my soul; and it was the same with him. When he had rubbed me all warm, he let me go, and we looked at each other with eyes of still laughter, and our love was perfect for a moment, more perfect than any love I have known since, either for man or woman. (pp. 222–3)

In terms of its biographical origins, this episode seems to fuse Lawrence's feelings for Chambers and for Neville, importing into this story of Cyril/Lawrence and George/Chambers the memory of Neville at the reservoir; but it also fuses the two incidents with Neville, in that Lawrence has drawn upon the posing episode for Cyril's rapt attention to George's physique, and for George's teasing reference to Cyril's slender body being 'like one of Aubrey Beardsley's long, lean ugly fellows'.

The episode is obviously homoerotic, but that term belies the complexity of Lawrence's imagination, which offers the reader a range of modes of perception, not all of them mutually compatible. The example of the larks suggests that Cyril wants a brother – though it is primarily the warmth produced by their physical contact which stirs his longing and his loneliness. The reference to Beardsley suggests a purely aesthetic mutual appreciation – though nothing associated with Beardsley could be said to be altogether pure. George grasps Cyril as if he were a child (like Neville comforting Lawrence at the reservoir), but also as if he were a woman whom he loved. More than the brotherly companionship and the warmth, it is specifically the contact of their two naked bodies which gives Cyril so much pleasure and to some degree satisfies a longing which he calls 'vague' and 'indecipherable' – which appears to be Lawrence's attempt to prevent further definition and deciphering by the reader.

Lawrence is evading definition, but (to put it more positively) he is trying to fashion a language for a form of male love which would combine comradeship with physical pleasure, without using words which would only imprison his characters in contemporary stereotypes. His awareness of the sensitivity of this task is evident in the revisions which he made to this passage in the manuscript. The account of George swimming on his back, naked, originally described how 'his white breasts and his belly emerged like cool buds of a firm fleshed water flower' (p. 386), but Lawrence cut this; in the published text the reader no longer gazes so precisely at the man's body, nor is that body's texture evoked, and we lose the romanticized (perhaps Pre-Raphaelite) suggestiveness of the comparison with water-flowers. Lawrence also toned down Cyril's admiration for George's body, cutting out his admission 'I was delighted with him' and his heady description of the 'round generosity of his limbs, the fulness of his broad, smooth breasts, and the heavy splendour of his trunk' (p. 432). In the published text George simply 'saw I had forgotten to continue my rubbing' (p. 222), but in the manuscript George 'saw me watching him, in my admiration forgetting to continue my rubbing' (p. 432). Cyril looks at George standing 'in white relief against the mass of green' (p. 222), but originally Lawrence had imagined this in more overtly aesthetic terms, with Cyril turning George into a classical work of art, 'standing up like a white cameo' (p. 432). Also cut was a passage which suggested that the mood which followed the rubbing-down was one of special intimacy:

> When I ask him a brief question, my voice is low, and full of rare intonation, so that he answers the words with a quiet "yes"; but the intonation he answers with his eyes, that have the softness of wet flowers. (p. 386)

The excision of this passage removes an important element of tenderness from the masculinity which Lawrence is attempting to imagine, though the idea that a man's eyes might have the softness of wet flowers could well have struck readers as more risible than moving. A more significant loss is the suggestion that the physical contact between Cyril and George had been the prelude to, and the means of achieving, a deeper emotional bond, a state in which words fall away, made redundant by a lover's sensitivity to tone and glance. Perhaps Lawrence recognized that he had crossed the Rubicon here, and decided to retreat.

Despite its title, *Women in Love* is much concerned with how two men might fashion an intimate relationship. On the last page of the novel Rupert Birkin and his wife Ursula reflect on their future after the death of their friend Gerald Crich. Rupert confides: 'Having you, I can live all my life without anybody else, any other sheer intimacy. But to make it complete, really happy, I wanted eternal union with a man too: another kind of love' (p. 481). To Ursula this is 'an obstinacy, a theory, a perversity . . . false, impossible'. But in the last line of the book Rupert replies, 'I don't believe that'. At various points in the novel Lawrence focuses on the rapport between Rupert and Gerald, but the most extended discussion of this occurs in the 'Prologue' which Lawrence wrote in Cornwall in April 1916 but dropped from the final published text. In this 'Prologue' Rupert and Gerald are brought together by one William Hosken (was Lawrence's imagination dwelling on William Hocking?) when the three men go for a climbing holiday in the Tyrol. Lawrence uses religious language for the bond which is forged between them: it is a 'transfiguration', a 'transcendent intimacy' (pp. 489–90) even though – or perhaps because – the spoken, social contact between them is so slight. 'They knew they loved each other, that each would die for the other' (p. 490), but this knowledge is scarcely conscious, let alone articulated: Lawrence is using the special idiom which is so typical of him, particularly in *The Rainbow* and *Women in Love*, for describing what passes in the unconscious of his characters over long periods. When the ordinary social round brings Rupert and Gerald together in England, Rupert feels 'a passion of desire for Gerald' which embraces his 'cruder intelligence', 'limited soul' and 'unlightened body'; Gerald in return feels a tenderness towards the physically weaker man. Again, all this takes place 'in the other world of the subconsciousness' while at the observable, social level the two remain mere acquaintances (p. 493). Much as one may admire Lawrence's effort at imagining the unacknowledged growth of feeling in his characters, it does incur a special difficulty in the case of relations between men, in that neither Rupert nor Gerald is ever made to reflect on the connexion between their feelings and those forms of relationship between men which in that period were stigmatized and punished. Rupert and Gerald seem to accept their intimacy without relating it to the vocabularies and definitions current in contemporary society. In this respect Lawrence makes them inhabit an hermetically sealed linguistic world. The use of the word 'desire' to describe Rupert's feelings about Gerald may seem not to indicate a specifically sexual desire, since it is Gerald's intelligence and soul which attract Rupert, along with his 'unlightened' body: soul responds to soul. But as the 'Prologue' continues, Lawrence writes that while Rupert felt at home with women, 'it was for men that he felt the hot, flushing, roused attraction which a man is supposed to feel for the other sex'; 'the male physique had a fascination for him, and for the female physique he felt only a fondness, a sort of sacred love, as for a sister' (pp. 501–2). It is male beauty which excites Rupert in the street, and chance encounters in railway carriages or on the beach stay with him, haunting his memory (p. 503). When a Cornish type of man comes into a restaurant, Rupert watches fascinated, 'as if the satisfaction of his desire lay in the body of this young, strong man' (p. 505). But Lawrence characterizes these feelings as a source of 'despair . . . deep misery . . . the greatest suffering . . . the bondage and the torment' (p. 505); and these are only spasmodic, recurring desires, not any settled tendency or longing; his periods away from them are times of freedom and strength. They are not a source of self-definition, nor do they lead into relationships.

This sexual tension in Rupert is less prominent in the published novel than one might expect from this cancelled 'Prologue', and Lawrence focuses on the search for some form of blood-brotherhood which might link Rupert and Gerald together in a mutually-sustaining emotional bond without any overt eroticism or sexual expression. This is imaged most directly in the nude wrestling scene in the chapter called 'Gladiatorial'. It takes place in a private space, a locked library in Gerald's comfortable house, and is therefore an encounter which Lawrence imagines happening safely within the homosocial space of the English gentry – though the realism of this assumption is open to question.

The conversation which leads up to the wrestling bout is tense with half-sensed possibilities, and the conversation shifts unsettlingly in its tone (pp. 266–8). Rupert's unexpected arrival relieves Gerald of his loneliness and boredom, but when Gerald says that he has been wanting 'the right somebody' to relieve his solitude, Rupert replies, 'The right woman, I suppose you mean'. He says this 'spitefully'. Gerald wonders about having a round of boxing with Rupert, but when he assures Rupert that this would be purely friendly, Rupert's reply – 'Quite!' – is said 'bitingly'. Gerald keeps looking at Rupert with 'a sort of terror' in his eyes and 'a queer, smiling look'; 'I feel that if I don't watch myself, I shall find myself doing something silly' he says. What would be 'queer' and 'silly' in this context? At this period 'queer' can carry a homosexual significance, but need not, and Lawrence seems to leave the implications fluid. The elliptical exchanges, the fluctuations in tone, and the unexpected intensity with which certain words are spoken reveal undercurrents of feeling, uncertainties which the two men cannot articulate in any other way.

When the two men have stripped naked to begin wrestling, each is aware of the other's body but 'not really visually': Rupert is for Gerald a presence rather than a visible object (p. 269). Lawrence shifts the emphasis away from the gaze of the involved observer, trying instead to fashion a mode of knowledge and emotional connexion which inhabits the body in a new way, and so must inhabit language in an unaccustomed and at times awkward way. The account of their wrestling match has many features which suggest a sexually charged encounter, and which even – with the repetition of 'penetrate' – suggest intercourse:

[Birkin's grip] seemed to penetrate into the very quick of Gerald's being . . .

They seemed to drive their white flesh deeper and deeper against each other, as if they would break into a oneness . . .

[Birkin] seemed to penetrate into Gerald's more solid, more diffuse bulk, to interfuse his body through the body of the other . . . It was as if Birkin's whole physical intelligence interpenetrated into Gerald's body, as if his fine, sublimated energy entered into the flesh of the fuller man . . . into the very depths of Gerald's physical being. (p. 270)

At the end of the bout Rupert kneels over Gerald, slides forward over him, and their hands clasp. Later Rupert tells Gerald that he is beautiful.

In this episode Lawrence is using some vocabulary which would be entirely appropriate in a scene of sexual intercourse. The energy with which the two men wrestle so 'rapturously' must be partly sexual, and one cannot wholly discount a Freudian sense for that word 'sublimated' (its basic meaning is simply 'refined'). At the same time, it would be a misreading to view the passage simply as disguised or displaced sex, for Lawrence is attempting to fashion a new language for a new kind of male relationship which would stand alongside marriage between a man and a woman and have a comparable emotional intensity; it therefore needs a comparable physical expression. Lawrence's problem lies in imagining an uninhibited expression of this which does not stray into what his readers would interpret and classify as homosexual intercourse. Lawrence's characters show no embarrassment about their encounter: for them there seems to be no worrying line of demarcation between the acceptable and the unacceptable. Yet Lawrence says that the wrestling had an unfinished meaning (p. 272). Such indefinition is crucial, inviting the reader to complete the text, while challenging him to make that completed and interpreted text something new and different, a break with the commonplaces and constraints of the period.

E.M. FORSTER AND *MAURICE*

Forster's early stories and novels often fashion opportunities for characters to escape from the cautious lives which they had been leading under the constraints of Edwardian middle-class morality.

In *Where Angels Fear to Tread* (1905), Lilia marries an impoverished Italian while on holiday, scandalizing her family; in *A Room with a View* (1908) Lucy breaks off her engagement with the supercilious aesthete Cecil and marries a man who had once stolen a kiss from her in Florence to the outrage of her chaperone. Though these free spirits are both women, they are part of Forster's hesitant dream of a more liberated life; besides, homosexual undertones can be seen in both books, in the mutual attraction – and then the almost murderous fight – between Lilia's brother Philip and her husband, and in *A Room with a View* when the clergyman Mr Beebe watches George and Freddy romping naked in the woodland pool before joining them. More suggestive is 'The Story of a Panic' (1904), where the boy Eustace breaks out of his English reserve on holiday in Italy, discovering Pan-like freedoms which include an intimate relationship with the young waiter Gennaro. The Italian dies, however: there is always a caution and often a self-punishment in Forster's attempts to imagine anyone acting on his homosexual desires, even in the more overt stories which were published after Forster's death. The rescuer from afar easily turns into the destroyer in the stories 'The Other Boat' and 'The Life to Come', as Forster himself recognized (Furbank, *E.M. Forster*, ii, 303).

But it was in *Maurice* (written in 1913–14, intermittently revised, but only published posthumously in 1971) that Forster made a sustained attempt to imagine homosexual relationships. The novel tells how Maurice Hall and Clive Durham fall in love; how Clive turns away from Maurice – and from men – to marry; and how Maurice finds love again with Clive's young gamekeeper, Alec Scudder. Forster does not resort to a mythologized, liberating Italy, but there are elements in the book which set the story in a special kind of world which is not quite congruent with the England of actual possibilities.

Clive and Maurice meet as undergraduates at Cambridge, itself always a somewhat unreal space. Gradually they grow to recognize that within the language of undergraduate friendship and posturing, unusual feelings are making themselves apparent. When they first meet, their awkwardness shows that they had already registered each other's existence and attractions: Clive flushes, Maurice keeps saying that he must be going when he does not need to, and his voice goes out of control. The idiom of their friendship develops through displays of affection which are at first recognizably within the confines of good form; they walk arm in arm; Maurice sits stroking

Clive's hair; when they rag each other their friends can join in their horseplay. The approach which the two make to a disclosure takes a detour through theological debate which stands as a prologue to, and an anticipatory metaphor for, the revelation of their emotions. Clive causes trouble at home by refusing to attend church at Easter, which is for his mother more of a social than a spiritual scandal. Clive argues Maurice into relinquishing many Christian notions which he had held without quite knowing why, foreshadowing his similar role in bringing Maurice's sexuality into the open. When Clive locks his door to prevent their being disturbed and tells Maurice, 'You wanted to get it and you're going to' (p. 47), Maurice turns cold and then crimson, but all he gets is a theological argument. Soon, however, their world begins to move on to the dangerous edge. Lying 'breast against breast' their cheeks are just meeting when they are interrupted by some boisterous acquaintances (p. 55). Their move out of the socially acceptable forms of intimacy into a private world of exclusive and fobidden desire keeps stalling. The discovery of these feelings has been made possible by the idealism and the freedom of language and behaviour which Cambridge fosters, and yet their private space can exist only precariously even within this environment. There is no secure time and place for speech, nor do the two have their own idiom. When Clive eventually tells Maurice 'I love you', he blurts it out even though there are other people around. And Maurice's reply is an anthology of the clichés of his class: 'Oh, rot! ... you're an Englishman ... Don't talk nonsense ... a rotten notion really' (p. 56). But with whose voice is Maurice speaking?

There is a problem concerning authenticity which runs through the book, as the coherence of Maurice's 'I' is called into question. The agony produced as a result of his brusque rejection of Clive's love 'worked inwards, till it touched the root whence body and soul both spring, the "I" that he had been trained to obscure' (p. 57). This agony forced Maurice to recognize his feelings for Clive. 'No one might want such love, but he could not feel ashamed of it, because it was "he", neither body or soul, nor body and soul, but "he" working through both' (p. 60). Nevertheless, Maurice continues to be divided against himself, and when he composes his autobiographical analysis for the hypnotist whom he hopes will cure him of homosexual feelings, he imagines that someone had been reading it over his shoulder, or that he had not written it personally. He 'seemed a bundle of voices' (p. 154). When he goes to the window of his room in Penge and cries 'Come!', Forster asks 'Whom had he called?', but he might equally have asked, 'Who called?'.

While Maurice does not have a voice and a language of his own, Clive has fashioned a language for himself from his study of the Greeks. It was a reading of the *Phaedrus* that had shown him his 'malady' in a new light, as a passion which could be directed (like any other) to good or bad ends. This gave him the language of self-acceptance, but required a rejection of Christianity. It is via the Greeks that Clive courts Maurice, paving the way by remarking that the Dean ought to lose his fellowship for hypocritically telling his translation class to omit 'a reference to the unspeakable vice of the Greeks' (p. 50). Clive tells Maurice to read the *Symposium* during the vacation, and prefaces his declaration of love by referring to it, expecting that this will enable Maurice to understand him straight away. But we are not told what Maurice made of the *Symposium*; he cannot use it as a text through which to interpret Clive's feelings and shape his own response, and he falls back on a stock reaction. Later, when trying to tell Clive that he loves him, Maurice stumblingly uses Clive's language, saying, 'I have always been like the Greeks and didn't know' (p. 62), but when Clive challenges him to explain, he is at a loss for words. Greece never provides a shared ideal, a shared idiom for the pair. When their relationship becomes one of mutual, declared love, its terms are prescribed by Clive, who has schooled himself through a selective interpretation of the Greeks to believe that such love must entail sexual abstinence: 'the love that Socrates bore Phaedo now lay within his reach, love passionate but temperate' (p. 91) – love without sex. Maurice, however, has no use for Greece, and his interest in things Greek vanishes when he begins to love Clive (p. 99). As the novel progresses, the uses of Greece turn ironic: it is on holiday in Greece – sitting in the theatre of Dionysus, of all places – that Clive turns from homosexual to heterosexual desire (if 'desire' is not too strong a word for what Clive is capable of). The unhelpful doctor whom Maurice consults is called 'Jowitt'. Clive's jocular description of the village cricket match as 'the Olympic Games' grates on the reader when that match has been a stage in the hesitantly developing relationship between Maurice and Alec.

The space which Clive and Maurice inhabit is the Cambridge of undergraduate romance; their love belonged to Cambridge, and when they start careers in London it is as if prison closed around them. Forster says little about the life which Clive and Maurice share in their two years in London; it is a time of unfulfilled sexual desire on Maurice's side, but for Clive apparently the realization of his bloodless Hellenic ideal. Clive's home, Penge, is a decaying estate which Clive and Maurice manage to make into an imitation of Cambridge, but only temporarily. Life cannot for ever be an imitation of Cambridge. Throughout the book Forster mixes elements of romance with elements of realism – that is to say, he imagines time and space both in terms of romance (the narrative as a form of quest, with time and space stylized for symbolic purposes) and in terms of realism (times and places recognizably habitable, where the social arrangements of the everyday world must be negotiated). Throughout the text the social realities of 1912 – Maurice's suburbia, Clive's country estate, work in the City – are shot through with flashes of romance, gestures which speak of a longing to break out of the constraints of the commonplace and into a different kind of narrative in which homosexual desires can be fulfilled. Maurice's two recurrent adolescent dreams transport him into such a world: in the first the gardener's boy comes towards him, naked; in the second he longs for a friend, someone to die for: 'they would make any sacrifice for each other, and count the world nothing' (p. 26). Cambridge seems to enjoy a perpetual early summer, the air heady with the sounds and scents of May, but this is a May which owes more to Elizabethan lyrics than to the actual climate of the fens. When Clive mentions Greek homosexuality to Maurice, the breath of liberty touches him in the middle of a college court which is, inevitably, sunlit. When Maurice commits himself to Clive he does so like a true chivalric hero by climbing in through his window at dawn; and when Maurice in his turn is liberated from the stultifying atmosphere of Penge, it is by Alec scaling the wall and climbing through Maurice's window.

But at times the romance geography of the novel is clearly an impossible construction which only underlines Maurice's frustration. In the midst of his despair after breaking up with Clive, Maurice imagines a space where men could love and live together: 'He was an outlaw in disguise. Perhaps among those who took to the greenwood in old time there had been two men like himself – two. At times he entertained the dream. Two men can defy the world' (p. 120). The dream is repeated when he is talking to the hypnotist, who had suggested that he move to France or Italy where homosexual relations were legal; Maurice replies with a nostalgic vision of a mythical space where outlaws and Athenians mingle: 'It strikes me there may have been more in that Robin Hood business than meets the eye. One knows about the Greeks – Theban Band – and the rest of it' (p. 185; corrected from Gardner, p. 206). To Clive, the world where he had once greeted Maurice as a 'shade from the old Hellenic ships' is now merely 'the land through the looking-glass' (p. 152).

The relationship of Maurice and Alec is partially realized in a recognizable social world, where Alec, as a servant, is initially treated with a mixture of brusqueness and condescension, and where there is no possibility of the two men making that gradual mutual discovery which would nurture and disclose feeling. Alec approaches Maurice by means of the forms available to him as a servant, declining a tip, enquiring whether Maurice would like to bathe and make use of the boat which he has prepared. Strolling one evening in the shrubbery, Maurice collides briefly with Alec in the darkness, and muses on episodes which have involved Alec: 'it was as if an electric current had passed through the chain of insignificant events so that he dropped it and let it smash back into darkness' (p. 164). He makes no conscious use of this half-recognition. Alec belongs to the outdoors, and details place him in a new version of the romance world. His eyes are associated with the flowers which Maurice sees, and Alec himself with the scent of fruit. Their meetings move between realistic and symbolic spaces, and some places take on both colourations, like the boathouse at Penge, owned by Clive but colonized by Alec and prepared as a comfortable setting for making love to Maurice. In spite of Alec's urging, Maurice postpones coming to the boathouse, unable to trust Alec, and afraid to enter the paradise to which Alec (both literally and metaphorically) holds the key. Alec has virtually no history (he is caught in the almost static class system) and we know virtually nothing about how he came to accept his sexuality, how he decided to take the initiative and cross the class barriers between himself and Maurice, or how his homosexual feelings co-exist with an interest in girls. Alec remains not quite imaginable, a need rather than an individual.

The diversion into romance relates also to the way the sexual relationships are realized, for Forster repeatedly recoils from the physical expression of love. In part this is a failure of imagination which may be due to a lack of experience, for when writing *Maurice* Forster had no personal experience of sex, and after sleeping with a man for the first time (in 1917) he reflected that he would have written the second half of *Maurice* rather differently if he had had such knowledge at the time (Furbank, ii, 40). Perhaps; but Forster's coyness is not confined to the descriptions of Maurice and Alec in bed together, it extends to his inability to describe the male body as the object of desire with anything approaching the passionate eye of Lawrence. There is virtually no description of Alec. Furthermore, there is a strong seam of denigration which runs through the novel, defining homosexual desire, and particularly its physical expression, through the vocabulary of disgust. This is not just a matter of the characters struggling against the social hostility which they have internalized: it is part of the vocabulary through which the author himself conceives these experiences. Maurice's awakening into a recognition of the nature of his feelings for Clive is accomplished through pain, and we are told that he has awoken too late for happiness (at the age of twenty); moreover, the exploration of horrible abysses in his nature still awaits him, years in the future (p. 60). The mutual recognition of love between Maurice and Clive is like the action of a poison (p. 62). When Forster reflects on the absence of physical sex between Maurice and Clive, he praises abstinence: Maurice regrets that their one day of privacy and freedom at Cambridge had not been spent in each other's arms, but Forster reproves him: 'He was too young to detect the triviality of contact for contact's sake' (p. 78). (Could Forster not manage to guess that lovers might seek something more in sex than 'contact for contact's sake'?) Lytton Strachey was surely right when he told Forster that Maurice would never have refrained from sex during those years in London with Clive, and that Maurice and Alec would split up after six months (Furbank, ii, 15). When Forster records Clive's view that their relationship was perfect because it avoided the two extremes of 'saint or sensualist' (p. 91) it is hard to hear any authorial irony in the tone. There is a moment when Maurice stands gazing down at a sleeping youth, Dickie Barry, who is a house guest, and for once Forster gives us a description of the male body which invites an erotic response:

> He lay with his limbs uncovered. He lay unashamed, embraced and penetrated by the sun. The lips were parted, the down on the upper was touched with gold, the hair broken into countless glories, the body was a delicate amber. (p. 129)

The word which Forster makes Maurice use to describe his attraction to Dickie is simple: 'Lust' (p. 132). The night which Maurice and Alec share at Penge leads to Maurice being scared that Alec will blackmail him; historically this is a plausible fear, but it is revealing that Forster should make this Maurice's overwhelming response to his first sexual encounter, and that he should extend Maurice's panic into this generalization: 'Physical love means reaction, being panic in essence, and Maurice saw now how natural it was that their primitive abandonment at Penge should have led to peril' (p. 198). This uses 'panic' partly with the sense of Forster's myth of Pan as the god who symbolizes sexual desire which can disrupt a life but may also be the force which forges new connexions. It is, however, always something which intervenes from outside rather than being the development of an acknowledged part of the individual. Forster has not really allowed his language to register the force of desire between men, nor does his narrative explore the ways in which sexual desire is interwoven with other forms of love and companionship to make up the fabric of a relationship. A recoil from his own sexuality is skewing the picture.

Forster's difficulties with conceptualizing the sexual relationship between Maurice and Alec are evident in his revisions to the novel. In the earliest version of *Maurice* there is a brief description of Alec as he climbs through the window of Maurice's room, 'an athlete, beautiful and young, who desired him and whom he desired'. This generalizes Alec's physical attractiveness into a safe formula, with echoes of Greek statuary and heroes of the public school playing fields, while that last phrase has a syntax and cadence reminiscent of Whitman. Then Forster continues:

> All broke. They forgot society and the law and the fruitless knowledge that they were unlike most men. The world became mist, its censure a murmur of leaves. Locked in the glimmering night they established perfection, perfection of a sort, perfection for a time. (Gardner, p. 214)

Curiously, this passage focuses not on the couple so much as on society's disapproval: apart from that first terse sentence indicating their abandonment of all restraint, the men's emotions and their physical pleasure find no place in this text. The final sentence starts positively, but becomes grudging and disparaging: 'perfection of a sort ... for a time'. The early version of the novel made Maurice tell himself in quite grotesque terms that 'he had abused his host's confidence and defiled his house in his absence, he had insulted Mrs. Durham and Anne so foully that were they to know of it they might go insane' (Gardner, p. 215). It was only in his various revisions that Forster gave some substance to the links between Maurice and Alec: he added the brief encounters in the shrubbery to register Maurice's growing awareness of the gamekeeper, the night which they spend in the hotel in London, and – his final revision to the novel in 1959 – the passage at the end of chapter 45 when Maurice returns to the boathouse at Penge and finds Alec waiting for him (Gardner, pp. 214–21).

At the end of the book the various imagined worlds are brought together, not for Maurice and Alec but for Clive. In the garden at Penge, Maurice takes leave of Clive, refusing him any part in his future with Alec. Clive hardly knows when Maurice left him:

> Maurice had disappeared thereabouts, leaving no trace of his presence except a little pile of the petals of the evening primrose, which mourned from the ground like an expiring fire. To the end of his life Clive was not sure of the exact moment of departure, and with the approach of old age he grew uncertain whether the moment had yet occurred. The Blue Room would glimmer, ferns undulate. Out of some eternal Cambridge his friend began beckoning to him, clothed in the sun, and shaking out the scents and sounds of the May Term. (p. 215)

Here Forster fuses the book's various places, and various kinds of place. All the times and spaces come together in Clive's imagination – an imagination which is more poetic here in old age, registering his loss, than it had ever been in youth, when it was the imagination rather than the body which took possession of Maurice. Maurice and Alec have disappeared. In a discarded epilogue Forster showed the two men some years later, as woodcutters in an idyll of love sustained against the world's hostility by their withdrawal into the greenwood. But, as Forster recognized in his terminal note to *Maurice*, this is unimaginable, not least because the idyll would have coincided with the First World War.

WILFRED OWEN AND THE POETRY OF THE FIRST WORLD WAR

The war of 1914–18 threw together men from different social milieux in conditions of unaccustomed intimacy and horrific stress. Mutual dependence, strong loyalty and intense affection forged a comradeship which spoke a language that is not always distinguishable from the language of love. It would be wrong to see an erotic motivation in every expression of devotion and loss, but it would also be wrong to disguise the sexual feelings which inspired the writing of some of the war's major poets: Rupert Brooke, Robert Graves, Ivor Gurney, Wilfred Owen and Siegfried Sassoon all had strong homosexual inclinations. For many years their writings and lives were edited to obscure this: Wilfred Owen's brother Harold destroyed some letters and censored others, while some of Owen's more obviously homoerotic poems were not printed until 1983; Sassoon contributed to the burning of Owen's letters, and his own homosexuality was carefully excluded from his extensive published memoirs; Graves's autobiography *Goodbye to all that* (1929) is similarly disingenuous. Such reticence is understandable, but need not be perpetuated.

War forced men into a world which was almost entirely without women. G.A. Studdert Kennedy in 'Passing the Love of Women' (*Lads*, pp. 147–8) contrasts the love of a woman which draws a man to heaven with 'your comrade Love' which is stronger precisely because it draws a man back into hell, into an incomparably more intense life. Robert Nichols's 'The Secret' (*Lads*, pp. 148–9) evokes the predicament of a man who cannot respond to a woman's tenderness because between them come other memories: to touch a woman's hand recalls the weight of wounded male limbs, and there can be no possibility of a woman's embrace for one who has 'kissed a dead man's face'. In fact, Nichols's speaker actually says that he has no *need* of a woman because he has experienced this extraordinary form of intimacy with men. This is a self-contained world of traumatized memory, compounded of nightmares and gentle epiphanies, which no one else can enter. There is nothing necessarily erotic about the memory which haunts Nichols's speaker, but other poets do bring this note into their verse. When Sydney Oswald in 'The Dead Soldier' (*Lads*, pp. 144–5) reads the dead body of a youth whom he had loved, the sexual nature of his longing is clear from the 'sweet red lips' and the 'goodly harvest of thy laughing mouth' which his gaze contemplates. So too Herbert Read in 'My company' imagines that the dead soldier caught on the wire in no man's land will have his lips eaten by worms:

> It is not thus I would have him kissed,
> But with the warm passionate lips
> Of his comrade here.

> (*Lads*, p. 98)

While the language which most frequently informs the eroticism of this war poetry is derived from the Uranian or decadent poetry of the late nineteenth century, in the case of Geoffrey Faber this way of seeing is rethought. In his sonnet 'Mechanic Repairing a Motor-Cycle' (*Lads*, pp. 129–30) the poet watches the mechanic, standing over him conscious that 'Black dirt and oil and loose blue clothing hide/ What can be hidden'. Then in a moment of further illumination the sun's rays strike the youth's neck and highlight a beauty which is all the more attractive for being unconscious of its own perfection, unlike the proud, golden lads of ancient Greece: 'Here's soil and sweat, and youth shines godlike through'. Faber's homoerotic gaze has been educated to appreciate Grecian beauty, but something else, something distinctively modern draws him; there is a counter-aesthetic at work here rejecting the cult of the beautiful surface and the myth of purity: instead he is stimulated by the dirt which signals the lad's working-class status, and his modernity as a man conversant with machines. One might compare Edward Carpenter's moment of discovery on a railway journey:

> my eyes from their swoon-sleep opening encountered
>   the grimy and oil-besmeared figure of a stoker . . .
> And the firelight fell on him brightly as for
>   a moment his eyes rested on mine.
>
> That was all. But it was enough . . .
> The quiet look, the straight untroubled unseeking eyes,
>   resting upon me – giving me without any
>   ado the thing I needed.
> [Indeed because they sought nothing and
>   made no claim for themselves, therefore
>   it was that they gave me all.]

> (*Towards Democracy*, pp. 140–1)

By contrast Faber's gaze is not returned; he is an isolated observer who does not wish to imagine comradeship or love across class boundaries: the pleasure of the gaze is sufficient.

The aesthetic from which Faber distances himself was still a powerful influence on the work of Wilfred Owen. It is difficult to map any clear line of development in Owen's writing. The canon of his poetry has been carved by successive editors out of a mass of manuscript drafts and fair copies which often give no indication as to which version had the poet's final approval. Many poems were left as fragments. Some of the most interesting evidence as to how Owen struggled with the expression of homosexual desire in verse lies half-buried in the manuscript record of rough drafts, discarded phrasing and unfinished poems, but there is also a homoerotic strain which informs some of his finished and most moving poems, contributing to their passionate perception of wasted potential.

Many poems articulate an unfulfilled longing checked by a fear of venturing into this dangerous territory. An early piece called 'The time was aeon' quotes (and implicitly rejects) St Paul's demand that one crucify the flesh and its desires; the flesh is symbolized by Owen as a flawless naked boy who cannot be described in detail because thought too soon becomes passion: evidently at this date too elaborate a description of this figure would arouse unwelcome feelings. Owen probably drafted the poem at Dunsden in 1912–13 (aged 19–20), while he was a lay assistant to the vicar. This was the period when he was turning against the evangelical Christianity of his upbringing, and at the same time taking what the vicar seems to have regarded as too close an interest in some of the local boys, including Vivian Rampton. A fragment from 1914 (*Complete Poems and Fragments*, pp. 437–8) records a parting after two years' companionship (probably with Rampton), as the poet observes in his friend 'the secret change from boy to man', and in himself 'metamorphoses not less strange'. In these jottings Owen wonders whether it would have been better if he had never seen his face, and if the boy had never 'touched my hand', or 'known my voice', or – in a lovely phrase which speaks of both physical closeness and emotional disclosure – 'heard my heart'. In another fragment from the same year (pp. 439–43) Owen imagines a lonely youth reading on a windy night; sometimes the wind would shriek like 'demented girls' but then 'fell rhy[th]mical and calm/ As 'twere the slumber-breath of vigorous boys/ Warm-sleeping knee to knee and cheek to cheek'. Owen hesitated over 'vigorous', alternatively envisaging the boys as 'strong', 'healthy', 'ruddy' or 'lusty'. Later the wind sounds like a sobbing boy 'hurt by some sorrow of impossible love'. The listener finally hears the wind saying that it must wander on, with nowhere to stay. Though these jottings were never brought into focus as a coherent poem, it is sufficiently clear that the wind is partly an image for desire breaking into the youth's isolation, yet carrying uncertain promises: perhaps offering the satisfaction of lusty boys sleeping together, but perhaps only bringing continued loneliness.

The dream of meeting the ideal male partner appears in several poems where the longing remains unrewarded. In the fragmentary 'Lines to a Beauty seen in Limehouse' (pp. 481–4) the only element in the description which identifies the person addressed as male is the word 'god', but this is enough to imply that the lines which enviously imagine this dockland beauty 'Taking strange pleasures . . . / Where love is easy, and no customs bind' suggest sex between men. Owen dwells on his uncertainty about the meaning of their glances, for he does not know whether the beauty was still observing him as he turned his head: 'was there a watching in your eye's aversion' he wonders. The sonnet 'How do I love thee?' says that the poet cannot woo in the traditional ways used by other men, but instead loves as Shakespeare loved; such courtship will entail only pain without the prospect of satisfaction, loving 'Most gently wild, and desperately for ever'. Other poems bring consummation closer. 'To the Bitter Sweet-heart: A Dream' is addressed to a girl, and says that Eros had promised to give him her hand, but has instead given himself to the poet as his 'passion-friend', so requiting his quest for love more amply than he had ever envisaged. 'Storm' dwells on the thrilling danger of opening himself to another man: 'His face was charged with beauty as a cloud/ With glimmering lightning', while the poet shakes like a tree which is about to draw down 'the brilliant danger'. If the desired man's face does let loose its lightning, then the poet's sap will be consumed and his heart will open. Onlookers may cry out in horror, but the poet will rejoice in the glory of his fall. In these early poems and fragments the recurring theme is unfulfilled longing for a male lover, and a recognition (part in fear, part in hope) that such an encounter would unleash a storm.

In several cases the drafts reveal homoerotic material which Owen removed from the final texts. Its presence in the early versions reveals the original agenda for these poems, and shows how Owen policed his own thoughts. In 'Six o'clock in Princes Street' the poet observes the crowds, and reflects that he would not go 'tiring after beauty' and 'following gleams unsafe' if he dared to 'go side by side with you'. The 'you' addressed here is not identified, and it is not clear whether the daring would involve sharing love or sharing war. A draft reveals that Owen noticed 'plenty of handsome men in kilts & trews' (p. 256), but they do not feature in the finished text. In 'Music' Owen explains that other forms of emotional excitement are feeble compared with love; the final text does not specify the gender of the body which he has touched 'into trembling cries', but the manuscript shows a vacillation between 'his eyes' and 'her eyes' (p. 248). 'Maundy Thursday' ends with the poet kissing not the crucifix but the 'warm live hand' of the acolyte who holds it; in the manuscript the boy's hand is more sensuously described as 'soft' and 'sweet' (p. 265). The poem 'Purple' imagines the rosy skin of Venus, but in the draft it is the boy Eros whose skin is rose or white or 'mauve-marbled' (p. 272). Through the manuscripts runs a vein of homoerotic sensibility, partly shaped by the aesthetics of late Victorian pederasty, which Owen often removed from his completed texts.

There are, however, several poems which more explicitly imagine sexual pleasure with a male lover. The fragments of a poem on Perseus (pp. 464–71) give the female speaker eroticized descriptions of the male body, his skin 'gold-brown' and 'richened with misty mauve', his mouth 'carmine' and the whole body 'dangerously exquisite, from toe to throat'; his touch is 'electrical;/ Acutely pleasurable; as is said/ To be the spasm of death'. Although these drafts are confused, Owen was experimenting here with different viewpoints, hesitating over the gender of a speaker's lover ('I loved her/him perfectly') and imagining the experience of an herm-aphrodite. 'The Wrestlers' describes the contest between Heracles and Antaeus, emphasizing the muscularity of the two male bodies, and the scene is given an overtly homosexual frame by the presence of Heracles' lover Hylas, who realizes that the way for Heracles to defeat Antaeus is to lift him clear of his mother the earth who is sustaining him, and then crush him. Owen wrote these lines at Craiglockhart Hospital in 1917 at the suggestion of his doctor who thought that the myth spoke to Owen's condition, since like Antaeus he had lost contact with the earth which nourished him and was being crushed by a herculean war machine. But Owen interpreted the story differently, showing that Heracles wins by listening to his lover. Moving from classical to quasi-medieval material, the 'Ballad of Lady Yolande' (pp. 472–80) tells the story of a lady in love with her fifteen-year-old page, who is 'white as ivory bone/ Whan [sic] by the stream he strips'; she stood him on a stool, put her arms around his knees, and then the page 'let her lips so soft and cool/To kiss him where she please'. This ballad reminds us that the dominant influence on Owen's poetry was Keats, but in this case it is Keats via Wilde. In another chivalric fantasy the poet speaks in his own voice to his 'Page Eglantine', saying that he has no wish to drink or suck his pipe if the page himself will be his wine that night.

Besides these poems which envisage encounters in legendary frameworks are others with contemporary settings. 'It was a navy boy' recounts a meeting in a railway carriage. Between the lines of the conversation the narrator appraises the sailor-boy's beauty, from his golden hair and his shapely lips to his 'silken muscles'. The draft is more blatant than the final text, and shows the poet studying the boy's 'close-girt loins' and imagining him home in bed (pp. 219–21). The poem captures the doubleness of much homosexual experience in the two simultaneous encounters, the one a polite, shared conversation, the other Owen's parenthetical erotic reading of the sailor who remains unaware of his interest. The verse dialogue 'Who is the god of Canongate?' dramatizes some teasing conversations with rent boys with names like 'the Flower of Covent Garden' and 'Violet Eyes' who work 'up secret stairs men mount unshod'. What it is that the poet seeks up those stairs is unmistakable, as he asks:

> But will you fade, my delicate bud?
> No, there is too much sap in my blood.
>
> Will you not shrink in my shut room?
> No, there I'll break into fullest bloom.

Another homosexual fantasy is 'The Rime of the Youthful Mariner'. The speaker is a sailor who recalls (not without some suggestion of masochistic pleasure) how he has been flogged with a knotted rope, and had his wrist tied with a twisted cord; the men who hurt him on those occasions have been punished, but there is one sailor to whom he wishes no harm:

> One bound my thighs with his muscled arm,
>   Whose weight was good to bear.
> O may he come to no worse harm
>   Than what he wrought me there.

The fragment 'Reunion' (pp. 518–19) was never worked into a finished poem, but it celebrates in buoyant rhythm the ecstatic physical union of two men heedless of the world's hostility:

I saw you, I sought you,
I sought you, I caught you,
And we were two,
Were two against the world's taboo.

We wreathed us. We breathed us
We embraced us, we enlaced us.
And we were one,
Against the anger of the sun.

These poems display a range of erotic interests, from rent boys with flower-names to muscular sailors, and are written in a variety of voices. Though influenced to some degree by the sensually aesthetic dreams of Uranian poetry, his objects of desire are such as could be met in the streets of Edinburgh or London in war time.

The poems in which Owen wrote directly about the suffering of his comrades contemplate their ruined bodies with a pity and outrage which is often informed by a loving tenderness and an awareness of paradises lost. But the ways in which his homoerotic sensibility was brought into the war poems are complex, and from the evidence of the drafts this thread of feeling was one which Owen found difficult to manage, unsure of how it might be allowed to speak in poems intended for publication. In 'Has your soul sipped' the poet distances himself from the sensuous pleasures of peace, finding sweeter than all of them 'that smile/ . . . On a boy's murdered mouth' where 'All his life's sweetness bled/ Into a smile'. The use of 'sweetness' in this poem is curious. The boy's smile might seem to render superficial or trite those sweetnesses which the poem has been recalling – the pleasures of the dawn, the moon, roses, nightingales, all the familiar repertoire of love poetry and the common currency of that civilization which has sent this lad off to die. But though the smile may be sweeter than these, it is not of a wholly different order; the word 'sweet' still applies, and it is moreover 'a strange sweetness', a phrase which would not be out of place in Pater or Wilde. The decadent relish of life as a series of sensations has established the terms through which the smile on the boy's lips is appreciated. The poet's final attention to the 'bitter blood' is unsettling: 'bitter' is not just a transferred epithet (blood which makes me bitter), or a rebuke to crass ideas that sacrifice is sweet ('*Dulce* et decorum est . . .'); it is also a word which registers the taste of the blood. Owen's language may not seek the sadistic pleasure evoked in Symonds's 'Midnight at Baiae', but as a medium for the sensuous appropriation of the boy it is incompletely distanced from this homoerotic aesthetic, particularly in the draft where the lips themselves are called 'sweet' (pp. 232–4).

Owen's uncertainty over how to use his awareness of the soldiers' beauty is apparent in some of the drafts. In sketching 'Dulce et decorum est' he initially tried to emphasize the awful waste of men by contrasting the tormented face of the gassed soldier with his face as it had once been, 'like a bud, / Fresh as a country rose, and pure, and young' (p. 297), an idealization which he eventually rejected. In other jottings (p. 528) he wondered how to be 'true to the more earlier moulds & beauty', to 'traditioned perfectness' and 'the first purities', and contemplated 'the old significance of statues'. The classical ideal of 'eternal youth' in its 'pinioned-sandals' as handed down in works of art could, it seems, neither be set to use nor set aside. The fragment 'As bronze may be much beautified' begins with the argument that as bronze acquires a beautiful patina by being buried in the earth, so bodies in the dust 'fade/ Fairer'. But men's bodies are not bronze statues, nor are they pearls washed brighter by the sea: the desire to imagine the transformation of the dead into a new kind of beauty fails, because Owen has come to the limits of aestheticism. The simile peters out, and the poem cannot be completed.

But however problematic this language was for Owen, it nevertheless enabled some of his most poignant writing when he could find how to allow the idioms of male love into his war poetry. In 'I saw his round mouth's crimson' (surely Owen's finest poem) the tender precision of the gaze on the boy's face registers so poignantly the disappearance of life from the features:

> I saw his round mouth's crimson deepen as it fell,
>   Like a sun, in his last deep hour;
> Watched the magnificent recession of farewell,
>   Clouding, half gleam, half glower,
> And a last splendour burn the heavens of his cheek.
>   And in his eyes
> The cold stars lighting, very old and bleak,
>   In different skies.

The poem's gently devastating power comes from the kind of rapt attention which a lover would give to a face. It summons up those tropes of love poetry which praised the beloved's crimson lips, saw heaven in his face, and thought his eyes like stars. The resources of love, and of love's language, are emptied out as life drains away from the body.

HOMOSEXUALITY AND PACIFISM: *DESPISED AND REJECTED*

In the spring of 1918, while the war was still raging, Rose Laure Allatini published a novel called *Despised and Rejected* under the pseudonym of A.T. Fitzroy. The book was suppressed on publication as it contained a dangerous mixture, a sympathetic account of both homosexuality and pacifism. It illustrates what might be said, but not safely published, in 1918, forming an instructive contrast to *Maurice*, and is of particular interest in that it offers a woman's view of homosexual relations between men, for as well as being written by a woman, the novel sees the central male character increasingly from the point of view of his closest female friend.

The principal character is Dennis Blackwood, a young composer. He is close to his mother, but they do not share confidences, and though she realizes that there is something different about him she cannot identify what it is. She can read her two other sons like open books, but not Dennis: his text is hidden. That he is an artist might be the explanation, but she cannot really satisfy herself that this accounts for her gnawing intuition that he is unhappy, and that there is something which he is not telling her. She never does identify it. Dennis and his father dislike each other, and the son recoils from all that his father represents, from 'the whole coarse overbearing masculinity of the man' (p. 30). Dennis's sexuality is never disclosed to his parents, and instead his struggle to establish his difference from them is articulated through two other passions: the first is his music, the second his pacifism.

At school Dennis had to hide his musical ability, and resented that the other boys did not have to 'wage this perpetual war against part of their own selves' (p. 79). When a Jewish boy, Eric, a gifted violinist, tries to befriend Dennis he backs away, leaving Eric and his music to the mockery of the other boys: 'I dared not let myself get fond of Eric, or I might have been swept away to heaven knows what headlong flights of – "differentness"' (p. 83). But the pull of music could not be resisted, much as Dennis fought against it. The passion for music, unsuccessfully repressed at school, continues to be a sign of his difference in adulthood, and the occasion when he and his friend Crispin refuse to gratify Mrs Blackwood's circle by playing for some amateur theatricals prefigures his refusal to play the game in other respects later on.

Those quotations in which Dennis describes his experiences at school come from the letters which he writes to Antoinette de Courcy. At their first meeting Dennis recognizes that there is something different about her, and cautiously begins to explore what he senses may be common ground. Admitting that he is a square peg in a round hole, he suggests ' "Like yourself . . ." ' and still his eyes held hers, as if seeking some response, some sign by which he might know that she knew the answer to his riddle' (p. 52). (The ellipsis here and in subsequent quotations from this novel is in the original text, whose frequent use of this punctuation reveals the difficulty which both characters and novelist have in putting this subject into words.) Antoinette is sexually attracted to women, and the reader's recognition of her lesbian feelings forms a necessary detour in the novel's approach to defining Dennis, for it is only after we have understood her difference that we are led to identify his. Dennis recognizes Antoinette's sexuality, and creates an opportunity for telling her about himself, but while he is waiting for some sign that the recognition is reciprocated the moment passes, and the disclosure which the novel has been promising is not made. Instead of Dennis making a descriptive confession, finding some label for himself, the revelation to the reader comes about in quite a different way.

On a walking holiday in Cornwall Dennis stops at the mining village of Crannack, and in the evening he sees light coming from the blacksmith's forge:

The door of the smithy stood wide open. Dennis, rather dazzled, sat down upon a ramshackle fence on the opposite side of the road. Two swarthy-faced men stood facing the forge, and a third, a muscular-looking giant was holding by the bridle a great cart-horse, that impatiently pawed the ground and shook back its mane.

A youth was at work at the anvil. He was stripped to the waist, and in the leaping light of the flames, his body seemed white and slender. Dennis reflected that it was a most effective picture: in the midst of the clammy surrounding darkness, this great square of blazing heat and light; crimson glow illuminating the men's dark faces, the glossy coat of the horse, and the boy's black head; and showing every ripple of the muscles under the fine skin, as he raised his arms to hammer the red-hot iron into shape. (pp. 96–7)

Dennis's first response is aesthetic, but the picture which he sees is more like a painting by Joseph Wright of Derby or Ford Maddox Brown than by Tuke. It turns out that this youth, Alan Rutherford, is not the working-class icon we would expect in Forster or Lawrence, but is actually an Oxford graduate whose father has sent him off to learn mining engineering, and who is meanwhile becoming a crusader for the improvement of the workers' conditions. Trying his hand at the smithy is merely a recreation for him. However, Alan drops a red-hot horseshoe on his foot, which gives Dennis the chance to intervene and help him back to his lodgings. As Alan limps along, Dennis looks at the boy. (Alan is regularly called a 'boy' throughout the novel, though Dennis is only 26 and Alan must be in his early twenties: it is evidently essential that as the object of desire he should be thought of as a mere lad.) Dennis admires the 'clean line of the jaw and throat', and sees him as a young knight setting off to combat the evils of the world. As he bandages Alan's foot the boy winces, evoking in Dennis a pang of tenderness and the reflection that Alan's mother must 'love to stroke back the dark hair from his forehead'; he watches 'this finely-strung creature with the tanned face, sensitive level brows, and great black eyes that burned with a smouldering fire' (p. 103).

Both men feel that, against all the odds, they have discovered a kindred spirit, but have they discovered any stronger feelings? When Alan asks Dennis to play the piano for him, Dennis refuses; he senses that the 'play' which Alan seeks may not simply be musical, and he resolves to leave. He is too deeply stirred by Alan to be able to face his feelings, still less put them into words, and spends the night composing music which he leaves with the boy the following morning as the only explanation which he can give for his hasty departure. It is only when he has fled from Alan that the novel gives us the first explicit account of Dennis's sexuality, describing how his flight is motivated by the terror which had possessed him since adolescence, and which had motivated his rebuttal of Eric at school. Despite his resistance to social pressure in other ways, Dennis has internalized society's hatred of his kind, yet he also tries to ward off its terminology:

Abnormal – perverted – against nature – he could hear the epithets that would be hurled against him, and that he would deserve. Yes, but what had nature been about, in giving him the soul of a woman in the body of a man? (p. 107)

As the train carries him away from Alan it carries him away also from

> that which all his life long he had sought, and from which he now must flee, in order that it might not become shameful.
>
> Shameful – strange that such a word might ever be applied to love such as his for Alan; love that had grown up in one night of happiness, and that every instinct bade him welcome with glad lips and eyes and heart. (p. 108)

Returning to his mother, he finds that his first social duty is to attend a fancy-dress ball, but in his distraction he turns up in ordinary clothes; he is the only one not in disguise, but at the same time the only one whose life is to be a perpetual masquerade.

With the coming of war Dennis takes a decision which places him outside the rest of society. His refusal to volunteer, and his subsequent refusal to be conscripted, is a principled course of action in its own right, but it also functions in the novel as an analogy for sexual difference. Dennis's pacifism is consonant with his earlier opposition to conformity for its own sake, and his revulsion from England's philistine chauvinism dressed up as chivalry. One of the reasons why Dennis will not fight is that he cannot bear the thought of killing boys like Alan. He is convinced that Alan will join up and be recklessly brave, and becomes haunted by a vision of him lying dead on the battlefield.

Dennis roams the streets of London looking for Alan, but also registering every chance resemblance in the faces which he scans; he is drawn into a nightmare as the city dissolves into a futurist painting accompanied by the dissonant music which is now the only sort which he can compose:

> Deeper and deeper into the crazy depths of the nightmare – nightmare set to his own horrible music, and filled with strange faces, figures, voices; and, almost like a futurist picture, with bits of streets, buildings, bridges, where he had caught a glimpse of this one and that. . . . There was danger in his present mood, as there had been danger that night at Crannack. (p. 160)

The painting is no longer one which places the viewer in a secure position, allowing him a steady and satisfying gaze at the desired object; instead Dennis is trapped within a futurist painting of multiple perspectives, fragmentary forms, and distorted faces.

For help Dennis turns to Antoinette, and as their friendship develops his nightmare fades, but only at the cost of him denying his true desires. In an ironic image the bathing pool and the shared homoerotic delight which it had often represented has become a snare:

> he had been sinking, as a person sinks into a dark, weed-clogged pool. The weeds still clung about him: there were several things from which he must avert his mental gaze – or, better still, he must pretend that they were not there. The picture of a boy's lean body, lit by the glow of a forge, was one of them. (p. 169)

Dennis asks Antoinette to marry him, but he is seeking marriage only as a reassuring sign of normality, and as a bulwark against other feelings. Eventually he ends the pretence, and breaks off their engagement. Returning to his previous restlessness he lives on the dangerous edge, seeking Alan, encountering other men but always veering away: 'courting danger and the thrill of danger from a flung glance or smile or whispered word . . . and with burning cheeks and beating heart, fleeing danger . . . and courting it again' (p. 185). He dreads receiving the understanding and the contact which London offers, because that would present him with a freedom which he dare not accept: he is held back from acting on his sexual desires by a desire to be like other men, together with some kind of fear or fastidiousness which the novel calls 'the aesthete in him' which insists on a perpetual struggle against his instincts. Though the book does not put it in quite these terms, the aesthete is the enemy of the artist, and so long as Dennis recoils from what he can only see as a world of dissonance he will have no music in him.

A less threatening form of understanding is offered by the pacifists, and although Allatini can only hint at a homosexual milieu in her references to the faces in the streets, she describes in detail the pacifist subculture of rebels and outcasts who find common cause and share congenial meeting places. It is in the pacifist tea-room that Dennis once again meets Alan. Alan has become a highly articulate opponent of the war: this is where his courage and crusading spirit have led him, not to a quasi-chivalric death on the battlefield. In the first clear indication of his sexual orientation and his feelings for Dennis, Alan speaks not in an intimate, self-disclosing language but in the fervent words of an evangelist about their shared nature: Dennis must be true to himself, not 'pervert' himself into something which he can never be. In a plea which half-reveals, half-disguises an invitation to physical expression, Alan urges Dennis not to 'make our love an abstraction. Believe me, you'll only succeed in making it unnatural' (p. 250). When Dennis exclaims that it is surely unnatural already, Alan responds:

> Why will you persist in regarding it as something vicious and degenerate? For people made as we are it's natural and it's beautiful to love as we love, and it's perversion in the true sense to try and force ourselves to love differently. (p. 250)

It is in the company of Antoinette that Dennis meets Alan, for she has joined the pacifist cause too; she has also belatedly fallen in love with Dennis. She has to sit watching the two of them together, and her gaze rests on Alan as she tries to account for his hold over Dennis:

> It was not difficult to see wherein Alan's attraction lay: he *was* attractive, no doubt of it, with his feverish dark eyes and sensitive well-cut mouth. He gave her the impression of a very high-spirited race-horse. She could quite well imagine how he would appeal to Dennis. . . . this terrible boy against whom she was utterly powerless, for he seemed to possess all the fascination of her own sex as well as of his. (pp. 266–7)

The novel increasingly focuses on Antoinette's plight, and it is through her struggle to understand desire between men that the novel leads its readers along the same path. Whereas Dennis's mother wants to understand him but is too conventional to manage it, Antoinette can; but this understanding has its cost, for when Dennis explained to her about his nature, he had also shown her that her own feelings about women were more unusual than she had realized: the revelation of his sexuality has entailed the revelation of her own.

When Alan's appeal for exemption from military service is refused, he knows that he will be arrested and sent to prison. His last evening of freedom is spent with Dennis. Beforehand Antoinette finds herself imagining what will happen between the two men, 'Alan's provocations. . . . Dennis's battles against desire that might prove stronger than himself'. Whereas only a few days earlier she had found all this so hard to comprehend, it now seems easy to move 'in these forbidden regions' because 'the taint was in herself too' (pp. 274–5). When the evening comes, Alan tells Dennis that in a past life, in ancient Greece or Rome, they had been comrades in battle and comrades in love. Overcome by a sense of Alan's youth and vulnerability in the face of their uncertain future, Dennis 'tried to master the choking sob that rose in his throat. But at that note in Alan's voice all his laboriously built-up self-control and restraint gave way. . . .' (p. 289). As the text dissolves into dots it is clear that Dennis gives way to more than tears: this is the first, and last, occasion on which he allows his sexual feelings for Alan to find physical expression. Later, as they part on the doorstep, Alan murmurs, 'I'm glad it's been like this – the last time' (p. 290).

This consummation comes as a revelation to Dennis, who, separated from Alan but seeing now with his eyes, regards his previous war with himself as futile:

> his life was one stupendous aching regret that what had happened that last night had not happened sooner. The senselessness of all his repression and self-denial stood revealed to him. (p. 304)

Having liberated himself, through sex with Alan, from that 'imagined aestheticism' (p. 304) which had warred against his instincts, he pours himself into his music, which loses its dissonance and becomes the medium for expressing his love.

The novel refuses to engage in a Forsterian fantasy of escape to a gay greenwood; its focus is resolutely on what is realistic in a blinkered society mired in war. Alan is brutally treated in prison, his body tortured in a straitjacket and his mind cramped by solitary confinement; soon Dennis too is arrested and imprisoned. *Despised and Rejected* does not imagine a future for the two together, but the note on which it does end is a moving vision of a society which values such men; indeed, a society in which progress depends on them. Barnaby, the crippled journalist, is speaking to Antoinette:

> Perhaps these men who stand mid-way between the extremes of the two sexes are the advance-guard of a more enlightened civilisation. They're despised and rejected of their fellow-men today.

What they suffer in a world not yet ready to admit their right to existence, their right to love, no normal person can realise; but I believe that the time is not so far distant when we shall recognise in the best of our intermediate types the leaders and masters of the race. (p. 348)

That phrase 'intermediate types' suggests that Allatini has been pondering Carpenter's philosophy. Barnaby sees such types as the 'bad specimens' produced by a workshop as part of the process of developing a new product, for Nature is working towards something new:

> the human soul complete in itself, perfectly balanced, not limited by the psychological bounds of one sex, but combining the power and the intellect of the one with the subtlety and intuition of the other; a dual nature, possessing the extended range, the attributes of both sides, and therefore loving and beloved of both alike. (p. 349)

Beside Allatini's capacity to imagine personal and social possibilities, Forster's seems rather limited.

The novel's inability to envisage that Alan and Dennis might live together and share their love is probably an act of realism rather than a failure of imagination or sympathy, but there are some important aspects of their sexuality which are left unconsidered, particularly Alan's feelings and his sense of himself. We are shown in detail Dennis's struggle against his desires, and then against the self-hatred which he has internalized; but what was Alan's story? Nothing is said about how he grew up, and how he came to be so confident in his sexuality, so untroubled in taking the initiative towards physical consummation. His self-possession and energy, which are part of his attractiveness, are expressed through his commitment to the pacifist cause, but the psychology underlying this is left unexplored. The narrator never analyses Alan's feelings about Dennis, either during their first meeting at Crannack or during their time in London. We do not see the world through his eyes, or understand it through his heart; he remains the object of desire, always slightly remote, always slightly idealized. But to rephrase these observations more positively, Allatini has taken a great imaginative leap in making the desirable youth something more than a pretty boy at play, in giving him an adult's intelligence and social awareness, and in refusing to burden him with a tortured history.

Indeed, *Despised and Rejected* is remarkably free from most of the stereotypes which had emerged in the previous fifty years, and when some of these are deployed they are usually rethought. Dennis is made a sensitive, artistic type, close to his mother and distanced from his father, but his determination not to conform makes him far from effete, and his artistry becomes a strong resource for personal expression and cultural dissent. In his rage against himself Dennis thinks that he has a woman's soul in a man's body, but that idea is also rethought later into a source of strength and attraction when Barnaby says that Dennis has both a woman's passion and a man's in his love for Alan, a combination of tenderness and virility (p. 347); Alan seems to Antoinette to combine the attractions of both sexes; and the future of the race is finally envisaged as resting on some kind of bisexuality. The familiar motif of inequality in years is reworked, since the two men are close in age; and although Alan is the younger, and the one whose physical attractions are spelt out, he is given an adult energy and competence rather than a boyish innocence and vulnerability. What does make Alan vulnerable is not his sexual purity but his social idealism. Chivalry, a notion which had been appropriated by Uranian poets such as Revd Dr E.E. Bradford in his collection *The New Chivalry* (1918), is also brought into the text and transformed, as Alan and Dennis discover the true cost and the practical consequences of that form of chivalry which their ideals demand. Comradeship is translated into a pacifist comradeship. Alan's social origins set him apart from the Forsterian ideal, for he is not a working class hero, even though the scene in which he is first presented to Dennis and the reader momentarily suggested this. The novel also avoids invoking the resources of pastoral, for although Alan and Dennis meet in Cornwall it is in a mining village where life is dour: this is no idyll. The book soon switches to London, to the companionships of urban life but also to the city as a nightmare in which Dennis is offered dangerous freedoms. After Alan has been sent to gaol, Dennis feels that nothing holds him any longer, and half-wishes to escape to somewhere like Ireland, 'to live in truth the life of the outlaw and outcast that he was' (p. 304). But this would not be an escape into pastoral freedom and fulfilment, quite the opposite: it would be a symbolic realization of his marginality.

The kinds of looking which the book offers also refreshingly re-work the previous literature of the homoerotic gaze. Dennis may first see Alan as part of a picture, but he quickly breaks through the frame and enters a narrative. Increasingly the excluded onlooker is Antoinette, and her puzzled and longing gaze often becomes the gaze of the reader. The line of sight which the novel offers therefore places us in an unusual position: apart from the scene in the smithy (and then only briefly) the book hardly ever offers homoerotic pleasure, and instead readers are placed close to Antoinette's viewpoint – that of a woman who is sexually attracted to other women, who loves a man who values her as a cherished companion but is himself in love with another man whose attractions she understands. Thus the reader is led to experience the possibility of new kinds of relationship within and between the sexes, even though these are viewed tragically and cannot be brought to fruition in a society which is at war with itself as well as with Germany.

This attempt at imagining new forms of relationship is part of Allatini's presentation of an alternative culture. It is not a fringe group, nor one which relies upon a specialized homoerotic code or canon (the only unusual book mentioned is *Towards Democracy*, which has a political as well as a sexual significance); rather, it is a community which occupies the moral and cultural high ground. The pacifists are a collection of writers and musicians, they have cosmopolitan sympathies, and their opponents' culture is exemplified by Crispin's uncle and aunt who eject his grand piano from their house because it is German. In contrast to the Little Englanders' cry of 'rope 'em all in' (p. 189), which applies equally to amateur theatricals and to war, this group has forged a new kind of community and fellow-feeling.

THE SECOND WORLD WAR:
LOOK DOWN IN MERCY AND *THE CHARIOTEER*

Walter Baxter's *Look Down in Mercy* (1951) and Mary Renault's *The Charioteer* (1953) explore the emergence of a homosexual relationship within the context of the comradely feelings which war generates. In both cases the protagonists face problems in conceptualizing themselves, their feelings and their actions as they cross the boundaries between comradeship and sexual desire, and venture on the twin processes of trying to understand themselves and trying to interpret the signs of another man's interest. War has loosened some social constraints, throwing up new kinds of time and space where desire may find expression, but class distinctions still have an important influence over what turns out to be imaginable.

Look Down in Mercy is set in Burma and India. The book begins with two soldiers taking a shower, and straight away the reader is invited to read the nude male body. It is not an erotic reading but an interpretation of two bodies as signifying different kinds of masculinity. The men share a comradely space, and both carry the traces of military service in India which has left its mark in the form of a tan, but their bodies are made to signal a difference in the two men's sensibility: Anson's skin is 'fresh', his mouth 'generous', and his features have an expression of youthful charm and sincerity; Goodwin, however, lacks the attributes of youth, has a coarse skin, a lined face and an expressionless mouth. A moral reading is rapidly established. The two are close comrades, though perhaps not exactly friends; they are, in army slang, 'muckers', and as their commanding officer, Captain Kent, uses the term he wonders exactly what it covers. The relationship between Anson and Goodwin is tense: when Goodwin gets drunk he resents the physical contact of Anson's arm which is steadying him, and roughly implies that there is an unwelcome sexual invitation in that gesture: 'stop mauling me about for Christ's sake, I don't like it, I want a woman' (p. 20). Goodwin's own sexuality is complex, for when he visits a brothel he only derives satisfaction from the girl he is with when Anson is standing near the cubicle waiting for him, and he realizes that what he really wants is for Anson to come inside and watch. When Goodwin murders a sleeping watchman outside the local temple, the attack is described in terms which mark this as being in part a sexual act:

His whole body suddenly seemed to come alive . . . He reached the body and straddled it gracefully . . . He smiled gently at the terrible paroxysms of the body as it writhed in the blanket . . . The thin writhing body between his open legs, the sense of power, moonlight, a golden face, if only Anson was watching; he felt a slowly swelling pressure of desire that took its tempo from the twisting body against which he now pressed his own, exquisite pleasure that made him whimper; in that split second between the unbearable pleasure breaking and the flood of relief he dug inwards and upwards with his thumbs and felt the neck snap. (p. 25)

Though the victim later turns out to be a woman, at this particular moment both Goodwin and the reader think that it is a man, and so the episode has an inescapable element of homosexual sadism.

Anson distances himself from Goodwin and is relieved to be made Captain Kent's batman. The relationship of master and servant, officer and private, gradually becomes something more. Through a series of glances Baxter registers the exceptional feeling which the two men develop for each other, but these are not the glances of a privileged observer safely contemplating the object of his pleasure, they are recognitions extorted by shared danger. Lying in the dust under machine-gun fire, Kent sees his immediate surroundings with an unusual intensity: 'He looked at the ground and could see each individual grain of dust, they were of exquisite beauty, glittering and many-coloured. The soft hair on Anson's cheek was powdered with it and there was a broad smear of dust, wet and black with sweat, that divided his lips from the gold of his skin' (pp. 82–3). Kent's heightened perception is directed first at the beauty of the dust, then at the dust on Anson's cheek, then at Anson's skin; his eye registers the beauty of Anson's face in close detail (not as a whole, as an ideal form) and takes in its texture as well as its colour, gold but also soft, and sensuously black with sweat. It is not only their deadly predicament which has made Kent see Anson with this intensity, it is the physical contact which occurred when Anson threw his arm over Kent's shoulder to press him down underneath the bullets. A little later, when Kent prepares to rescue the injured Goodwin under fire, Anson offers to go instead, which prompts a moment when the eyes meet, and Kent makes a gesture which goes beyond an officer's normal care for his men:

He turned his head and looked at Anson, his eyes soft with gratitude. They looked at each other for what seemed a long time; the dust still glittered on Anson's cheek, the sweaty streak of dirt, a dried spot of blood on his chin, the pulse in his throat, all were beautiful and suddenly, without knowing why, Kent was calm and happy. He smiled and put up his hand and rubbed the smeared dirt on Anson's face with his finger. He could feel the roughness of the beard on his finger-tip.

"No," he whispered, shaking his head, "not you." The words were spoken without thinking, and immediately he was embarrassed. He went on quickly: "I want a batman, not a corpse."
(pp. 84–5)

In this second incident Kent has crossed a boundary, touching Anson and becoming embarrassed at his wish to protect him, suddenly having to invent a covering story. But the recognition is mutual: each has tried to prevent the other from risking his life, momentarily suspending the relationship of officer and subordinate, and a special intimacy has been established. As yet, however, the recognition is not explicit, and the intimacy is without a language of its own.

A shared space of physical privacy is gradually fashioned within the chaos of battle. In a rest period the two men lie down with Kent's head across Anson's chest, and Kent feels the wet shirt against the back of his neck. That night Kent and Anson sleep side by side, and Anson moves close to Kent to keep him warm. The following evening Anson makes a shelter for them, screened within a thicket, and here the physical contact through which the two men have helped each other to survive becomes something else:

> Moved by a compulsion that he did not understand, without considering the consequences, believing that what he was about to do was utterly disgraceful and criminal, he put his arms round Anson and pulled him closer. They lay still for a moment and then Kent lifted his shoulder from the ground and Anson put his arms round him. Kent was dimly aware that although his body might demand more, he himself did not: it was sufficient that they should rest in each other's arms. (p. 159)

The passage is framed by the explosion of mortars and the screams of a wounded man: the embrace is a protection against the horrors around them, and is altogether without words. This moment, which Baxter has so sensitively led up to in his evocation of the two men's increasing awareness of each other, seems to go no further than an embrace, but the American edition of the novel tells a different story:

> . . . he put his arms round Anson and pulled him closer. They lay still for a moment and then their mouths met. Kent lifted his shoulder from the ground and Anson put his arms round him. They lay pressed closely together and Kent was dimly aware . . . [etc] (p. 169)

The passage is prolonged in the American edition with an account of how the men's movements express both a tenderness and a care for each other's physical comfort:

They lay together for a long time and then Kent carefully moved his hand from beneath the blanket and brushed Anson's hair back from his forehead.

"Let's try and get some sleep," he whispered again, and felt Anson nod his head slightly. Very carefully, as though he was afraid someone might hear, he moved his body until he was almost lying on his back and Anson came closer until he could lay his head on the soft pad of muscles below Kent's shoulder. Kent put his arm back beneath the blanket, their hands met and their fingers interlocked. (p. 170)

The omission of these passages from the English edition may have been because the detail of the men kissing and linking hands was thought too provocative; in any case, it is notable that it should be this carefully delineated expression of homosexual feeling within a homosocial context which should be thought likely to offend: it blurs the very distinction which the British army still patrols.

How do the two men understand what has happened? Anson reflects that in other circumstances it would be surprising to discover that Kent was 'like that', but not here – implicitly, not here on the very edge of the world, on the edge of life itself. The narrative of their embrace focuses more on Kent's actions and on his confused half-awareness of what he is doing, but before he is given any chance to reflect on what has happened he is put through the trauma of being captured by the Japanese. Kent and Anson are tied up side by side, and to encourage Kent to answer questions about the disposition of the British forces they are made to watch as three of their comrades are strung up, stripped naked, and disembowelled. While these bodies are being subjected to such unspeakable mutilation, the bodies of Kent and Anson are acutely aware of each other, Anson's fingers touching and gently stroking Kent's hand in reassurance. As so often in this book, simple gestures which go just beyond comradeship speak instead of words. At the point in the narrative where one expected some explicit acknowledgement of Kent's feelings for Anson, there is a different revelation, the disclosure of Kent's weakness as he panics, allows his men to die, and desperately begs Anson not to leave him. It is this disclosure which brings the two men into a further stage of intimacy which is grounded on their new knowledge of Kent's cowardice and somewhat displaces the awareness of their recent sexual bond. When they escape, Anson gently takes care of Kent's wounded and humiliated body in locations which in other circumstances would have been redolent of erotic pleasure: they are alone together by a cool stream, with birdsong, sunlight, and a screen of leaves to give them privacy. When Anson takes off Kent's shirt and shorts it is simply in order to wash them. Yet the need for Anson to clean Kent's wounds and wipe his face brings a physical closeness which signals an emotional closeness. This practical intimacy between captain and batman would have been possible just as a result of the exigencies of war, but it is additionally a silent recollection of their earlier erotic intimacy which cannot be put into words. Even his cowardice is easier for Kent to talk about than their feelings for each other. Had he become a 'contemptible pervert'? Kent tells himself that the incident with Anson was due to his long absence from his wife, and that the attraction would disappear once he could sleep with women again. Nothing like it had happened before, and he cannot place himself in the same category as perverts, furtive old men peeping over the tops of urinals. Kent is unable to accept himself, unable to understand what that 'self' is, and unable to put his feelings into speech. Anson, by contrast, seems adept at the tender physical gesture, resigned to waiting silently for Kent to act, and able to accept whatever happens. In part this is a difference which runs along class lines, for the novel highlights the officer's experience, attending to his confused self-awareness while assuming that the batman has no such complexity. Like Scudder, Anson has no history, and no troubled subjectivity. He is principally imagined as the answer to the gentleman's needs, strong, tender and patient, ready whenever he is called, and prepared to leave when his superior says so.

Though their intimacy has been fashioned by the pressures of war, Baxter provides a quasi-domestic space for Kent and Anson to share at the bungalow where Kent is recuperating. Kent is uncertain about asking Anson to stay the night, and the two men partly preserve the distinctions of rank: 'Do you want me to go, sir?' says Anson, taking the initiative but maintaining deference. Kent is nervous and sweating, and he breaks a glass. Then he holds his hand out to Anson and they go silently into his bedroom. They have no words for their relationship, no names for each other, no shared idiom beyond Anson's subtle modifications of deferential army speech, and it seems as if neither quite knows what it is that has happened between them: 'they crossed the room like dreamers' (p. 217). Then, in the English edition:

They reached the doorway and he saw the light switch, and then the room was in darkness and they moved together.

In the darkness of the bedroom they stripped off their clothes swiftly, laying them on the floor at their feet, noiselessly taking off their boots as though the faintly showing mosquito net held a sleeper who must not awake. Lying down side by side on the bed they encircled each other with their arms, until Kent was aware that he was cold and pulled up a sheet and one thin blanket. (p. 217)

In the American edition there is an extra phrase at the end of that first sentence: 'and their mouths met' (p. 233). The American edition continues to provide more details:

Lying down side by side on the bed they bound themselves together with their arms. A gentle, almost unintentional movement began, and their muscles crushed their bodies together.

At last Kent was aware that he was cold . . . [etc.] (p. 233)

English readers are shielded from the indications of passion in 'bound' and 'crushed', but are also deprived of the tenderness signalled by 'gentle', and the implication in 'almost unintentional' that this is still something which they are not quite understanding, something still kept from full consciousness. These are details, but in such a sensitive and complex area details reveal much about how such relationships can be imagined. Kent tells himself that 'he had committed the unforgivable sin' but at the same time feels that Anson is a protection against the darkness, and against 'the remorse that would come with the day' (p. 218). He feels tenderly towards him, but is still glad that Anson calls him 'sir' when leaving. In the morning Kent turns to Anson and asks:

"Are you sorry?" He spoke sadly, not looking at him.

"No of course not, I'm not sorry at all, why should I be? If I was going to be sorry I wouldn't have let it happen." He was quite ready to discuss the matter but not from the point of view of regrets, and he did not want Kent to begin feeling remorse. (p. 219)

Then in the American edition 'he gently rubbed his unshaven face against Kent's' (p. 235), and when dressed he 'smiled and touched Kent's fingers through the net' (p. 235). The American edition gives

Anson a gentleness and sensitivity in the use of such simple physical gestures through which he can reach out to Kent while not trespassing into speech. The loss of these passages in the English edition does not simply tone down the description of the love-making, it removes the physical signs through which the two men, led by Anson, establish a contact which escapes words.

Baxter has shown how the comradeship of war becomes transmuted, hesitantly, into something else when time and place permit. But how can such a relationship be continued? What form of closure could the narrative bring about? The end of the novel differs drastically in the two editions. Kent is staying alone in a hotel in Delhi, recuperating from his punishing escape from Burma. He sees no way forward, and drifts towards suicide. He drinks a bottle of brandy, and kneels on the window ledge, ready to throw himself out. About to topple over, he vomits, tries to scramble back into his room, but overbalances. 'As his body began to plunge towards the drive he held his arms in a grotesque attitude as though to break his fall and cried out; but not for mercy' (p. 288). There the English edition ends, with Kent falling to a death which at the last minute he has tried to avert: divided against himself to the last, his self-hatred overcomes any other feelings.

But the American edition ends quite differently. Kent falls back into the room, and gradually becomes stronger and happier. Typically he cannot formulate a coherent understanding of himself, but some things have become clearer. 'He felt that he had vomited up all the causes of his sadness as he knelt on the window sill. He knew that he had solved nothing and he persuaded himself that there was nothing to solve, all he had to do now was to go on living and be with Anson' (p. 308). There is *naïveté* in Kent's conclusion, but it is at least the *naïveté* of hope and trust rather than despair. One cannot quite imagine a sequel to this novel, or envisage the circumstances in which that simple idea 'be with Anson' might be realized, for the conditions in which Anson and Kent have come together have been specifically produced by the Burmese war, and the two have been too reticent in their overt expressions of feeling for the full individuality of each man to become apparent. But the American edition of the novel at least turns away from self-hatred towards some kind of future.

Like *Despised and Rejected*, *The Charioteer* is another remarkable novel of love between men in wartime written by a woman, and once again without that nervousness about crossing boundaries which seems to attend male writers' approaches to the subject. The novel is set in England just after the evacuation from Dunkirk, in which Laurie Odell (known as 'Spud') has been wounded. Its title refers to the *Phaedrus*, a talismanic text for Laurie who had acquired his copy at school in an episode which resonates through the novel. The head prefect, Ralph Lanyon, is about to make a hasty departure from the school following the discovery of his affair with a younger boy. Laurie cannot believe that the accusation is true, and intends to lead a campaign on Ralph's behalf until Ralph calls him into his study to stop him. The interview moves into territory which Laurie finds difficult to interpret: 'he felt like someone who tries to read a book when the pages are being turned a little too quickly' (p. 33). He is made aware that the allegations against Ralph are true, but he still regards Ralph with hero-worship. Indeed, that feeling modulates into something else as he glimpses Ralph not simply as the head prefect but as a human being. They keep looking at each other, trying to read but also sometimes to evade each other's gaze; two conversations mingle, one a spoken exchange about Laurie's impetuosity, the other an unspoken one about what can happen between men. As the latter emerges into speech,

> Lanyon seemed about to step forward; and Laurie waited. He didn't think what he was waiting for. He was lifted into a kind of exalted dream, part loyalty, part hero-worship, all romance. Half-remembered images moved in it, the tents of Troy, the pillars of Athens, David waiting in the olive grove for the sound of Jonathan's bow. (p. 32)

The move which Ralph eventually makes is to give Laurie a translation of the *Phaedrus*, accompanied by a warning: 'It doesn't exist anywhere in real life, so don't let it give you illusions. It's just a nice idea' (p. 33). Laurie is conscious that as the book was passed over their hands had touched, but he cannot quite grasp the undercurrents of Ralph's conversation. He senses that he is being deprived of the opportunity for a more intimate understanding, but Ralph insists that although he has been watching Laurie for some time he will not interfere in his life: 'Look, if you want to know, one reason why not is because it would mean too much. To me, too, if that's any satisfaction to you'. As the conversation (whose complex currents Renault charts so deftly) exhausts itself in the silence which must presage parting, Laurie cannot act on Ralph's signals to leave. So Ralph says:

> What is it, then? Come here a moment. Now you see what I mean, Spud. It would never have done, would it? Well, goodbye. (p. 34)

What action is covered by this speech? Some gesture (an embrace? a kiss?) moves the conversation out of the register of an interview between head prefect and fifth-former into an expression of intimacy – but an intimacy which is immediately consigned to the past, achieved precisely in order to demonstrate its impossibility.

The near-recognition, the half-disclosure, in this conversation is the first of many in the book, for Renault understands the importance of the glance, the hint, the allusion in eliciting recognition in a milieu where sexual relations between men are not just part of a myth but now have become realizable with a new freedom in a society shaken up by war. There are various moments when such glances are crucial, one being the episode when Laurie is lying wounded and close to death on the boat which is evacuating him from Dunkirk; seeing a bearded sailor bending over him he murmurs, 'Sorry, dearie. Some other time' (p. 39). This is at once a disclosure and a misrecognition. Only much later does he discover that this sailor was Ralph.

In hospital Laurie falls in love with Andrew, a young Quaker and conscientious objector who is serving as a medical orderly. The moment of revelation so familiar in idealized settings takes place here in much less glamorous circumstances:

> In the open doorway of the lavatory the boy who had been scrubbing the floor sat back on his heels and smiled.
> Laurie stopped in his tracks, balanced himself between the crutch and the bathroom doorpost, and smiled back . . .
> The boy put down his floorcloth, wiped his hand on the seat of his trousers, and with the back of it pushed the hair away from his eyes. It was fairish, the colour of old gilt. He had a fair skin which was smoothly tanned, so that his grey eyes showed up very bright and clear. He was working in old corduroy trousers and a grey flannel shirt with rolled sleeves. (p. 58)

This entranced reading of Andrew's body does not exclude the exotic touch ('old gilt') but is placed firmly within the mundane, and rapport is established between the two by Laurie preventing another soldier from maliciously upsetting Andrew's bucket over the clean floor. Their relationship develops as friendship, and any disclosure of something deeper proves difficult as Laurie is uncertain about Andrew's likely response. Laurie tries to test the ground by alluding to Tchaikovsky being 'queer', but Andrew does not understand, simply taking the word to mean 'mad'.

They do not share a language, but they do come to share semi-private spaces in which their languages mesh without ever quite fusing. One day Andrew joins Laurie in a nearby orchard, his 'Garden of Eden', and a conversation ensues in which the two men both meet and miss each other. They discuss hell and salvation, but unlike the undergraduate theological discussion in *Maurice*, this one broaches matters which lie at the heart of each man's self-understanding, Andrew's as a Quaker, and Laurie's as a soldier who has just been delivered from the hell of war. As Renault remarks, 'intensity can be a powerful solvent of thin and brittle protective surfaces' (p. 83), and we are offered the possibility that the depth of disclosure brought about by this probing of moral and theological views will lead the two men into disclosures of another kind. As Laurie looks at Andrew, who is sitting in the sun with his shirt off, Andrew suddenly says, 'We can't go on like this, can we?'. Laurie's heart races, but what Andrew means is that they have never discussed his reasons for not fighting, and Laurie's view of pacifism. Later in the conversation there is another moment of near-recognition:

> As soon as Laurie turned he looked away, not furtively but rather shyly. Something about his face had taken Laurie back a bit; during his last term at school . . . he had sometimes caught the tail-end of looks like that. But this time it seemed too much that it should be true, and he dared not believe in it. (p. 87)

So Laurie lapses into the day's 'undemanding stillness'. As they leave he quotes Milton's lines on Adam and Eve expelled from paradise; Andrew completes the quotation with 'They hand in hand, with wandering steps and slow,/ Through Eden took their solitary way', but he does not complete its application by joining hands with Laurie. As they walk back to the hospital, the sight of two horses being led home reminds Laurie of the copy of the *Phaedrus* in his locker, now covered in blood and stained by seawater, but still intact, still a text which has power.

Prompted to return to the *Phaedrus* after this failure to achieve a mutual recognition, Laurie is reading the book in a secluded patch of woodland when he is interrupted by Andrew. The conversation is electric with tension from the start, and when Andrew asks Laurie to describe the subject of the *Phaedrus*, and then to read it to him, it seems as if Laurie is on the edge of a disclosure. But he explains that the book is about rhetoric, summarizes the speeches on love without indicating the gender of the lovers, and says that the work is too long to read aloud. He cannot give voice to this text in Andrew's presence, and cannot manage even that elliptical disclosure which Ralph had made by means of the same text. All through their friendship Laurie assumes that Andrew could not cope with the prospect of a sexual relationship with another man, however strong his feelings for him might be. Andrew recognizes this attitude, without recognizing quite what it signals, and when they are alone in the hospital kitchen he tries to broach the point:

> "Only you keep things to yourself sometimes. Well, of course. It's just a way you look with it. 'No, he couldn't take that.' You oughtn't to think of me as a person whose head has to be stuck in a bag. That ought to be the last thing, if you see what I mean." When Laurie didn't answer, he said with difficulty, "It makes me feel, in a way, jealous, without knowing what of." (p. 286)

At this moment Laurie feels that there is nothing in himself from which Andrew needs to be protected, and kisses him. Immediately, just as Andrew 'was looking up with a kind of strangeness which was only the threshold of some feeling not yet formed', a nurse interrupts them. Andrew's half-formed feelings are not brought into the light; the significance of the kiss is never discussed.

The story of Laurie and Andrew is played out against the resumed story of Laurie and Ralph. As a result of giving a young doctor a blatantly cruisy smile, Laurie finds himself invited to an all-male party at the doctor's flat which turns out to be both a birthday party and a lonely hearts' club. Much as Laurie finds some comfort in recognizing in the doctor 'a speaker of his own language; another solitary still making his own maps' (p. 135), he is uncomfortable in the company of the predatory and temperamental queens who dominate the doctor's world, and reacts against being defined in their terms. He feels that the word 'queer' is a confining gesture, 'shutting you away, somehow; roping you off with a lot of people you don't feel anything in common with' (p. 176). Into the room walks Ralph Lanyon. In a medieval romance he would be a 'helper' figure who in his first encounter with the hero gives him a magic book, and in their second meeting rescues him from death without being recognized. Now they meet for the third time, and as in all good fairy-tales the third encounter is the decisive one.

Their deepening relationship resumes and completes the conversation which had begun in the head prefect's study seven years earlier. As Laurie sprawls in front of Ralph's fire listening to his sailor's yarns, his happiness seems as intense – but also as fragile – as if 'some legend, dear to one's childhood but long abandoned, were marvellously proved true' (p. 268). Images of heroism cluster round Ralph now as they had done in their schooldays. After they have spent a morning clearing out the relics of childhood from the cupboard in Laurie's old bedroom, Laurie's loving gaze transforms Ralph into a storybook hero:

> Through the open shirt showed a spearhead of tan which, more than a year after he had last worn tropical whites, was still burned into his fair skin. Laurie thought again that he was built like the hero of a boy's adventure story; strong-looking, but not with the set look of a man's strength; the hollows over the collar-bones and in the pit of the throat had still the softened edges of youth. One could imagine him, Laurie thought, stripped to the waist in all the classic situations, fishing in lagoons or pinioned bravely defiant to a tree. (p. 332)

But this is also the morning after Ralph and Laurie have made love for the first time. Heroism of a kind not found in the storybooks, the courage to work through conflicting loves and loyalties, is now demanded of them.

Romance and realism meet in *The Charioteer* in a way which is quite different from Forster's vision in *Maurice*. Powerful though the heroic images are, they are poignantly altered when translated into the wartime adult world. Ralph may be a handsome naval officer, but he has had part of his hand shot away, which prevents him resuming the career which alone had given purpose to his life. He may be the donor of a Platonic text on love, but he makes it clear to Laurie that he had gone to the doctor's party for the same reason as everyone else – he was looking for sex. He may be a helper figure, but his habit of trying to run people's lives causes Laurie difficulties. Andrew too is only in part an ideal figure: for all his moral opposition to fighting, he is not above thumping one of the queens, and cannot in the end trust himself or Laurie sufficiently to talk through the misunderstandings which separate them. Renault is fully alive to the attractions of ideal homoerotic love, but has more practical intelligence than Forster in understanding how one fashions a viable life in the world as it actually is. Laurie's love for both Andrew and Ralph does not simply pose him with a choice, it sets him the task of understanding what each man needs, and what kind of love each is capable of giving and receiving. Twists in the plot sow misunderstandings between the three, and push the novel close to tragedy as they abandon the attempt to make love work out: Ralph prepares to commit suicide, and Andrew goes off to care for victims of the blitz in the East End; both are heroic gestures but compromised by the despair from which they spring. Laurie appears ready to abandon both of them, and sends Andrew his copy of the *Phaedrus*, first tearing out the endpaper where the names of Ralph Lanyon and Laurie Odell are joined, and throwing it to the winds. But *The Charioteer* actually ends with all three characters realizing their own versions of the Platonic ideal. Andrew admits that his relationship with Laurie has made him know himself, and self-knowledge is exactly the goal of the Socratic philosopher. Laurie returns to Ralph in time to prevent his suicide, and the two are reconciled, but only because Laurie decides to tell a crucial lie. Love requires ideals, but also practicality. Greek love both is and is not a myth, and Renault shows how it can indeed come about in a recognizable world, albeit translated into a new idiom and inevitably making compromises with the world around it. The final sentence, in which the two horses rest together for the night, looks like a quotation from the *Phaedrus* but is not; it is actually adapting Plato's images to mark the union of Ralph and Laurie amid the uncertainties of wartime Britain. The old book has been mutilated and discarded, but its text is completed once again as the two men are brought together. Dorian Gray was poisoned by a book; Laurie Odell was saved by one. And when Laurie had learned all he could from the book, he gave it away, and set off on his own path.

Orientations:
A Select Bibliography

This bibliography is intended as a guide to further reading, both primary and secondary. It is organized in sections which correspond to the chapters of the book, with numbered paragraphs to facilitate cross-reference. Unless stated otherwise, the place of publication is London.

Abbreviations

ELH	*English Literary History*
JH	*Journal of Homosexuality*
PFL	*Pelican Freud Library*
PMLA	*Publications of the Modern Language Association of America*
VN	*Victorian Newsletter*
VS	*Victorian Studies*

There is no comprehensive bibliography of gay literature and criticism, though Ian Young's *The Male Homosexual in Literature: A Bibliography* (Metuchen, NJ, 1975) presents a wide-ranging list, arranged only in alphabetical order. There is an *Encyclopedia of Homosexuality*, (ed.) Wayne R. Dynes, 2 vols (1990), and a dictionary of *Gay and Lesbian Literature*, (ed.) Sharon Malinowski (1994) which covers writers since 1900.

The Penguin Book of Homosexual Verse, (ed.) Stephen Coote (Harmondsworth, 1983) is a useful anthology. There are several rather uneven anthologies of fiction: *The Faber Book of Gay Short Fiction*, (ed.) Edmund White (1991); *The Penguin Book of Gay Short Stories*, (ed.) David Leavitt and Mark Mitchell (Harmondsworth, 1994); and *In Another Part of the Forest*, (ed.) Alberto Manguel and Craig Stephenson (1994). There is an anthology of writings on Sodom in *The Book of Sodom*, (ed.) Paul Hallam (1993).

1 THE TEXTURE OF THE PAST

1.1 General Surveys. The most useful historical survey is H. Montgomery Hyde, *The Other Love: An Historical and Contemporary Survey of Homosexuality in Britain* (1970), somewhat dated, but still valuable. *Hidden from History: Reclaiming the Gay and Lesbian Past*, (ed.) Martin Bauml Duberman, Martha Vicinus and George Chauncey (Harmondsworth, 1991), is a wide-ranging collection of essays with many good contributions. Robert Aldrich's *The Seduction of the Mediterranean: Writing, Art and Homosexual Fantasy* (1993) offers a survey of writers and artists who have used the Mediterranean for the exploration of homosexual desire.

1.2   Theories of Sexuality. Recent work on the theory of gender and sexuality includes David F. Greenberg, *The Construction of Homosexuality* (Chicago, 1988), which ranges widely across many cultures and periods; Thomas Laqueur, *Making Sex: Body and Gender from the Greeks to Freud* (Cambridge, MA, 1990); and Judith Butler, *Gender Trouble: Feminism and the Subversion of Identity* (1990). Michel Foucault's influential study *The History of Sexuality* was unfinished at his death; the portions which have appeared in English are *Volume I: An Introduction* (1979), *Volume II: The Use of Pleasure* (1986), on ancient Greece, and *Volume III: The Care of the Self* (1988), on ancient Rome. Some of his interviews which discuss gay politics and the relation of the individual to the structures of power are printed in *The Foucault Reader*, (ed.) Paul Rabinow (Harmondsworth, 1986) and in Michel Foucault, *Politics, Philosophy, Culture: Interviews and other writings 1977–1984*, (ed.) Lawrence D. Kritzman (1988).

1.3   General Literary Studies. Books which bring together literature and theory include three by Eve Kosofsky Sedgwick: *Between Men: English Literature and Male Homosocial Desire* (New York, 1985), *Epistemology of the Closet* (Hemel Hempstead, 1991) and *Tendencies* (1994). Jonathan Dollimore's *Sexual Dissidence: Augustine to Wilde, Freud to Foucault* (Oxford, 1991) is stimulating but not well organized. John Boswell's *Christianity, Social Tolerance, and Homosexuality: Gay People in Western Europe from the Beginning of the Christian Era to the Fourteenth Century* (Chicago, 1980) draws its material from the middle ages, but has wider implications because of its thesis that 'gay people' is a viable category through different historical periods. James Creech's *Closet Writing/Gay Reading* (Chicago, 1993) discusses the theory and practice of reading, focusing on Herman Melville. Kevin Kopelson's *Love's Litany: The Writing of Modern Homoerotics* (Stanford, 1994) discusses modern English and French texts.

1.4   Collections of Essays. There have been several collections of essays on homosexuality and literature, notably *Literary Visions of Homosexuality*, (ed.) Stuart Kellog (New York, 1983); *Displacing Homophobia: Gay Male Perspectives in Literature and Culture*, (ed.) Ronald R. Butters, John M. Clum and Michael Moon (Durham, NC, 1989); *The Pursuit of Sodomy: Male Homosexuality in Renaissance and Enlightenment Europe*, (ed.) Kent Gerard and Gert Hekma (New York, 1989); *Inside/Out: Lesbian Theories, Gay Theories*, (ed.) Diana Fuss (1991); and *Sexual Sameness: Textual Differences in Lesbian and Gay Writing*, (ed.) Joseph Bristow (1992).

1.5   Freud's Myths. The library edition of Freud's work is *The Standard Edition of the Complete Psychological Works of Sigmund Freud*, (ed.) James Strachey, 24 vols (1953–74); most of the works which are accessible to the lay reader are collected in the Pelican Freud Library ('PFL'), to which the references have been keyed where possible. Freud's understanding of homosexual behaviour is set out in his *Three Essays on the Theory of Sexuality* (1905) (PFL vol. 7), and in *Leonardo da Vinci and a Memory of his Childhood* (1910) (PFL vol. 14); see also his case study of Schreber (1911) in PFL vol. 9. There are strong homosexual undercurrents in *The Freud/Jung Letters*, (ed.) William McGuire (1974; abridged 1979) and *The Complete Letters of Sigmund Freud to Wilhelm Fliess 1887–1904*, (ed.) Jeffrey Masson (Cambridge, MA, 1985). For other letters see *Letters of Sigmund Freud 1873–1939*, (ed.) Ernst

L. Freud (1961). Peter Gay's biography *Freud: A Life for our Time* (1988) is thorough and lucid, with a good introductory bibliography.

1.6 Plato's Myths. The best guide to ancient Greek practice is Kenneth Dover, *Greek Homosexuality* (1978); also valuable are Bernard Sergent's *Homosexuality in Greek Myth* (1987) and David M. Halperin's collection *One Hundred Years of Homosexuality and other essays on Greek Love* (1990), where the title essay is of wide interest. Dover's edition of Plato's *Symposium* (Cambridge, 1980) has a good short introduction and excellent notes. The best translation of the *Symposium* is by R.E. Allen in *The Dialogues of Plato: Volume II* (New Haven, 1991), from which quotations are taken, though his comments on homosexual practices in the introduction and notes are unsympathetic. Walter Hamilton's Penguin translation (Harmondsworth, 1951) is reliable; for Shelley's see § 4.7. *Phaedrus* is quoted from R. Hackforth's translation in the Bollingen edition of *The Collected Dialogues of Plato* (Princeton, 1961). References to both dialogues follow the Stephanus system of numbering common to different editions and translations.

2 THE RENAISSANCE

2.1 Renaissance Literature and Society. The most important book in this field is Alan Bray's pioneering *Homosexuality in Renaissance England* (1982), supplemented by his 'Homosexuality and the signs of male friendship in Elizabethan England', *History Workshop* 29 (1990) 1–19. For historical material see also Caroline Bingham, 'Seventeenth-century attitudes toward deviant sex', *Journal of Interdisciplinary History* 1 (1971) 447–68 and B.R. Burg, 'Ho hum, another work of the devil', *JH* 6 (1980–1) 69–78. For literary works Bruce Smith's *Homosexual Desire in Shakespeare's England* (Chicago, 1991) is a learned, subtle and stimulating account of the imaginative resources available to Renaissance readers. Other books worth consulting are James M. Saslow, *Ganymede in the Renaissance: Homosexuality in Art and Society* (New Haven, 1986), chiefly on Italian art; Gregory W. Bredbeck, *Sodomy and Interpretation: Marlowe to Milton* (Ithaca, 1991); and Jonathan Goldberg, *Sodometries: Renaissance Texts, Modern Sexualities* (Stanford, 1992). Rictor Norton's *The Homosexual Literary Tradition: An Interpretation* (New York, 1974) is primarily focused on the Renaissance, and has good local readings, though his overall concern with finding echoes of the myth of Hercules and Hylas is unconvincing. Collections of essays on Renaissance literature include *The Pursuit of Sodomy* (see § 1.4); *Homosexuality in Renaissance and Enlightenment England*, (ed.) Claude J. Summers (New York, 1992); *Renaissance Discourses of Desire*, (ed.) Claude J. Summers and Ted-Larry Pebworth (Columbia, MO, 1993); and *Queering the Renaissance*, (ed.) Jonathan Goldberg (Durham, NC, 1994). Satires against effeminacy are discussed by Susan C. Shapiro in ' "Yon plumed dandebrat": male "effeminacy" in English satire and criticism', *Review of English Studies* 39 (1988) 400–12. Raymond-Jean Frontain has an illuminating essay on the appreciation of male beauty in representations of David in 'Ruddy and goodly to look at withal', *Cahiers Elisabéthains* 36 (1989) 11–24. There is a useful article by Giovanni Dall'Orto on ' "Socratic love" as a disguise for same-sex love in the Italian Renaissance' in *JH* 16 (1988) 33–65.

2.2   Renaissance Drama. The erotic dimension to the use of boy actors for women's parts has been discussed by Lisa Jardine in *Still Harping on Daughters: Women and Drama in the Age of Shakespeare* (Hemel Hempstead, 1983) ch. 1; by Phyllis Rackin in 'Androgyny, mimesis, and the marriage of the boy heroine on the English Renaissance stage', *PMLA* 102 (1987) 29–41; by Jean E. Howard in 'Crossdressing, the theatre, and gender struggle in early modern England', *Shakespeare Quarterly* 39 (1988) 418–40; by Stephen Orgel in 'Nobody's perfect: or why did the English stage take boys for women?' in *Displacing Homophobia* (see § 1.4); and by several contributors to *Erotic Politics: Desire on the Renaissance Stage*, (ed.) Susan Zimmerman (1992): see especially Stephen Orgel's 'The Subtexts of *The Roaring Girl*', Lisa Jardine's 'Twins and travesties' on *Twelfth Night* and Peter Stallybrass's 'Transvestism and the "body beneath": speculating on the boy actor'. The contemporary controversy is charted by J.W. Binns in 'Women or transvestites on the Elizabethan Stage?: an Oxford controversy', *Sixteenth Century Journal* 5 (1974) 95–120; and Michael Shapiro, 'Lady Mary Wroth describes a "boy actress" ', *Medieval and Renaissance Drama in England* 4 (1989) 187–94. The question is discussed in relation to ideas of the self and magic by Laura Levine in *Men in Women's Clothing: Anti-Theatricality and Effeminization, 1579–1642* (Cambridge, 1994).

2.3   Editions of Renaissance Texts. The primary texts discussed in this chapter are quoted from the following editions. **Poetry:** Barnfield from *The Complete Poems*, (ed.) George Klawitter (Selinsgrove, 1990), though there are also older editions by A.B. Grosart (1876) and Edward Arber (Birmingham, 1882); Beaumont's *Salmacis and Hermaphroditus* from *Elizabethan Minor Epics*, (ed.) Elizabeth Story Donno (1963) which also contains James Shirley's *Narcissus*; Crashaw from *The Complete Poetry*, (ed.) G.W. Williamson (New York, 1974); Marlowe's poetry from *The Complete Poems and Translations*, (ed.) Stephen Orgel (Harmondsworth, 1971); Spenser from *Spenser's Minor Poems* (ed.) Ernest de Selincourt (Oxford, 1910). **Prose:** Sidney's *The Countess of Pembroke's Arcadia* survives in two versions: 'The Old Arcadia', (ed.) Katherine Duncan-Jones (Oxford, 1985) and the unfinished 'New Arcadia' with part of the old to complete it, (ed.) Maurice Evans (Harmondsworth, 1977). **Plays:** Middleton and Dekker's *The Roaring Girl*, (ed.) Paul A. Mulholland (Revels: Manchester, 1987).

2.4   Renaissance Literature: Further Reading. Other relevant literary texts are: Beaumont and Fletcher's play *Philaster*, (ed.) Andrew Gurr (Revels; 1969), for the role of the page Bellario; Ben Jonson's play *Epicoene*, (ed.) R.V. Holdsworth (1979), which includes various homosexual innuendos; John Lyly's play *Gallathea* shows two girls (dressed as boys) falling in love with each other: see Anne Lancashire's edition of his *'Gallathea' and 'Midas'* (Regents; 1970). Other plays by Middleton with occasional homoerotic material include *More Dissemblers besides Women*; *No wit, no help like a woman's*; and *The Widow*; for these one needs the edition of *The Works* by A.H. Bullen, 8 vols (1885–7), which also includes the verse satire *Microcynicon* by 'T.M.'. For the complex autoeroticism and homoeroticism of Andrew Marvell's poetry see Paul Hammond, 'Marvell's Sexuality', forthcoming in *The Seventeenth Century*.

2.5 The Story of Edward II. Raphael Holinshed's account of Edward II is quoted from his *The Third Volume of Chronicles* (1587), pp. 318–21. Marlowe's *Edward II* is quoted from the edition by Charles R. Forker (Revels: Manchester, 1994), which includes a good survey of the play's stage history and of critical opinion; also useful are *The Complete Works of Christopher Marlowe: Volume III: Edward II*, (ed.) Richard Rowland (Oxford, 1994) and *Christopher Marlowe: The Plays and their Sources*, (ed.) Vivien Thomas and William Tydeman (1994). Drayton's *Peirs Gaveston Earle of Cornwall* is quoted from volume one of *The Works of Michael Drayton*, (ed.) J. William Hebel (Oxford, 1931). Also worth consulting is *The Life and Death of Edward the Second* (1628–9) in *The Poems of Sir Francis Hubert*, (ed.) Bernard Mellor (Oxford, 1961).

3 SHAKESPEARE

3.1 Texts of Shakespeare. Shakespeare's works are quoted from the Arden editions, except for *The Two Noble Kinsmen* which is cited from the Penguin edition by N.W. Bawcutt (Harmondsworth, 1977), and the *Sonnets*, which are cited from the Penguin edition of *The Sonnets and A Lover's Complaint*, (ed.) John Kerrigan (Harmondsworth, 1986). Kerrigan's judicious introduction, notes and bibliography make this the best edition of the *Sonnets*, though that edited by William Ingram and Theodore Redpath (1964; second edition 1978) has a precise and thoughtful explanatory commentary which remains valuable. The Variorum edition of the *Sonnets*, (ed.) Hyder Rollins, 2 vols (Philadelphia, 1944) has an extensive summary of earlier commentators' interpretations, and includes a section devoted to the debate over the question of homosexuality in the poems (ii, 232–9).

3.2 Studies of Shakespeare's *Sonnets*. Many of the studies listed in § 2.1 and § 2.2 provide a framework for understanding Shakespeare's handling of emotional relations between men. There is a good discussion of the *Sonnets* in Smith (see § 2.1). A book which is entirely devoted to arguing for the homosexual content of the *Sonnets* is Joseph Pequigney's *Such is my Love: A Study of Shakespeare's Sonnets* (Chicago, 1985), while Martin Green's *The Labyrinth of Shakespeare's Sonnets* (1974) offers a close reading of the sexual elements in the sonnets' language. Books which discuss the homosexual dimension more briefly, but are generally informative and stimulating, include G. Wilson Knight, *The Mutual Flame* (1955); J.B. Leishman, *Themes and Variations in Shakespeare's Sonnets* (1961); and Joel Fineman, *Shakespeare's Perjured Eye* (Berkeley, 1986).

3.3 Studies of Shakespeare's Plays. Discussions of the homoerotic elements in Shakespeare's plays include Smith (see § 2.1); and Joseph Pequigney, 'The two Antonios and same-sex love in *Twelfth Night* and *The Merchant of Venice*', *English Literary Renaissance* 22 (1992) 201–21. Many recent studies of gender and sexuality in Shakespeare are pertinent to the question of close relations between men, though they may not focus directly on the homosexual dimension; amongst the best are Janet Adelman, 'Male Bonding in Shakespeare's Comedies', in *Shakespeare's 'Rough Magic'*, (ed.) Peter Erickson and Coppelia Kahn (Newark, 1985) 73–103; and Adelman's *Suffocating Mothers: Fantasies of Maternal Origin in Shakespeare's Plays, 'Hamlet'* to *'The Tempest'* (New York, 1992); Peter Erickson, *Patriarchal Structures in Shakespeare's Drama* (Berkeley, 1985); Joel Fineman, 'Fratricide and cuckoldry: Shakespeare's doubles', *Psychoanalytic Review* 64 (1977) 409–53; and Coppelia Kahn, *Man's Estate: Masculine Identity in Shakespeare* (Berkeley, 1981).

4   FROM THE RESTORATION TO THE ROMANTICS

4.1   Restoration and Eighteenth-Century Literature and Society. The social world of eighteenth-century homosexuality has been well described by Rictor Norton in *Mother Clap's Molly House: The Gay Subculture in England 1700–1830* (1992), and in a series of articles by Randolph Trumbach: 'London's sodomites: homosexual behavior and western culture in the 18th century', *Journal of Social History* 11 (1977–8) 1–33; 'Sodomitical subcultures, sodomitical roles, and the gender revolution of the eighteenth century', *Eighteenth-Century Life* 9 (1985) 109–121 (reprinted in *'Tis Nature's Fault: Unauthorized Sexuality during the Enlightenment*, (ed.) Robert Purks Maccubbin (Cambridge, 1985)); 'Sodomitical assaults, gender role, and sexual development in eighteenth-century London', *JH* 16 (1988) 407–429; 'Sodomy transformed: aristocratic libertinage, public reputation and the gender revolution of the 18th century', *JH* 19 (1990) 105–124 (also printed in *Love Letters*, see § 4.3); 'Sex, gender, and sexual identity in modern culture: male sodomy and female prostitution in enlightenment London', *Journal of the History of Sexuality* 2 (1991) 186–203. Dennis Rubini writes on 'Sexuality and Augustan England: sodomy, politics, elite circles and society' in *JH* 16 (1988) 349–381. G.S. Rousseau provides an invaluable survey of eighteenth-century literature in 'The pursuit of homosexuality in the eighteenth century: "utterly confused category" and/or rich repository?' in *Eighteenth-Century Life* 9 (1985) 132–168, reprinted in *'Tis Nature's Fault* and in Rousseau's collection *Perilous Enlightenment: Pre- and Post-modern Discourses: Sexual, Historical* (Manchester, 1991), which includes several other relevant essays. There is a brief treatment of homosexuality in Peter Wagner's *Eros Revived: Erotica of the Enlightenment in England and America* (1988). Louis B. Crompton's *Byron and Greek Love: Homophobia in 19th-century England* (1985) is not only an illuminating study of Byron's life and work, but a valuable guide to eighteenth- and early nineteenth-century homosexuality, with extensive material on Jeremy Bentham's enlightened writings. G.J. Barker-Benfield's *The Culture of Sensibility: Sex and Society in Eighteenth-Century Britain* (Chicago, 1992) provides a context for contemporary ideas of masculinity, which are also explored by Carolyn D. Williams in *Pope, Homer, and Manliness* (1993).

4.2   Restoration Poetry. The most useful edition of Rochester's works is generally *The Complete Works*, (ed.) Frank H. Ellis (Harmondsworth, 1994), but this excludes 'Régime de vivre' and *Sodom*, which are available in *Complete Poems and Plays*, (ed.) Paddy Lyons (1993), from which my quotations are taken. For the letters (and a good biographical sketch) see *The Letters of John Wilmot, Earl of Rochester*, (ed.) Jeremy Treglown (Oxford, 1980). Harold

Weber has an essay on ' "Drudging in fair Aurelia's womb": constructing homosexual economies in Rochester's poetry', *The Eighteenth Century* 33 (1992) 99–117. Aphra Behn's poems are quoted from *The Works of Aphra Behn: Volume I: Poetry*, (ed.) Janet Todd (1992).

4.3 The *Love Letters*. *Love Letters Written between a Certain Late Nobleman and the Famous Mr Wilson* was probably first printed in 1723, though no copy of that edition seems to survive; there is a copy of the 1745 edition in the Bodleian Library. The 1745 text was reprinted (ed.) Michael S. Kimmel (New York, 1990), but grossly corrupted by many misprints which often make the work unintelligible; my quotations have been corrected from the 1745 edition. Kimmel's edition includes an important historical essay by George Rousseau (reprinted in his *Perilous Enlightenment* – see § 4.1).

4.4 Restoration and Eighteenth-Century Drama. *The Soldier's Fortune* is quoted from *The Works of Thomas Otway*, (ed.) J.C. Ghosh, 2 vols (Oxford, 1932). Thomas Baker's *Tunbridge Walks* (1703) and Nathaniel Lancaster's *The Pretty Gentleman* (1747) are cited from the first editions; for *Miss in her Teens* see *The Plays of David Garrick: Volume 1*, (ed.) Harry Pedicord and Fredrick Bergmann (Carbondale, 1980). George Granville's *The Jew of Venice* is quoted from the first edition (1701) but is also available in *Five Restoration Adaptations of Shakespeare*, (ed.) Christopher Spencer (Urbana, IL, 1965). Other relevant plays are Sir John Vanburgh's *The Relapse* (1697) and Thomas Southerne's *Sir Anthony Love* (1691). For studies of the fop and molly in the drama see Susan Staves, 'A few kind words for the fop', *Studies in English Literature 1500–1900* 22 (1982) 413–28, and Laurence Senelick, 'Mollies or men of mode?', *Journal of the History of Sexuality* 1 (1990) 33–67.

4.5 Eighteenth-Century Fiction. Tobias Smollett is quoted from *The Adventures of Roderick Random*, (ed.) Paul-Gabriel Boucé (Oxford, 1979); see also *The Adventures of Peregrine Pickle*, (ed.) James L. Clifford (Oxford, 1964), ch. 49. John Cleland's *Memoirs of a Woman of Pleasure* [*Fanny Hill*] is now one of 'The World's Classics' (ed.) Peter Sabor (Oxford, 1985).

4.6 'A Language that is foreign': Byron, Beckford and others. Byron is quoted from his *Poetical Works*, (ed.) Frederick Page (Oxford, 1970), though some relevant poems have been added to the canon in *The Complete Poetical Works*, (ed.) Jerome J. McGann, 7 vols (Oxford, 1980–93). Crompton's book (see § 4.1) is the best guide to Byron, but see also Jean H. Hagstrum, *Eros and Vision* (1989) ch. 10. William Beckford's *Vathek* is available in many editions; the most useful one, from which I quote, is by Roger Lonsdale (Oxford, 1970). This omits the 'episodes', which are not easy to find; they are inserted into the main novel in the edition of the original French text by Guy Chapman, 2 vols (1929), from which I have translated my quotations of them. *The Journal of William Beckford in Portugal and Spain 1787–1788*, (ed.) Boyd Alexander (1954) and *Life at Fonthill 1807–1822*, (ed.) Boyd Alexander (1957) offer some of Beckford's letters and diaries. Among several biographies the most recent is Brian Fothergill's *Beckford of Fonthill* (1979). Mary Shelley's *Frankenstein* is quoted from the Penguin edition (Harmondsworth, 1992), and Goethe's *Elective Affinities* from the translation by R.J. Hollingdale (Harmondsworth, 1971). Amongst other primary texts worth consulting are Thomas Gray's poems and letters; for a sympathetic essay see Hagstrum's *Eros and Vision*, ch. 8.

4.7 'A Language that is foreign': Hellenism. A good introduction to contemporary fascination with Greece is provided by the anthology *English Romantic Hellenism 1700–1824*, (ed.) Timothy Webb (Manchester, 1982); there is also *The Seduction of the Mediterranean* (see § 1.1). Winckelmann is quoted from *Winckelmann: Writings on Art*, (ed.) David Irwin (1972). Richard Payne Knight's *An Account of the Remains of the Worship of Priapus* (1786) can be read at a special desk in the British Library under the watchful eyes of the staff; for studies of Knight see *The Arrogant Connoisseur*, (ed.) Michael Clarke and Nicholas Penny (Manchester, 1982) and Rousseau in *Perilous Enlightenment* (see § 4.1). For Shelley see James A. Notopoulos, *The Platonism of Shelley* (Durham, NC, 1949), a detailed study with the texts of Shelley's translation of *The Symposium* and his essays on Greek culture; for his notes on sculptures see *Shelley's Prose, or The Trumpet of a Prophecy*, (ed.) David Lee Clark (Albuquerque, 1954). These are also available in *Shelley on Love*, (ed.) Richard Holmes (1980), from which quotations are taken.

5 THE VICTORIAN PERIOD

5.1 Victorian Literature and Society. *Manliness and Morality: Middle-class Masculinity in Britain and America 1800–1940*, (ed.) J.A. Mangan and James Walvin (Manchester, 1987) offers a wide-ranging collection of essays. Also useful is Joseph A. Kestner's *Masculinities in Victorian Painting* (Aldershot, 1995). Mark Girouard's *The Return to Camelot: Chivalry and the English Gentleman* (New Haven, 1981) charts the rise of chivalric ideals of masculinity, while Norman Vance's *The Sinews of the Spirit: The Ideal of Christian Manliness in Victorian Literature and Religious Thought* (Cambridge, 1985) is useful for the religious dimension to this ideal. Victorian anxiety about the unmanliness of Catholic and Anglo-Catholic religion is explored by David Hilliard in 'Unenglish and unmanly: anglo-catholicism and homosexuality', *VS* 25 (1982) 181–210 and Oliver S. Buckton, ' "An unnatural state": gender, "perversion", and Newman's *Apologia pro Vita Sua*', *VS* 35 (1992) 359–83. Two books chart the ways in which the Oscar Wilde affair changed contemporary understandings of masculinity: Ed Cohen, *Talk on the Wilde Side* (1993) and Alan Sinfield, *The Wilde Century* (1994). Richard Dellamora's *Masculine Desire: The Sexual Politics of Victorian Aestheticism* (Chapel Hill, 1990) explores the ambiguous sexuality expressed in the work of Pater and Swinburne, with briefer discussions of Tennyson, Hopkins and Ruskin. Linda Dowling has a short but illuminating discussion of the ambiguities of vocabulary for male relationships in 'Ruskin's pied beauty and the constitution of a "homosexual" code', *VN* 75 (Spring 1989) 1–8, and useful studies of *Language and Decadence in the Victorian Fin de Siècle* (Princeton, 1986) and *Hellenism and Homosexuality in Victorian Oxford* (Ithaca, 1994). The best introduction to the ways in which homosexual desires were expressed in this period is Brian Reade's anthology *Sexual Heretics: Male Homosexuality in English Literature from 1850 to 1900* (1970), while poetry which expresses admiration for boys is discussed by Timothy D'Arch Smith in his thorough and detailed study *Love in Earnest: Some Notes on the Lives and*

Writings of English 'Uranian' Poets from 1889 to 1930 (1970). Rupert Croft-Cooke discusses Swinburne, Symonds and Wilde in *Feasting with Panthers: A New Consideration of some Late Victorian Writers* (1967) but his approach is rather reductive. Christopher Craft's *Another Kind of Love: Male Homosexual Desire in English Discourse, 1850–1920* (Berkeley, 1994) discusses Tennyson, *Dracula*, Wilde and Lawrence.

5.2 'On the dangerous edge': Hughes, Collins and Stoker. Thomas Hughes's *Tom Brown's Schooldays* is quoted from the Penguin edition (Harmondsworth, 1971). The public school ethos is well documented by J.R. de S. Honey in *Tom Brown's Universe* (1977). Wilkie Collins's *Armadale* is quoted from the Dover facsimile (New York, 1977) of the original magazine publication. Bram Stoker's *Dracula* is quoted from the Penguin edition (Harmondsworth, 1993). For essays which explore the homosexual dimension to *Dracula* see Christopher Craft (§ 5.1) and Talia Schaffer, ' "A Wilde desire took me": the homoerotic history of *Dracula*', ELH 61 (1994) 381–425. Eric, Count Stenbock's 'The True Story of a Vampire' appears in his *Studies of Death* (1894; facsimile reprint New York, 1984) along with 'Hylas'.

5.3 'Forms for desire': homoerotic prose and poetry. *Don Leon* (1866) is quoted from the rare first edition; there is a copy in the Bodleian Library. Pater's *The Renaissance* (1873) is quoted from the edition by Adam Phillips (Oxford, 1986); see also 'Winckelmann' in that volume, 'Lacedaemon' in *Plato and Platonism* (1893), and 'Apollo in Picardy' in *Miscellaneous Studies* (1895). Bloxam's 'The Priest and the Acolyte' is quoted from Reade's *Sexual Heretics* (§ 5.1). Dolben's poems are quoted from *The Poems and Letters of Digby Mackworth Dolben 1848–1867*, (ed.) Martin Cohen (Avebury, 1981), which is more complete and accurate than *The Poems of Digby Mackworth Dolben*, (ed.) Robert Bridges (1915). Robert Bernard Martin's biography *Gerard Manley Hopkins: A Very Private Life* (1991) has a good account of his homoerotic feelings and his relationship with Dolben. For the homoerotic strain in Hopkins's poetry see Dellamora (§ 5.1), and Joseph Bristow, ' "Churlsgrace": Gerard Manley Hopkins and the working-class male body', ELH 59 (1992) 693–711.

5.4 Tennyson and Hallam. Tennyson is quoted from *The Poems of Tennyson*, (ed.) Christopher Ricks, second edition, 3 vols (1987), which has useful notes, including manuscript variants; the major poems are also available in the paperback abridgement of Ricks's edition, *Tennyson: A Selected Edition* (1989). The edition of *In Memoriam* (ed.) Susan Shatto and Marion Shaw (Oxford, 1982) has more detailed notes. The best biography is by Robert Bernard Martin, *Tennyson: The Unquiet Heart* (Oxford, 1980), but see also Christopher Ricks, *Tennyson* (1972). The diary of Sir Sydney Waterlow is quoted from the manuscript in the Berg Collection, New York Public Library, entry for 16 November 1907. For various interpretations of the feelings expressed in *In Memoriam* see (besides Martin and Ricks) the review in *The Times*, 28 November 1851, p. 8; Alan Sinfield's *Alfred Tennyson* (1986); and Christopher Craft (§ 5.1).

5.5 Walt Whitman. Whitman is quoted from the Penguin *Complete Poems*, (ed.) Francis Murphy (Harmondsworth, 1975). Whitman revised his poems repeatedly, so the textual problems are considerable: Murphy's text of *Leaves* *of Grass* is the 1891–2 'deathbed' edition, but earlier versions of some poems, and texts of poems excluded from the final edition, are also included. In 1867 Whitman removed three overtly homoerotic poems from 'Calamus': 'Who is now reading this', 'I thought that knowledge alone would suffice' and 'Hours continuing long' (*Complete Poems*, pp. 607–9). The manuscript of 'Once I pass'd through a populous city' shows that the subject of this poem was a man, but the lover's gender was changed before publication (*Complete Poems*, p. 798). There were also significant revisions to 'Song of Myself' and 'Sleepers' after the first (1855) edition of *Leaves of Grass*. This edition (which did not include *Calamus*) is available in Penguin Classics, (ed.) Malcolm Cowley (1959; Harmondsworth, 1976), cited in the text as '1855' with page numbers. For Whitman's contemporary reception see Harold Blodgett, *Walt Whitman in England* (Ithaca, 1934). The best introduction to Whitman's homosexual writing is by Robert K. Martin in *The Homosexual Tradition in American Poetry* (Austin, 1979), but see also Michael Moon, *Disseminating Whitman: Revision and Corporeality in 'Leaves of Grass'* (Cambridge, MA, 1991); Byrne R.S. Fone, *Masculine Landscapes: Walt Whitman and the Homoerotic Text* (Carbondale, 1992); and Tenney Nathanson, *Whitman's Presence: Body, Voice, and Writing in 'Leaves of Grass'* (New York, 1992).

5.6   John Addington Symonds. Symonds's *A Problem in Greek Ethics* was privately printed anonymously in 1883; the British Library copy has manuscript alterations by Symonds. His *A Problem in Modern Ethics* (1891) is anthologized in Reade (§ 5.1), as are some of his poems, including 'Eudiades' and 'Midnight at Baiae'. Amongst his volumes of verse is *Many Moods* (1878); see also *Gabriel*, (ed.) Robert L. Peters and Timothy D'Arch Smith (1974). Prose works include *In the Key of Blue and Other Prose Essays* (1892) and *Walt Whitman: A Study* (1893). His *Memoirs* appeared in 1984, (ed.) Phyllis Grosskurth, who has also written *John Addington Symonds: A Biography* (1964). See also his *Collected Letters* (ed.) Robert Peters and Herbert Schueller, 3 vols (1967–9). The *Bibliography of the Writings of John Addington Symonds* by Percy L. Babington (1925) includes homoerotic passages from the privately printed verse which Symonds excluded from the published texts. There is a discussion by R. St John Tyrwhitt of 'The Greek Spirit in Modern Literature', referring to Symonds and Arnold, in *The Contemporary Review* 29 (1877) 554–66.

5.7   Oscar Wilde. Wilde's writings are quoted from *Complete Works of Oscar Wilde*, (ed.) Vyvyan Holland (1966), except for *The Picture of Dorian Gray*, which is quoted from the Norton edition, (ed.) Donald L. Lawler (New York, 1988); this presents both the 1890 magazine text and the revised 1891 book version, with notes, contemporary reviews and critical essays, though it suffers from many misprints. See also *Selected Letters of Oscar Wilde*, (ed.) Rupert Hart-Davis (Oxford, 1979). The pornographic novel *Teleny* (1893), possibly partly by Wilde, is available (ed.) John McRae (1986). The best introduction to Wilde and his milieu is Neil Bartlett's *Who was that man? A Present for Mr Oscar Wilde* (1988), an imaginative exploration of the homosexual culture of nineteenth-century London from the standpoint of a gay man in the 1980s. The standard biography is Richard Ellmann's *Oscar Wilde* (1987). Transcripts of the trials are provided in *The Trials of Oscar Wilde*, (ed.) H. Montgomery Hyde (1948), while contemporary responses are collected in *The Oscar Wilde File*, (ed.) Jonathan Goodman (1989). Robert Hichens's satire on Wilde called *The Green Carnation* (1894) was reissued in 1992. Amongst an extensive critical literature on Wilde interesting recent work includes Joseph Bristow, 'Wilde, *Dorian Gray*, and gross indecency' in *Sexual Sameness* (see § 1.4); Ed Cohen (§ 5.1) and 'Writing gone Wilde', *PMLA* 102 (1987) 801–813; William A. Cohen, 'Willie and Wilde: reading *The Portrait of Mr W.H.*' in *Displacing Homophobia* (§ 1.4); Lawrence Danson, 'Oscar Wilde, W.H., and the unspoken name of love', *ELH* 58 (1991) 979–1000; Dollimore (§ 1.3); Dowling, *Language and Decadence* (§ 5.1) and 'Imposture and absence in Wilde's *Portrait of Mr W.H.*', *VN* 58 (1980) 26–9; Regenia Gagnier, *Idylls of the Marketplace: Oscar Wilde and the Victorian Public* (Stanford, 1986); Kopelson (§ 1.3); Sinfield (§ 5.1).

5.9 The Victorian Period: further reading. The major writers not discussed in this chapter whose work treads the dangerous edge in different ways (besides Hopkins: see § 5.3) are Charles Dickens in *David Copperfield* (1849–50), *Our Mutual Friend* (1864–5) and *Edwin Drood* (1870); and two Americans: Herman Melville (see particularly *Moby Dick* (1851) and *Billy Budd* (posthumously published 1924)), and Henry James (see *The Pupil* (1891) and *The Turn of the Screw* (1898)).

6   THE MODERN PERIOD

6.1 Modern Literature and Society. Social and political developments are well charted by Jeffrey Weeks in *Coming Out: Homosexual Politics in Britain from the Nineteenth Century to the Present* (1977). Jeffrey Meyers's *Homosexuality and Literature 1890–1930* (1977) is unsympathetic in tone; more positive and combative is Mark Lilly's *Gay Men's Literature in the Twentieth Century* (Basingstoke, 1993). For discussions of fiction see Kopelson (§ 1.3), and Claude J. Summers, *Gay Fictions: Wilde to Stonewall* (New York, 1990); for poetry, Gregory Woods, *Articulate Flesh: Male Homo-eroticism and Modern Poetry* (New Haven, 1987), which includes Lawrence, Auden and Gunn; for drama, John M. Clum, *Acting Gay: Male Homosexuality in Modern Drama* (New York, 1992; second edition 1994), and Nicholas de Jongh, *Not in Front of the Audience: Homosexuality on Stage* (1992). Byrne R.S. Fone writes on 'This other Eden: Arcadia and the homosexual imagination' in *Literary Visions of Homosexuality* (see § 1.4). An important influence on early twentieth-century views was Edward Carpenter, especially in his Whitmanesque poem *Towards Democracy* (1883; fifth edition 1931) and his anthology *Ioläus* (1902).

6.2 D.H. Lawrence. Lawrence is quoted from the Cambridge edition: *The Prussian Officer and Other Stories*, (ed.) John Worthen (1983); *The White Peacock*, (ed.) Andrew Robertson (1983); *Women in Love*, (ed.) David Farmer, Lindeth Vasey and John Worthen (1987); *The Letters*, (gen. ed.) James T. Boulton, 7 vols (1979–93). Also relevant are *Aaron's Rod*; *Kangaroo*; *The Plumed Serpent*; and the discussion of Whitman in *Studies in Classic American Literature*. The least unsatisfactory biography is still Harry T. Moore's *The Priest of Love* (1974), now superseded for the early life by John Worthen's *D.H.*

Lawrence: The Early Years 1885–1912 (Cambridge, 1991). There is some discussion of Lawrence's complex attitudes to homosexuality by Paul Delany in *D.H. Lawrence's Nightmare: The Writer and his Circle in the Years of the Great War* (Hassocks, 1979), and by Jeffrey Meyers in *D.H. Lawrence: A Biography* (1990), though Meyers's interpretation of both literary and biographical material lacks subtlety. Relevant contemporary testimonies include G.H. Neville, *A Memoir of D.H. Lawrence*, (ed.) Carl Baron (Cambridge, 1981); Frieda Lawrence, *The Memoirs and Correspondence*, (ed.) E.W. Tedlock (1961); Compton Mackenzie, *My Life and Times: Octave Five: 1915–1923* (1966); and *D.H. Lawrence: A Composite Biography*, (ed.) Edward Nehls, 3 vols (Madison, 1957–9). Much of the extensive critical commentary on Lawrence would be relevant to a study of his understanding of male sexuality, but for specific accounts of the homosexual elements in his writings see Meyers (§ 6.1) and Craft (§ 5.1).

6.3   E.M. Forster. E.M. Forster's principal homosexual works are *Maurice* (1971; quoted from the Penguin edition, Harmondsworth, 1972) and several stories collected in *The Life to Come and Other Stories* (1972), both published posthumously. 'The Story of a Panic' was collected in *The Celestial Omnibus* (1911) and in *The New Collected Short Stories* (1985). The standard biography is P.N. Furbank, *E.M. Forster: A Life*, 2 vols (1977–8). For discussions of *Maurice* see John Fletcher, 'Forster's self-erasure: *Maurice* and the scene of masculine love' in *Sexual Sameness* (see § 1.4); Robert K. Martin, 'Edward Carpenter and the double structure of *Maurice*' in *Literary Visions of Homosexuality* (§ 1.4); Alan Wilde, 'The Naturalisation of Eden' in *E.M. Forster: A Human Exploration*, (ed.) G.K. Das and John Beer (1979); and several essays in *E.M. Forster: Centenary Revaluations*, (ed.) Judith Scherer Herz and Robert K. Martin (1982), especially a discussion by Philip Gardner of the textual evolution of *Maurice*.

6.4   Wilfred Owen and First World War Poetry. For studies of the literature of the First World War which discuss the homoerotic elements see Paul Fussell, *The Great War and Modern Memory* (New York, 1975) and Adrian Caesar, *Taking it like a Man: Suffering, Sexuality and the War Poets: Brooke, Sassoon, Owen, Graves* (Manchester, 1993). For an imaginative recreation of these experiences see Pat Barker's trilogy of novels, *Regeneration* (1991), *The Eye in the Door* (1993) and *The Ghost Road* (1995). There is an excellent anthology *Lads: Love Poetry of the Trenches*, (ed.) Martin Taylor (1989), which includes a substantial introduction. Geoffrey Faber's poems were collected as *The Buried Stream* (1941); for Sassoon see Siegfried Sassoon, *The War Poems* (1983), and for Ivor Gurney his *Collected Poems* (Oxford, 1982). A.E. Housman was an important influence on the war poets: see his *Collected Poems* (1939). Owen is cited from *Wilfred Owen: The Complete Poems and Fragments*, (ed.) Jon Stallworthy, 2 vols (1983); this edition was adapted for a general readership as *The Poems of Wilfred Owen* (1985). Page references are given only for those drafts and fragments which are available solely in the two-volume edition. My quotations from drafts occasionally select words which Owen deleted, and I have sometimes had to make a choice between variants to produce a coherent phrase. There is a biography by Jon Stallworthy, *Wilfred Owen* (1974), and a more revealing study by Dominic Hibberd, *Wilfred Owen: The Last Year 1917–1918* (1992).

6.5   Homosexuality and Pacifism: *Despised and Rejected*. Rose Laure Allatini's *Despised and Rejected* (1918) was published under the pseudonym A.T. Fitzroy; its publisher C.W. Daniel was prosecuted for prejudicing army recruitment and the novel was withdrawn; details are given by Jonathan Cutbill in his introduction to the 1988 reprint.

6.6   The Second World War and the 1950s. Besides Walter Baxter's *Look Down in Mercy* (1951; American edition New York, 1952) and Mary Renault's *The Charioteer* (1953), other books which describe the war and the post-war period include Rodney Garland's novel *The Heart in Exile* (1953); Rodney Ackland's play *Absolute Hell* (written in the 1950s, published 1990); *Quaint Honour*, a play about a boys' public school by Roger Gellert (pseudonym for John Holmstrom) (1953); Christopher Isherwood's memoirs *Christopher and his Kind* (1977); Stephen Spender's autobiographical fiction *The Temple* (written 1929; revised 1985–6; published 1988), which contrasts interestingly with his earlier memoir *World within World* (1951); John Lehmann's *In the Purely Pagan Sense* (1976), an autobiographical fiction; James Gardiner, *A Class Apart* (1992) assembling letters, diaries and photographs by Montague Glover; and Keith Vaughan's *Journals 1939–77* (1989). In America the most notable texts from this period include James Baldwin's *Giovanni's Room* (1956); Gore Vidal's *The City and the Pillar* (1948); and Tennessee Williams's plays *Cat on a Hot Tin Roof* (1955; altered for its Broadway performance and again for the film) and *Suddenly Last Summer* (1958).

Index of Principal Topics

Index of Names

Page numbers in *italics* refer to the bibliography. The bibliography has been selectively indexed: all literary writers (and anonymous literary texts) listed in the bibliography are included in this index, but critics and scholars are only indexed if they are also cited in the main text, in which case the index will assist in tracing the source of citations.

WITHDRAWN